JANINE DI GIOVANNI was a war reporter for nearly three decades. She is the winner of a 2019 Guggenheim Fellowship and in 2020 was awarded the Blake-Dodd Prize from the American Academy of Arts and Letters for her lifetime achievement in nonfiction. She has won more than a dozen other international awards. She is a Senior Fellow at Yale University's Jackson Institute for Global Affairs and the former Edward R. Murrow Fellow at the Council on Foreign Relations in New York City. She is a columnist for *Foreign Policy* and *The National*. She has written and reported from the Balkans, Africa, and the Middle East, where she witnessed the siege of Sarajevo, the fall of Grozny, and the genocides of Srebrenica and Rwanda in 1994, as well as more than a dozen other active conflicts. She has published eight other books. She lives between Manhattan and Paris and has one child.

janinedigiovanni.com

'The book illustrates the fine balance in which many of these communities now hang, examining how violence, economic instability, persecution, and emigration are leading to the dissolution of cultures forged both by land and by religion' *New Yorker*

'Janine di Giovanni, a former winner of the Courage in Journalism prize, is a shining example of the dwindling band of investigative reporters' independent.co.uk

'Di Giovanni writes elegantly, her reporting informed partly by being a Christian herself' *Daily Telegraph*

'The individuals di Giovanni interviews provide a rich portrait of these threatened communities, and of the wider societies they inhabit' *Harper's Magazine*

'*The Vanishing*, a mosaic of oral histories, paints a picture of the religion almost lost but preserved through collective memory in the Promised Land where Jesus Christ once walked' *Vanity Fair*

'With beautiful evocations of the power of faith in trying times … It's refreshing to hear from a correspondent who participated in, rather than merely observed, one of the most fundamental aspects of life in the Middle East: religious practice … di Giovanni does Middle Eastern Christians a service by highlighting their recent struggles' *Wall Street Journal*

'Janine di Giovanni is a humane and persistent witness who knows when to stand out of the way, has a unique ability to be both unflinching and tender and, most importantly, never forgets that war is always a human tragedy. And because the story of Arab Christians is also the story of the Arab Middle East, the book is a record of the painfully fractured region, the consequences of war and foreign intrusion, of which its peoples, of all faiths, but particularly its minorities, have suffered most' Hisham Matar

'Profoundly moving' Mark Tully

'Janine di Giovanni's beautifully written and deeply researched study of Christian communities in Iraq, Gaza, Syria, and Egypt is important not only for what it reveals about those vital but largely effaced communities, but also for its careful examination of an issue that is far more complex – as so much is in the Middle East – than typically presented or understood … A compelling and powerful study' Sara Roy

'*The Vanishing* is unique because di Giovanni is not seeking a solution, and indeed knows there may not be one. As a war reporter for 30 years she knows the reality of man … I like *The Vanishing* because it's true, and people in the West need to read the truth, even if they don't like it and can't do anything about it' *First Things*

'Each book of hers should be required reading … In addition to contextualising the conflicts, Janine shared the human stories … She exposes what we find so hard to confront in humanity' *Tablo*

'Gorgeously written and deeply felt' Elle Hardy

'This is an interesting work of journalism that mixes personal reflection with a patchwork of reportage' *Prospect Magazine*

'It's a beautifully written book, it's personally reflective and it takes you, the reader, and indeed Janine herself, through her reporting experiences. We're taken through some of the most testing and upsetting times in geopolitical events, but also we look in the face of the issue of a vanishing culture and a vanishing religion that seems so high profile in countries like Australia' *ABC Radio Melbourne's Morning*

'A moving and insightful portrait of the Middle East's shrinking Christian population' *Catholic Herald*

'A distillation of vivid notes taken while covering the past two turbulent decades in the Middle East … A wake-up call for worldwide Christianity' *Church Times*

'*The Vanishing* is neither a chronological record of Christian withdrawal nor a geopolitical analysis of religious trends. Instead, di Giovanni offers a kind of requiem for a disappearing religious culture, a tale rendered all the more heart-wrenching for having been written during some of the worst months of the COVID-19 crisis. The book skilfully manages to combine an overview of the rise and precipitous fall of Christianity in its ancient homelands, moving accounts from believers sticking it out there, and a deeply personal grieving over the withdrawal of the faith from its birthplace' *Christianity Today*

'*The Vanishing* is unique because di Giovanni is not seeking a solution, and indeed knows there may not be one. As a war reporter for thirty years she knows the reality of man: there will always be another war, there will always be slaughter and destruction. She writes because this is the twilight of Middle Eastern Christianity, because just maybe we'll remember their stories' *First Things*

'Di Giovanni's mesmeric narrative is an elegant balance of journalism and history that also includes semi-autobiographical reflections of the role faith plays in her own life. Seeking to illuminate those "worlds and communities of people who might, in one hundred years' time, no longer be on this earth", di Giovanni grants life forever on the page to those vanishing now … This is a rewarding, thoughtful and somber journey into the Middle East to find the last 'holdouts' of the Christian faith in Iraq, Syria, Gaza and Egypt' *Shelf Awareness*

'Di Giovanni writes with poignant authenticity as she weaves her own deeply personal faith experiences with those of a parade of Middle Eastern citizens who populate the history she recounts of Iraq, Gaza, Syria, and Egypt, places foundational to early Christianity … di Giovanni's many interviews and own observations detail heartrending circumstances that have wreaked irreparable harm to families, towns, and countries. The words of one Syrian expat, "Our present is a failure, but our past is glorious," illustrate di Giovanni's difficult, essential undertaking' *Booklist*

'In this informative work of journalism and memoir, war reporter Di Giovanni *Ghosts by Daylight* recounts her travels through the Middle East with a focus on rapidly shrinking Christian minority groups …The propulsive account is marked by the author's keen eye for detail and the stories of the people involved … perfect for anyone interested in the Middle East, or in how humans live through war' *Publishers Weekly*

'In her latest poignant book, veteran war correspondent and Guggenheim fellow di Giovanni focuses on Christian communities struggling to survive in the region where the religion had its birth … The author presents a distinctly personal and subjective account full of empathy and humanity amid upheaval' *Kirkus*

'Evocative portraits of Christians in the Middle East, struggling to survive in a region reeling from war, occupation and dictatorships' *The Markaz Review*

THE
VANISHING

THE TWILIGHT OF CHRISTIANITY IN THE MIDDLE EAST

Janine di Giovanni

BLOOMSBURY PUBLISHING

LONDON · OXFORD · NEW YORK · NEW DELHI · SYDNEY

BLOOMSBURY PUBLISHING
Bloomsbury Publishing Plc
50 Bedford Square, London, WC1B 3DP, UK
29 Earlsfort Terrace, Dublin 2, Ireland

BLOOMSBURY, BLOOMSBURY PUBLISHING and the Diana logo
are trademarks of Bloomsbury Publishing Plc

First published in 2021 in the United States by PublicAffairs,
an imprint of Perseus Books, LLC, a subsidiary of Hachette Book Group, Inc
First published in Great Britain 2021
This edition published 2022

Bloomsbury Publishing Plc does not have any control over, or responsibility for,
any third-party websites referred to in this book. All internet addresses given
in this book were correct at the time of going to press. The author and publisher
regret any inconvenience caused if addresses have changed or sites have
ceased to exist, but can accept no responsibility for any such changes

A catalogue record for this book is available from the British Library

ISBN: HB: 978-1-5266-2583-0; TPB: 978-1-5266-2584-7; PB: 978-1-5266-2585-4;
EBOOK: 978-1-5266-2581-6; EPDF: 978-1-5266-4585-2

2 4 6 8 10 9 7 5 3 1

Typeset by Amy Quinn
Printed and bound in Great Britain by CPI Group (UK) Ltd, Croydon CR0 4YY

To find out more about our authors and books visit
www.bloomsbury.com and sign up for our newsletters

For Luca Costantino. My mainstay and ballast.

And the last remnants, memory destroys.

W. G. Sebald, *The Emigrants*

We photographers deal in things which are continually vanishing, and when they have vanished there is no contrivance on earth which can make them come back again. We cannot develop and print a memory.

Henri Cartier-Bresson

CONTENTS

X

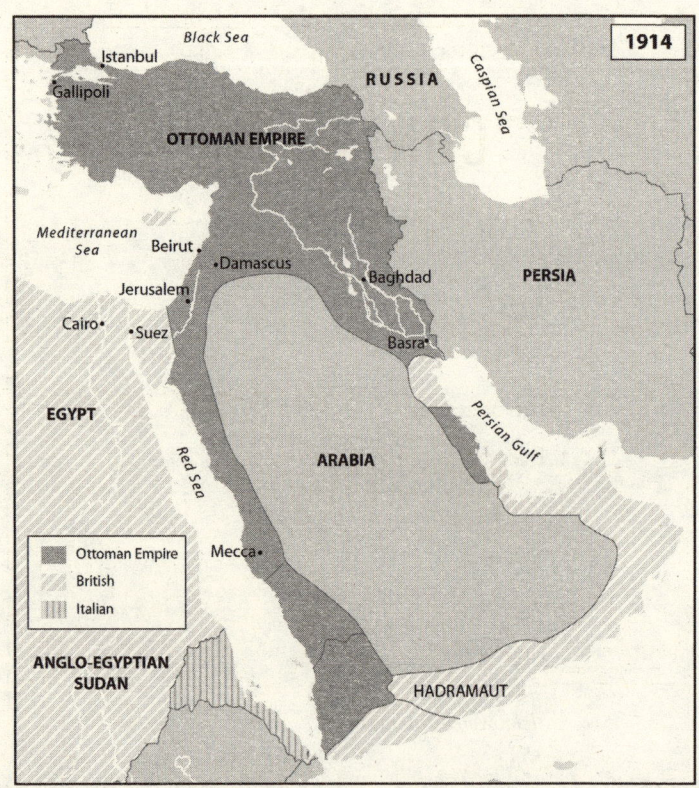

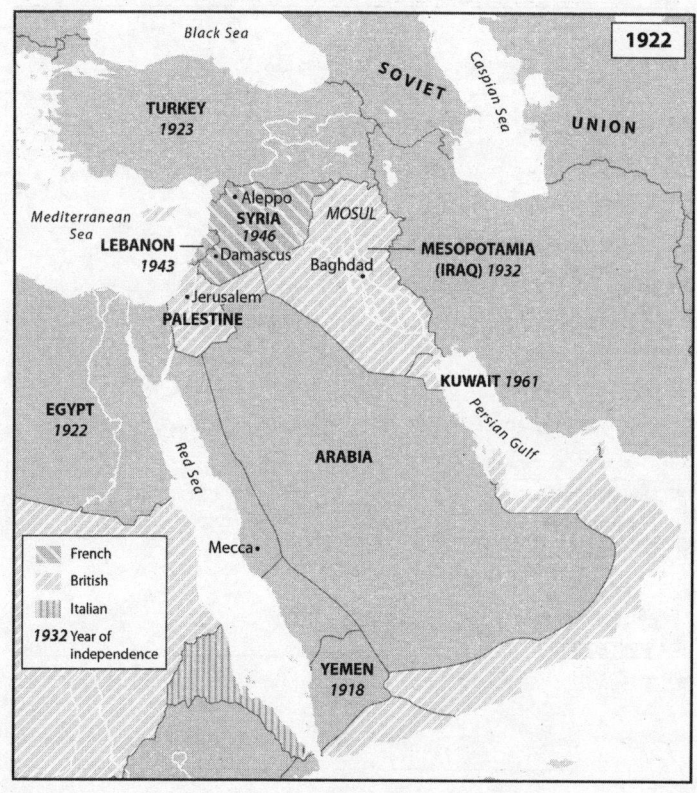

1922

Black Sea

SOVIET

Caspian Sea

UNION

TURKEY
1923

Mediterranean
Sea

• Aleppo
SYRIA
1946
• Damascus

MOSUL

MESOPOTAMIA
(IRAQ) 1932

Baghdad •

LEBANON
1943

• Jerusalem
PALESTINE

KUWAIT 1961

EGYPT
1922

Red Sea

ARABIA

Persian Gulf

Mecca •

French
British
Italian
1932 Year of
independence

YEMEN
1918

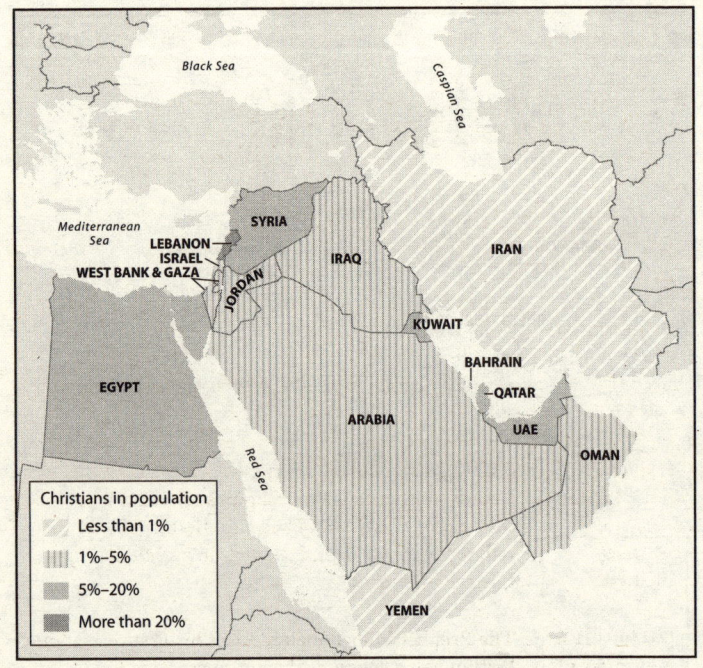

Christians in population

- Less than 1%
- 1%–5%
- 5%–20%
- More than 20%

TIMELINE

6–4 BCE: Founding of Christianity	Jesus Christ is born in Bethlehem in the modern-day West Bank, leading to the formation of Christianity. The new religion spreads quickly in the region, reaching Syria, Iraq, and Egypt in the first century CE.
313: Edict of Milan	The Roman emperor Constantine issues the Edict of Milan, which establishes religious tolerance across the empire. Christianity becomes Rome's official religion a decade later, including in its Middle Eastern provinces.
610: Founding of Islam	The Prophet Muhammad receives his first revelation. Within half a century, Muslim rulers from the Arabian Peninsula control much of the Middle East. Christians are considered a protected but second-class community.
1839–1876: Tanzimat Reforms	The Ottoman Empire, which controls much of the Middle East, introduces the Tanzimat reforms. Christians are deemed equal citizens under the law, opening up new opportunities but also fostering resentment among Ottoman Muslims.
1914–1923: Armenian Genocide	In the years during and following World War I, the Ottoman Empire carries out a genocide against ethnic Armenians. The genocide results in over a million deaths and leads many Armenian Christians to flee south to the Levant.

1916: Sykes-Picot Agreement	The United Kingdom and France agree to divide the Ottoman provinces in the Levant between them. The British establish mandates in Palestine, Jordan, and Iraq, while the French take control over Lebanon and Syria. Christians often receive preferential treatment from the European powers but nevertheless play an active role in nationalist movements.
1948: The Nakbah	Israeli forces defeat a joint army from the surrounding Arab states, consolidating the establishment of the state of Israel. Around seven hundred thousand Palestinians—including Christians—are forced to flee their homes to live in refugee camps in neighboring countries, where many of their descendants still live today.
1952: Gamal Abdel Nasser Coup	Gamal Abdel Nasser stages a coup against King Farouk in Egypt. His socialist reform policies strip wealthy Egyptian Christians of their land, and his Arab nationalism leads many Christians to emigrate or turn inward to their communities.
1970: Hafez al-Assad Coup	Hafez al-Assad, a member of the secular nationalist Ba'ath Party, stages a coup in Syria. As a member of the Alawite minority, he relies on support from Syrian Christians. His son Bashar takes over after Hafez's death in 2000.
1971–2012: Papacy of Shenouda III	Pope Shenouda III serves as head of the Coptic Church in Egypt. During his tenure, both the power of the papacy and the size of the Coptic Church grow significantly.
1979–2003: Saddam Hussein Presidency	Saddam Hussein, a member of the secular nationalist Ba'ath Party, comes to power in Iraq after forcing his predecessor to resign. He institutes a brutal dictatorship that targets the country's Shia majority and Kurdish minority, but his regime protects Christians in exchange for loyalty.

1981–2011: Hosni Mubarak Presidency	Hosni Mubarak takes over as president of Egypt after Anwar Sadat's assassination in 1981. He develops a close relationship with Pope Shenouda III, who demands increased rights for Egyptian Copts in exchange for their support.
1987–1991: First Intifada	A series of massive Palestinian protests against the Israeli state, the *intifada*, or "uprising," takes place in the West Bank and Gaza. Almost two thousand Palestinians are killed.
2003: American Invasion of Iraq	American forces help overthrow Saddam's regime in 2003, leading to a decade-long armed conflict in Iraq. As a result of the violence and rising sectarian tensions, the vast majority of the country's Christians emigrate.
2006: Election of Hamas	Hamas, a militant group deemed a terrorist organization by several Western countries, wins a majority in the 2006 Palestinian parliamentary elections. The election leads to a rift between the Fatah party in the West Bank, backed by the Palestinian Liberation Organization (PLO), and Hamas in Gaza. Conditions deteriorate even further in Gaza, and the few Christians left believe that Hamas does not adequately protect their rights.
2011: Arab Spring in Egypt	Massive protests in Egypt—part of the Arab Spring that started in Tunisia—lead to Mubarak's resignation in February 2011. In spite of Pope Shenouda III's relationship with the president, many Egyptian Christians join the protests.
2011– Present: Syrian Civil War	The Arab Spring inspires protests in Syria against the Assad regime. Assad cracks down quickly and violently on the dissenters, leading to a civil war that has left hundreds of thousands dead and millions displaced, either internally or as refugees abroad. Many Syrian Christians flee the country.

2012–2013: Muslim Brotherhood Rule in Egypt	The Muslim Brotherhood wins the first election after Mubarak's ouster, and Mohamed Morsi becomes president. Most Egyptian Christians strongly oppose the Muslim Brotherhood, and violence against Christians increases.
2013: Rise of ISIS	The Islamic State in Iraq and Syria, a Sunni terrorist group, attempts to build a caliphate based on a fundamentalist Salafi doctrine. The group manages to take over territory in Iraq and Syria roughly equivalent to the size of the United Kingdom and launches an ethnic cleansing campaign against the region's Christian communities. The group loses the vast majority of its territory within a few years.
2014–Present: Abdel Fattah al-Sisi Presidency	The Egyptian Armed Forces overthrow Morsi and the Muslim Brotherhood, and General Abdel Fattah al-Sisi takes over as president, installing an authoritarian and oppressive government.

INTRODUCTION

MARCH 19, 2020
ST. JOSEPH'S DAY
PARIS, FRANCE

I BEGIN THIS BOOK ON THE FIRST DAY OF SPRING IN PARIS, CLOSE TO THE TIME when the trees throughout the city blossom and the buds scatter on the sidewalks like stars.

It is the feast of St. Joseph, the name day of my closest brother. When I was very small, we celebrated it with cream-filled pastries called *zeppole di San Giuseppe* and token gifts. We had family dinners, where siblings and cousins and aunts and uncles lined both sides of a deep walnut table covered with a lace cloth my grandmother had crocheted.

My brother has been dead for five years now, but I still think of Joseph, see him, talk to him, walk alongside him, every day. We were only two and a half years apart. As children, people thought we were twins. We hunted frogs together at a creek near our house. We built snow forts from ice, our red mittens freezing to the snow. I once beat up an older boy who was tormenting my brother, breaking his nose by swinging my

1

backpack at his face. Although I was younger and smaller, I was stronger. My love for my older brother was fierce and visceral.

The day he died, I thought, *Who will be the keeper of my childhood secrets? Who will remember what I knew, what I have forgotten?* The telephone number of our childhood home. An afternoon at an old-fashioned cinema around Christmastime, watching the film *Oliver.* Learning how to ride waves in the Atlantic Ocean on a windy August morning before a hurricane. I still wonder where he has gone.

In the same way, religion provides shared memory, a set of rituals that endure, patterns that can be passed down: our shared intimates, our secrets.

My writing begins from quarantine inside the home of a kind friend who has taken me in. Genevieve is giving me shelter in a large room in the 7th arrondissement of Paris, not far from the Seine, with a long wooden desk pushed against a wall and high windows that open to the sky and nearly reach the tops of the trees. In happier times, she has told me, a man who worked in the theater made the long white curtains that look as though they open onto a stage.

From my "stage"—my room—I see a beautiful courtyard in the middle of our eighteenth-century building, a large *hotel particulier* where a single family, very wealthy, once lived in great luxury. Now most of the residents of this apartment complex have fled Paris, retreating to their country homes, to friends, to anywhere they believe to be safer.

Outside, beyond the heavy iron door that springs open onto rue de Grenelle, the streets of Paris are empty. In the morning, before the police who ask for your *attestation de sortie* papers arrive, I go for walks in the quiet.

This is a time of death, of *La Peste* across the world. In my small corner of it, my *quartier,* I see the bolted doors of the lovely church of St. Clotilde, the Catholic princess from Burgundy, who became the second wife of King Clovis I in 493 (history that every French schoolchild learns). In normal times, I sat in a corner of a café, watching children play. Now the square is closed.

I pass no one on my morning walk. It seems a time of physical but also emotional isolation, a time of tremendous sorrow. I feel a sadness so profound that I can hardly speak when I return to the apartment, placing my dusty shoes carefully outside and washing my hands with an eighteenth-century disinfectant called *eau de javel*. An old world is passing, a new one beginning.

From my window, I stare out to a courtyard edged with *tilleul* (linden) trees, now laden with pale green buds. Every morning at nine or ten, a mother of three—I think she is called Sabine—escorts her small children, aged about seven, nine, and eleven, to the courtyard to exercise. I can see the misery in their faces from being allowed out for such a short time; soon they'll be hurried inside to hide from the virus that is killing people across Europe and the globe.

One morning, the youngest one rushed to help me open the heavy door to pull my bicycle inside. He wore shorts and had an open, curious face.

"What is your name?" I asked him gently.

"Victor," he replied, smiling at me—me, a stranger in a long green coat and a face mask, wearing rubber gloves. So few strangers now, so few people coming from outside our courtyard.

Although it is a modern disease that began, possibly, with bats in China, it could just as easily be the fourteenth century, when *La Peste*, which came from fleas, ravaged Europe. There is a timelessness of suffering, of human despair. And of religious relevance.

Every day we are told something we must do and other things we must not do. Some of the advice seems more like faith than science. We must not go outside except to see the doctor or forage for food. We must wear masks, even ones we sew ourselves, and the kind of thick rubber gloves one normally uses for washing dishes. We must not touch those we love, must not speak on the telephone without wiping it with antiseptic cloths. We must not plan—we must cancel. We should only live minute to minute, something that, as modern, pulsing, busy people, we are not prepared to do. This strange time, riddled with uncertainty, has thrust us into the mouth of unknown peril. Suddenly we rely on old behaviors, on folk remedies that our ancestors might have used during the Spanish flu. But most of all, we are looking for signs and portents: that is, to God. I have prayer cards of Our Lady at my bedside table; I subscribe to an online novena that arrives in my email box every morning. But it does not quell the waves of fear that interrupt my thoughts.

At night, I cannot sleep. I lie in bed and worry, anxiety gripping me so strongly that my heart feels jumpy, as if in a strange new rhythm. I am separated from my son, who is with his father in the mountains. My mother, who is one hundred years old, is more than three thousand miles across the Atlantic. My friends are all in self-isolation, and the loneliness and fear I feel at four o'clock in the morning, *l'heure du loup*—the hour of the wolf, the hour when people die—overwhelms me.

At that dismal hour, I open the long windows and stare out to the empty courtyard with the shadows of the trees, and I try to see another light across the darkness. If someone else were awake, even a stranger, I would feel less frightened. But everything is dark. There might be no one left at all. I am alone and isolated.

In bed, I lie on my back and try to calm my bumping heart with my breath. Then I begin to pray. The meditation my mother taught me many years ago, the Rosary, forms words in my mind that I thought I had forgotten long ago. But they are still there. Our Father. Hail Mary. Blessed Be. I remember learning the chants as a child, holding my grandfather's black wooden rosary beads, which came with him from Naples on a boat, as he voyaged alone, without his family. The Hail Mary, for instance, which appeals to Our Lady's intercession, stretches back to the sixteenth century, and its opening words go back to the very roots of Christianity, to the first chapter of the Gospel of Luke. It is the most powerful of prayers for Latin Catholics, forming the basis of both the Rosary and the Angelus. Even as a child, my grandmother told me to use the prayer wisely, because if you truly needed something and prayed to Our Lady, she would ask her son: "And Jesus can never say no to his mother," my grandmother added.

The Hail Mary, the Our Father, the Glory Be. They are the prayers I hated as a child during Lent, when my classmates and I were forced to kneel for hours during Holy Week, passing caustic notes about the nuns or the priests and sighing dramatically at the length of time we had to spend on our knees. But these are also the prayers that have sustained me, consoled me, and guided me in the many years I have roamed the world to record and document wars.

Faith that I had lost came back to me at that time, after many years spent believing in nothing and no one. Christianity, like all the great faiths, has one resonating and alluring quality: it combines ritual, which soothes in anxious times, with a vast sense of belonging to something much larger and greater than yourself.

When I was a small child, my father once remarked that there were no atheists in the foxhole. I didn't understand what he meant until I began to live inside the vortex of wars and my life became suffused with danger. Now, I pray when I walk silently from my room to the outside world. I pray that I will be protected from danger, that I will be safe.

Danger is something I know well. I have operated in war zones, sometimes on autopilot, for three decades, mainly writing for *Vanity Fair* and *The London Times*. I know how to find my way out of a minefield and when to seek shelter during a bombing raid. I know how to get through just about any checkpoint in the Middle East, the Balkans, or Africa: Don't make eye contact. Have your papers ready. Be polite, but firm. Never get out of your car, especially if child soldiers wielding rocket-propelled grenades (RPGs) are aiming them at your heart.

But an invisible enemy, an angry and stubborn virus whirling its way around the globe, is a new concept, one that terrifies me beyond belief. My sixteen-year-old son has already left the city on the back of his father's motorcycle, fleeing south to a remote village in the Alps, leaving me crying on the pavement. Seeing him go, I felt bereft, abandoned, afraid, as if it were June 1940 and the occupation of Paris, with most of the population running away via the Porte d'Orléans, on foot or by cart or car. I've moved out of the apartment on rue Bonaparte, which belongs to my friend Myriem, where I was staying alone. It is a lovely, sun-filled place, with a view of the Church of Saint-Sulpice. I watched the light move through its arches as the sun took its course across the sky each day. The church's characteristically Baroque design makes it glow as if it were lit from heaven.

I've spent so much of my Paris life at Saint-Sulpice. My son received his First Communion there, and often, when my life has seemed sodden with confusion or sorrow—after the deaths of my two brothers, when I realized my marriage was breaking down, or when I was facing another painful period alone—I have sat for hours in the darkness at the back of the church, watching the light. Sometimes an organist would be practicing ahead of Sunday Mass. Tourists would come and stand near the marble fountains, staring at the three murals by Eugène Delacroix adorning the walls of a side chapel.

Inspired by St. Paul's Cathedral in London, Saint-Sulpice is dedicated to Sulpitius the Pious, a saint venerated in the Eastern Orthodox and Roman Catholic Churches, who is said to have extinguished a fire with a wave of his hand. It is a church of history: Victor Hugo was married at Saint-Sulpice; Charles Baudelaire and the Marquis de Sade were both baptized there. Like its more famous Parisian neighbor, Notre Dame, it caught fire in the spring of 2019. The doors were damaged, as were a stained glass window, a bas-relief, and a staircase.

The church survived the fire, later revealed by police to have been an act of arson, though it closed just over a year later for the pandemic. As restaurants and cafés around the city shut down and President Emmanuel Macron declared that the country was at war with the virus, I found myself at the barred doors of Saint-Sulpice. I climbed the stairs and tugged at the chains threaded through a lock, partially in disbelief. My chest felt heavy when I realized that the church, my sanctuary, was closed to me. I went home, bundled up most of my belongings, and took one of the few taxis on the street to the 7th arrondissement, in the parish of St. Clotilde, to live with my friend Genevieve, who is named after the patron saint of Paris.

After a week in Paris, no longer able to stand the anxiety, I packed my things again, leaving the room on the rue de Grenelle. I threw together my rubber gloves (the last pair on the shelves of the Monoprix on rue de Rennes), my homemade masks (which I had sewn from a piece of cloth), my eight boxes of Doliprane, and my medal of St. Christopher, the patron saint of travelers, and made my way to a mostly deserted Gare de Lyon. The few travelers wore masks and gloves; we stood a yard apart from one another.

I boarded one of the last trains to Grenoble, where my only child was sheltered deep in the mountains, in the family home of my ex-husband, whose ancestors have lived there for four hundred years.

When I arrived in Grenoble, the station was empty, with armed soldiers on the platform. My ex and my son were there to meet me and take me to the village. Our car, weaving into the mountain pass, was the only one on the road. In the darkness, we pulled up to the drive of a sixteenth-century house with thick walls, unheated rooms, and a fireplace large enough to cook a feast.

The mountains, of course, had not changed. But in the dozen years since I'd last been there, neither had the house: the old linens were still there, the squeaky beds, even a tube of hand cream I'd left in a bathroom drawer. On the wall of my room was a painting I'd always loved, *Le Retour au Pays*, the return to the countryside.

Judging from the dress of the people, the painting is probably from the 1850s; it's dusty and battered, with a frame half broken. It depicts a French sailor sitting in an old-fashioned kitchen. He's surrounded by villagers—a priest, a farmer, an old woman—with weathered but enchanted faces. There is a hearth, a fire. The sailor is telling a story, probably about his voyages to places they've never dreamed of. Now he has come home from his big world to their tiny one in the mountains.

I loved the painting long before I understood it. I wondered what stories he was telling them. But as I considered how he had been on voyages to all the corners of the world, I realized he is a character who has left the safety of his home, his village, to stretch his imagination and his world. And perhaps in a way that, in the natural order of things, he should not have.

My sense of time shifted in my months in the Alps, partly because time seemed to have stood still in the dozen years since I'd last been here. The villagers in this remote place always looked fairly ancient—in fact, their faces look a bit like those of the characters in *Le Retour au Pays*. Life has the same timeless-ness, COVID-19 or no COVID-19. The local farmer, Maurice, who married us (he also serves as mayor), still has his many cows, and he still rises at dawn. Cousins who kept rabbits that my son played with have passed on, but the woman who sells fresh eggs still sits in her garden on sunny days. When I go for walks, I pass the graves of cousins who fought in the Resistance during the war and were killed by Germans a few days before it ended in 1945.

RETREAT TO THE PAST

Here in the mountains, there is a gathering. We cook, work, and eat together. The pots and pans are scarred with years of the family meals that people eat in the mountains: *pot-au-feu, blan-quette de veau*. The rooms have crucifixes over the beds, fronds from Palm Sunday stuck to dusty frames, religious icons and medals. I am given a spare room, and I pile my bed with musty blankets and stained comforters. Exploring the rest of the house, I find a nursery with a wooden cradle inside. Long-gone cousins have left their mark in closets and cupboards. *A. Challet 1927* is written in dark blue ink on the inside of my wardrobe. Signs of generations of the spirits of the Molin family, stretch-ing back to the 1700s, seem to turn up everywhere. On one wall I rediscover the markings of relatives' heights, starting in the early 1920s and continuing up to my son's birth in 2004.

But it's not just the faith of cousins who have passed on that imbues the place. Living French cousins are sheltering in the house with us, and their faith, too, is deep and profound. They pray before meals, standing to sing, and they pray before bed. They do not eat meat on Fridays. At night, they gather around a single candle and sing in harmony so beautifully that I ask them what they are singing. "The song of the angels," they say. I fall asleep to their voices.

Before I sleep, I try to pray. I go back to other times of my life when there was danger and chaos, and where, through prayer, I found solace.

I attended schools run by Dominican Irish nuns, harsh women who wore wimples that covered their fleshy necks. They were cruel. They hit with rulers. They raged against abortion, homosexuality, and sex before marriage. They targeted the weaker children and exploited their pain: the sensitive ones, the ones from poor families. I annoyed them because I asked inappropriate questions and challenged their dogma. They sent me to the back of the room, expelled me from class to sit on a wooden bench in the principal's office, or simply ignored me.

Often, they talked of those who walked with the devil, which gave me my first sense of good and evil. Abortionists were evil, or anyone who opposed religion, or who tried to separate church and state. We prayed before our classes, before lunch, and when we left for the day. We memorized entire prayer books. Throughout, I sat at my wooden desk in the back row and let my mind wander. As the years passed, and the nuns faded from my memory, I forgot what the Transfiguration and the Annunciation meant.

My interest in religion as a political issue began to take shape during my years working in Bosnia during its civil war. I met a vast array of Christians in the former Yugoslavia: Croatian Catholics, Serbian Orthodox, Montenegrin Orthodox, Greek Orthodox, Assyrians, Melkites. I tried to understand their ancient roots. Who had arrived first? How did they maintain such tight-knit communities? Who emigrated, and who perished, because of their faith? I began to study and research the Christianity of the East and the differences between sects in dogma and practice, as well as the split between Constantinople and Rome.

My adopted godmother, Dessa Trevisan, was a devout Orthodox Serb. But she had been raised Roman Catholic and spent many years in Italy with one of her husbands. When I would go to Mass at the Brompton Oratory in London, I would always see her, tiny and wearing a fur coat, a few rows ahead of me. Whether she was Orthodox or Catholic hardly mattered: she was a believer. During the summer of 2005, a few years before she died, she took me to see the churches of ancient Montenegro. I suppose it was a way of trying to help me understand all sides of the Bosnian War—Muslim, Orthodox, and Catholic—on which I reported in the early 1990s.

During the war in Kosovo in 1999, I sat in a café in Podgorica, the Soviet-style Montenegrin capital, with an old general who had fought with Tito's partisans as a teenager, hiding in mountain caves and ambushing German and Italian soldiers. He told me a history of Montenegro. In his version, they have never been subjugated by the Turks. He said it was incorporated into the Serbian Empire in the late twelfth century, that it retained its independence from the Turks even after the Ottoman defeat of the Serbs at Kosovo Polje in 1389. That it was recognized as a state following the Congress of Berlin in 1878. That it was ruled by the Petrović-Njegoš family for some 222 years, until King Nikola I was dethroned in 1918 and fled into exile.

All of this faded history, pride, and fierce independence give Montenegro a mythic allure. There are countless legends, some of them true, others that might be fairy tales. He told me that Montenegrins are the tallest people in Europe, that most of Europe's stolen cars end up there, and that rich Russians are buying up the coast, turning it into a gaudy Porto Ercole.

In any case, it is a beautiful country, with its jagged Adriatic coastline, empty beaches, fierce canyons carved out of mountains, and tiny fishing communities, where families have not altered the pace of their lives for hundreds of years despite wars, dictators, and sanctions. There are former Venetian cities and sacred monasteries teetering on mountaintops, where the monks invite you to lunch. There is shellfish risotto and broiled lobster and delicious Montenegrin cabernet. There is a lethargy that is deeply Mediterranean.

I had come back to Montenegro in the late spring of 2005, while the rest of the continent lay under blankets of snow, to see Dessa, simply because I missed her. She lived then in Igalo, a suburb of Herceg Novi, an old Venetian port that was founded by a Bosnian king in 1382. Dessa had lived here quietly since she disappeared from London one winter a few years earlier.

One day we went to the seventeenth-century Savina Monastery, where in 1934 King Alexander of Yugoslavia, a critical figure in unifying that country, prayed and lit a candle before he sailed to Marseille and was assassinated. The candle is wrapped in a black ribbon and mounted in a glass box on the wall. The chair where he sat has a rope over it. A young boy, a novice monk, was sweeping the floor while singing Orthodox hymns. Another monk invited us to lunch and talked with us.

He had a shy, peaceful manner. I asked why the Orthodox altar was hidden behind a curtain. "Because we feel God, not see him," he told me. "That is the meaning of true faith."

FAITHFUL WANDERINGS

Faith meant two things to me: ritual and a sense of belonging. Regardless of where I was in the world, I felt a sense of being part of a larger community, no matter how difficult, dark, or dangerous the situation was. Even in a war zone, I could always find a church somewhere. Inside the church, there would be someone else kneeling in the gloomy light, trying to communicate with something higher. For me (though certainly not for my mother), it did not matter if the church was Catholic or Protestant, if it was a cathedral in Sarajevo or in a field in Rwanda. When I entered the space, I would feel at peace and no longer lonely.

Of all the places where I witnessed faith, the Middle East, where I began working nearly three decades ago, has given me the most insight into the notion of the divine and defined my own personal beliefs. My first trip to Jerusalem, nearly three decades ago, took place in the middle of a cold, wet spring in 1989. I arrived at Ben Gurion Airport in the chilly dawn, but by the time I got into a taxi, the light behind the hills was turning lavender and pink. Coming from dark, cold Europe, I was already entranced by Jerusalem before I entered the city gates. And so began my many years of roaming the Middle East, through wars, insurrections, assassinations, coup d'états, and my own personal tragedies and joys. In the background of my life are the many voyages I have taken in the region. In all of them, there were notebooks: sturdy leather-bound ones scribbled with the stories and histories of forgotten or vanishing people.

I also began to study the Christians of Gaza: their persecution, their fears for the future, and also the origins and history of their tiny community. I compared their predicament with that of other Arab Christians in Israel, who often found themselves caught between two worlds. On the one hand, those Christians inside Israel are Arabs, and therefore in solidarity with the Palestinian struggle, but they are also Israeli citizens by birth.

In Egypt, before and after 2011's January 25 Revolution in Tahrir Square, I tracked the plight of the Christian Copts, from ancient desert monasteries to their recent displacement. What would be their greatest enemy: emigration or discrimination? More than one million Copts have fled Egypt since the 1950s, largely to go to the United States, the United Kingdom, Canada, and Australia. For them, discrimination in Egypt means they cannot build churches for their worshippers. Laws on inheritance, marriage, and divorce bind them. They are absent from most high-level jobs in the military or government.

From Egypt, I researched the Eastern Christian Church south to Ethiopia and Sudan. In Africa, where I lived for a happy period of my life in the early 2000s, and then returned to report on the war in South Sudan and the formation of the world's newest nation in 2012, I would go to Mass largely to find my footing in a place where I felt lost and alone.

How does faith bind people and prevent them from vanishing? I think partly it is a question of the union, the sense of solidarity, that comes with faith.

But faith has also led to war, to bloodshed, and to genocide, as was the case in several conflicts on which I reported. Many years ago, in a hotel room in Zagreb, I read about Bishop Aloysius Stepinac, who at the time of his appointment as bishop of Croatia in 1934 was the youngest Catholic bishop in the world. He found himself involved with the Ustashe, an extremist insurgent group vying for Croat nationalism. They allied with the Nazis and fascist Italy.

The Ustashe carried out a brutal campaign against Orthodox Serbs, Jews, and Roma people, killing hundreds of thousands and overseeing forced conversions, all in the name of Catholicism. By 1942, Stepinac had condemned the actions of the Ustashe and reportedly tried to save many of the victims. But he was brought to trial after the war by the Yugoslav government and spent five years in prison. I remember reading somewhere that the intense existential loneliness he felt was partly due to his breach with the church. He had always felt connected to others by his faith. Now, dejected and expelled by his God, he was alone.

In Africa, especially in Côte d'Ivoire and Nigeria, the breadth of faith and the size of churches overwhelmed me. Northwest of Abidjan in Côte d'Ivoire, I drove to the Basilica of Our Lady of Peace, an inelegant 1980s structure built somewhat in the style of St. Peter's, in the capital city of Yamoussoukro. It was a

Sunday morning, hot and arid, and I woke as I did most mornings in Côte d'Ivoire, feeling as though I had a low-grade fever, perhaps a mild malaria. The drive took about three hours from our home in Deux Plateau, near the Vietnamese restaurant Nuits de Saigon (this is how people gave their addresses). While the size and the number of people in the church left me stunned, I was disappointed by the looming structure. It seemed too modern, too open to the skies, to be spiritual to me; it seemed more like a large market. It was not lovely. But the church had stained windows and a high dome, and what mattered was the concentration and power of the prayer. Thousands of people knelt and prayed together.

A few weeks after my trip to the basilica, a war broke out in the country. It happened very quickly, as happens so often with war. As I was lying in bed reading late at night, I heard shooting in my garden. It was a garden I loved, with fruit trees, a moldy swimming pool, and a writing studio painted lime green, and now there were soldiers with guns running across it.

Not long after, it bloomed into a full-blown war that spread beyond my garden, my fruit trees, my home. I left the house with the mangoes I often picked for breakfast falling all around the garden, thinking what a waste it was to lose all of that fruit someone could have enjoyed, taking only my passport and my computer, a few dresses, a pair of shoes. Everything else remained behind. That war went on for some years, and the churches were too difficult and dangerous to reach.

One afternoon, before I fled the country for safety, I went for a walk to a vegetable stand where in peacetime I had bought vegetables from a small girl crippled by polio. She was cheerful, always smiling, and sat in a chair wearing a brightly colored polka dot cotton dress.

The day I left, the vegetable stand was closed. The girl was gone, and so was the video shop where I used to rent DVDs.

People across the city were leaving. But on the way back I saw an older woman kneeling in the backyard of her home.

"What are you doing?" I asked her. She turned, and I saw her face, lined, weathered by the hard life of her country. She was the kind of woman I would see in the early mornings, walking on the red dirt roads at dawn, going to work, going somewhere.

"What are you doing?" I repeated, more gently.

"I'm praying," she said, pointing to a branch laden with ripe papaya, ready to fall. "God is there," she said. "He is still in that tree."

And that is what I have always believed: God, or whatever force of good people believe in, is still in that tree. Despite the wars, the misery, the pandemic.

But I cannot think about faith without thinking about how people survive when they have no notion of hope. How does faith exist in times and places where there is an endless vortex, a whirl of evil?

MERRIMENT LOST

"Djeznana," my friend in Sarajevo, Velma, once said, using the Bosnian pronunciation of my name. "Do you remember our first Christmas of war?"

Of course I remember, I answered her. I remember everything. You cannot forget.

On December 24, 1992, Christmas Eve, the city of Sarajevo was pitched in black silence, interrupted only by the occasional flare from a tracer round or the explosion of a shell. I woke early in my freezing room, unheated for many months. The icy air of the mountain city rushed through the plastic that covered my windows, which had been blown out by explosions.

Christmas Eve. On that morning, I was not so many years away from my own childhood, from the days when I had been unable to sleep from the joy that would arrive in the next few hours, when I would awake in my bedroom, run downstairs in bare feet, and find my mother and my aunts in the kitchen cooking complicated things, extraordinary things, recipes they had brought with them from Italy.

Now my day would be taken up with survival tactics, in a city under siege.

Tying my heavy snow boots and lining my body with layer upon layer of clothing to counter the chill, I descended to the cavernous dining room and had a breakfast of black tea and stale bread.

Then I started the walk from my hotel to Bjelave Hill, where a Catholic family I knew lived. The father had been tasked with searching for wood in a public park, and I joined him, walking carefully on icy streets down to the center of town. The yellow air stank of carbide from the bombs. We gathered wood in sacks, like medieval people, and carried it back up the hill. The people we passed were moving slowly and wordlessly, looking more like ghosts than humans.

The war had been going on for less than a year. It would continue for three more. Near the center of town, where we searched for wood, they had begun to bury the dead in a former soccer field. By the end of the war, it would be full.

For lunch, we ate rice with scraps of something that came from a can, and I walked home alone before nightfall. The family had traded cans of humanitarian aid food with a Muslim family, getting a tin of pork for some cooking oil. They were preparing, as best they could, a Christmas Eve dinner. I thought of my own parents, far away and six hours behind, preparing their own Christmas Eve dinner, which by Mediterranean Christian tradition must include seven fishes. Here, my friends, wrapped in coats and scarves and hats inside the house because of the deep and vicious cold, were thrilled that they could make *burek*, a traditional dish from this part of the world. It is a kind of filo pastry wrapped around meat and vegetables, or now, around whatever it was that came out of one of those cans. There was no cheese, there were no vegetables, nor the filo pastry they would have used in prewar times, but they tried.

Their home was like a church to me: a sanctuary, a place where I felt safe even if it was in one of the most exposed neighborhoods in Sarajevo. I knew the route well from their home to my own, a looming Holiday Inn on Sniper Alley with blasted-out windows, no water, no heat, no electricity, no phone. When I left the family, I found myself quite alone and suddenly realized where I was, how exposed I was to shells and mortars and bullets. I half-ran, half-walked down the hill, the cold seeping into my back, and I was pinned down by snipers only once, taking cover in the doorway of the shuttered bank. I ran in a zigzag pattern across the field behind the Holiday Inn before reaching the badly damaged back door of the hotel. Only then did I look down and see my shaking hands, trying to hold steady to light a match for a cigarette.

That night, I went to Mass on Sniper Alley, but rather than taking place at midnight, it was a secret time announced in whispers among Catholics only an hour before, so the bombers would not be able to send a mortar shell crashing into the church where a large crowd had come to pray. Still, it was emotional. With my friend Kurt (who would be killed eight years later, while we were working together in Sierra Leone) clutching my hand, we climbed up some stairs in the church to the place where, in better times, the choir had stood and the organist had played.

The Catholic soldiers had come down from the front lines to take Holy Communion, and they lined up first, their heads bowed, in their dirty uniforms and tattered sneakers. The people sang "Silent Night" in Bosnian as they shuffled forward. I was moved to tears and embarrassed to cry in front of Kurt, who was passionate, but stoic.

But I could not help it.

The priest laid the host on their tongues, then blessed them, making the cross on their foreheads. When they turned to go back to their pews, I could see their faces: children, really. Some gangly, others squat, short hair, long hair, hardly old enough to drive, to vote, to legally drink, to shave. And yet, they were fighting. And yet, most of them were probably going to die over the next three years. It was the first Christmas in my life that I was apart from my family, and that, too, made me weep.

In Sarajevo, even during the worst of the bombing, I would continue to make my way under sniper fire to Mass in the neo-Gothic Sacred Heart Cathedral near Marsala Tito Street in the Old Town. Despite the danger of leaving their homes, people always managed to make their way there: the old women in their tatty fur coats, the men in their Russian-style *ushanka* hats. And I remembered something I had read, something that had sustained me: no matter how alone you feel, when you enter a church, you are joined universally to people who share your faith.

There were other churches that I loved in that period of my life, other Catholic churches in Eastern Europe. In Zagreb one winter day, before setting off on a dawn humanitarian flight to Sarajevo, I walked to the cathedral in the Upper Town's Kaptol neighborhood. It had been the seat of the Croatian archbishop, and I wanted to light a candle as a way of calming my nerves before leaving for months in a war zone. Croatia had just finished its own war, and the shops and markets were empty of food. I had to search for a candle. Finally, at dusk, I made my pilgrimage to the cathedral and knelt near the altar.

It had endured so much. A thousand years before, King Laudislaus had moved the bishop's seat from Sisak to Zagreb for protection. Then the Ottomans invaded at the end of the fifteenth

century. Acts of God occurred—an earthquake in 1880, for example, that damaged most of the main structures—and more
violent history passed: two world wars and several Balkan wars.
But at the end of the twentieth century, in a dark time of yet another war, the cathedral was still standing. The church, despite
so much destruction, was still there. The interior was glowing,
lit by so many candles. I knelt by the altar and prayed. I knew I
was not alone.

I lived through the Bosnian War—many I knew did not—
and plenty of other conflicts that I went on to report. I believe, I
know, that partially it was faith that kept me alive.

The Atlantic published an essay in 2019 pointing out that in
America, the holy trinity of work, family, and religion, the bed-
rock of traditional Western society, was eroding. Millennials
were "nearly three times more likely than Boomers"—those
born between 1946 and 1964—"to say they don't believe in
God." Much of it was related to a "blanket mistrust of institutions of authority," a reasonable response to coming of age
during a global financial meltdown. Church attendance had
declined with the rise of the Internet. Rather than attending
community-based churches as a source of social interaction and
a place of spirituality, young men, in particular, were finding
spirituality online instead. The main thrust of the article was
that people were attempting to "renegotiate their relationship
with religion by picking and choosing elements of various religious traditions they found appealing."[1]

The Atlantic cited a Pew Research Center study. And yet the
Washington Post, citing a different Pew study, said Americans
were turning to their faith in the age of coronavirus:

A majority of Americans have prayed for the end of the pandemic, according to a poll from the Pew Research Center.

According to the survey . . . evangelicals are among the most likely to say that they have prayed for an end to the virus, with 82 percent saying they've done so. Among religious "nones"— those who describe their religion as "nothing in particular"—36 percent say they have prayed about the virus. And 15 percent of those who generally seldom or never pray say they have prayed for an end to the crisis.[2]

The two studies are not as far apart as they may at first appear. The *Post* article acknowledged that "older people are more likely to say they've prayed for an end [to coronavirus]," along with a number of other groups, including women, Blacks, Hispanics, Republicans, and evangelicals. Which, of course, still leaves out many Millennials, who in both studies lag behind other groups in reporting that they practice religion.

So that is where religion stands in the United States: a likely decline as a younger generation ages. What does this mean for our ever-evolving conception of faith in the twenty-first century? And what does it mean for how we understand the plight of people of faith around the world who—COVID-19 aside— struggle with issues very different from our own?

I began this book as a way of understanding how Christians in the Middle East, the birthplace of Christianity, have survived in the most turbulent of times. In a sense, it grew into a book about how people pray to survive their own most turbulent times.

More than 93 percent of the people living in the Middle East today identify as Muslim.[3] Islamic fundamentalist groups, in particular ISIS, have ravaged parts of Iraq and Syria and brought those countries' already decimated Christian populations to the verge of extinction. In Egypt, Christian Copts face legal and societal discrimination. In Gaza, which in the fourth century was entirely Christian, fewer than one thousand Christians remain.

I traveled to these places to try to record for history people whose villages, cultures, and ethos would perhaps not be standing in one hundred years' time.

But I also wanted to write about the people I met along the way, whose faith and resilience allowed them to survive, and to pay tribute to those who had vanished—some of whom had great faith, others no faith at all.

1

IRAQ

2002-2019

In the dying months of Saddam Hussein's regime in Iraq, the Ministry of Information, which controlled the movements of the press, granted my request to travel the country by car.

That long and melancholy voyage, shadowed by the coming American invasion, began in 2002. I usually had two companions on this trip: a driver, the kindly Munzer, a transplanted Palestinian Sunni whose family had emigrated to Iraq in 1948; and a translator, Reem, a woman from Babil Province, home of the capital of ancient Babylonia.[1] On some parts of the journey, there was also a bad-tempered minder accompanying us, graciously provided by the ministry. He was tasked with spying on us and taking detailed notes about where we went and whom we saw. But I only found that out later. He filed a daily report on our activities. Occasionally there was another translator as well. Ali moonlighted as a Martin Scorsese–worshipping film scholar. He and Munzer had a tumultuous relationship and sometimes came close to blows, so we tried to keep them separated.

Munzer had a 1987 Oldsmobile, nearly the same model that Hillary Clinton said she drove from Little Rock to Washington when her husband became president. I would load the car with fruit and water, a medical kit, and emergency supplies, and we would begin driving up and down, north and south, east and west across the country.

For me, these trips were accompanied by a sense of mournfulness because I knew even then, as we were traversing the endless highways constructed during Saddam Hussein's regime—Basra to Baghdad, Baghdad to Mosul—that I would never take those routes so effortlessly again. Although the invasion had not yet happened, the trip took place at a time when it was predictable, and everyone knew it. The highways, the villages, the way of life in the cities and in the countryside—all of this was sure to change.

But the war to come turned out to be worse than many expected. With the invasion of 2003 and the insurgent war that followed, Iraq itself would virtually disappear. The land of date trees, oases, and deserts would end up being marked by checkpoints and graves. But although I could not know then the extent of the anguish that would fall on this beguiling place, I was sure as we drove through those biblical ruins in the ancient land of the prophets, through languid farming villages and dusty cities, that they would be forever altered once the bombs started falling.

Part of what I had set out to do was to search for the descendants of ancient Christians. The biblical stories I had grown up with all seemed to begin in Mesopotamia, the land between two rivers, in what would become modern Iraq: Adam and Eve in the Garden of Eden, Abraham's flourishing birthplace of Ur, the stories of Daniel in the lions' den and Ezekiel in Babylon.

My childhood Bible had drawings of the Garden of Eden, full of immense trees with a man and a woman nearly naked, shaded by foliage. In the pastel children's Bible I was given for my First Communion, there were drawings of the couple fleeing the garden after tasting the forbidden fruit. The beautiful garden, sensual in its lushness, disappeared from their grasp forever. Then came yet another punishment, the flood.

The Garden of Eden was believed to have been in what was ancient Mesopotamia because of the description of four ancient rivers that kept it green and fertile. In the Book of Genesis, these rivers are clearly named: "A river flowed out of Eden to water the garden, and there it divided and became four rivers. The name of the first is the Pishon. . . . The name of the second river is the Gihon. . . . And the name of the third river is the Tigris. . . . And the fourth river is the Euphrates." Tracking biblical geography is complex, and I am not a biblical scholar. Modern locations remain uncertain. For instance, two rivers I know well, the Tigris and the Euphrates, which today run from Turkey through Iraq into the Persian Gulf, may not be in the same geographic location as the biblical rivers. The locations of the Gihon and the Pishon are unknown. After Genesis, they are never mentioned again in the Bible. And rivers are famous for changing their course over time.[2]

The biblical Eden might have been in any number of places other than Iraq—including Turkey, which also has portions of the ancient rivers running through it. And there are a legion of Eden-seekers, people who spend their entire lives searching for answers about where the garden may have been and what might actually have happened in it. They include scientists, archaeologists, biblical scholars, and crackpots.

Gihon might be the Nile, although some scientists have mentioned the Indus or the Ganges as possibilities. The Bible actually does not refer to the "Tigris"; it refers to "Hiddekel." Most Bible translations connect this to the Tigris and translate it as such. But some who have studied the issue maintain that they are quite different rivers. Some have even suggested that the biblical rivers were actually canals. The truth is, we know very little of the geographical features of the earth before the alleged devastating flood.

For certain, Abraham, the patriarch of Christianity, Islam, and Judaism, came from Ur of the Chaldees, a Sumerian city-state in Mesopotamia. Nowadays, Ur is called Tell el-Muqayyar, and it is near Nasiriyah, a town in Iraq about 225 miles south-east of Baghdad. It is here where, thousands of years after Abraham's death, in the last weeks of March 2003, US forces would fight Iraqis in a bloody effort to occupy their land. As we drove south of Baghdad several months before that war began, I was lost between both worlds. I would imagine life along the Euphrates in the time of Abraham, the swaying date trees, the merchants, the scribes and the temples, and then I would be brought to reality with thoughts about the upcoming war: how I was going to survive, what the landscape would look like once American troops arrived. This was part of the lure of Iraq for me: the certainties of its ancient past were wreathed by the imminent uncertainties of a chaotic present.

I was a war reporter who was supposed to be immune to fear, but that was not the truth. I was anxious, frightened, unnerved. I tried to hide it from my small team of travelers by taking notes, poring over maps—ancient and modern—and speaking to as many people as I could, most of whom were too terrified to speak, sensing the looming war. Like Adam and Eve's days in Eden, it was a time before a fall, and people were all too aware that the Iraq they knew, like Eden, could soon be out of their grasp—perhaps lost forever.

Still, the grandeur of the ancient places stunned me. Ur, Abraham's birthplace, was once the center of an affluent empire. Considered by many to be the world's first great cosmopolitan city, it dominated southern Mesopotamia after the fall of the

Akkadian Empire. Civilization reached a height in Ur around 2000 BCE, in the days when Abraham is thought to have lived.

The city had great wealth and nearly sixty thousand inhabitants. There were merchant ships, weaving establishments, and factories that produced wool clothing and carpets, which were exported. The Great Ziggurat, a massive four-thousand-year-old pyramid whose remains were rediscovered in the nineteenth century, rose above the city.

There were foreign quarters in Ur for traders, who came to the city from as far away as the Mediterranean, 750 miles to the West, and from the Indus civilization, called Meluhha by ancient Iraqis, 1,500 miles to the east. The marketplace was full of curiosities and the sounds of exotic languages. There was plenty of innovation. The creators of one of the earliest forms of writing, cuneiform, came from Ur. I slept in houses that were not so different from the ones that existed in ancient times—flat, square buildings with ladders to the roof, where we would sleep in summer to avoid the stifling, airless heat. In Abraham's day, men would gather in the courtyards to chat, bargain, and gossip, drinking from large urns with straws. In 2002, I saw men very much like their ancestors. They sat in the rooms drinking tea and smoking hookahs, while the women stayed in the kitchen or outside with the children. Technology, electricity, and medical science had come to Iraq, but traditions and society had a way of holding on.

Other prophets were said to have roamed across the region as well—or stayed there for a time unwillingly. Daniel, a heroic Jewish youth, most likely came from Jerusalem, but he was brought to Iraq in the time of the Babylonian captivity in the early sixth century BCE along with many of his fellow Jews. The Book of Daniel depicts the city under the Babylonian king, and later in the time of the Persian conqueror Cyrus, but also shows Daniel's righteousness and wisdom in the face of oppression, and depicts how God continues to work his plans when all seems to be lost. Some modern scholars argue that Daniel never existed; others claim he is buried in what is now modern Iran or Iraq.

Ezekiel, another Hebrew prophet in exile in Babylon, also lived during the reign of Nebuchadnezzar, around the time the Hanging Gardens of Babylon were built. He called himself a "sentinel for the house of Israel," sending messages of hope to the exiled Jews while warning them against idolatry. In his visions, he saw the rebirth of Jerusalem, but he also stressed the need to preserve Hebrew traditions in preparation for the day when God would lead them back to Israel, reporting how God spoke of the day that he would "[bring] them back from the peoples and [gather] them from their enemies' lands, and through them [vindicate] my holiness in the sight of many nations."[3] Ultimately, the prophecies of Ezekiel were about redemption. As I drove through Iraq in those final prewar days, what people seemed to seek most was solace. "Tell me a war is not coming," they would say to me. There was very little comfort I could give them without telling bald-faced lies.

The American invasion was planned for the early spring of 2003, but there was little solid information about it. We knew it was coming, though we were not sure when or how, what day, what hour. Rumors circulated through Baghdad before we left about how Saddam would light the city on fire, or how foreigners would be rounded up and put in Abu Ghraib prison.

It was with a kind of resigned relief that I heaved my bags and a few blankets and pillows into the trunk of the car as we set out. We were cut off from the world on those road trips. The Internet in Baghdad was carefully controlled, and there was no cellphone service. I did have a smuggled satellite phone, but it was illegal to use it, and the level of paranoia I felt from months of living under the Mukhabarat, Saddam's secret police, was fierce. I dressed in the dark, knowing that I was being filmed. Maids searched my room and went through my notebooks. If I had guests in my hotel room, I turned up the volume of the television to make it more difficult for anyone to hear us when we spoke. Most of all, I never really knew who I was talking to and what they might report back to save their own skin. I had to assume that every word was being monitored. Every night when I left the Ministry of Information, an official sealed my satellite phone with sealing wax, and every morning he removed the wax. This was so he could tell if I opened it or not and used it illegally overnight. The penalty for that was certainly deportation, but it could have been worse—jail. That was the way we lived in Saddam's Iraq—there was uncertainty, fear, and paranoia at an uncomfortably high level.

Throughout the trip, my goal was to meet people and write about all that I encountered. Although occasionally, Reem and I would watch Iraqi TV, mostly we talked to people and immersed ourselves in local gossip. There are rumors that inevitably come with the end of a regime. It was an overbearingly tense and claustrophobic time.

"What will happen when the Americans come?" I would ask Reem and Ali. In Baghdad, children were digging trenches, and sandbags were being piled on street corners. But no one wanted to look too far ahead. Reem usually stayed silent. Once, Munzer answered, "We will fight!"

We drove south to the sacred Shia cities of Najaf and Karbala. We drove north to Saddam's hometown of Tikrit, where we watched immense, pompous military parades. We spent Eid al-Fitr, the festival marking the end of Ramadan, with a farmer, who proudly slaughtered a goat in front of us in an alleyway—a gruesome killing—and then served it to us for lunch. Once,

Reem and I went to the Imam Hussein Shrine in Karbala. Reem went inside and came back with a green ribbon for me. "It means," she said solemnly, "you get a wish."

Reem knew what I wanted. I was getting married in August. I bowed my head, closed my eyes, and wished for a happy marriage, for safety, and for a healthy child someday.

Along the way on our long days of traveling, we met Iraqis from many different sects and tribes. Iraq is an extraordinarily diverse country. We stayed with Yazidis and with blue-eyed Assyrians, and we met Sunni Arabs, Shia Arabs, Turkmen, Chaldeans, Circassians, Armenians, Jews, and Kurds.

All of these groups had reason to fear the coming American invasion, but the fear among the Christians was particularly acute. The Christian community has been present in Iraq since the time of Thomas the Apostle, whose finger bones were said to be discovered in Mosul in 1964 during the restoration of a church. Thomas reportedly brought the religion there in the first century CE. The Assyrians of the time quickly adopted Christianity, making the Eastern Aramaic speakers still living there one of the oldest Christian communities in the world. It coexisted with the local religion for a few hundred years until the latter began to die out. The Christians themselves, however, began to be persecuted in the seventh century with the arrival of Islam.

The community persisted despite massacres by the Mongols and Mamluks in the thirteenth century and the widespread destruction ordered by the Turco-Mongol conqueror Tamerlane approximately one hundred years later. In recent years, persecution has triggered an exodus. Before the war, when I was living in Baghdad, there were nearly 1.4 million Christians in Iraq, mainly Catholic Chaldeans. Today, there are between 250,000 and 300,000 left, according to a report published by Samuel Tadros, a Senior Fellow at the Hudson Institute, a conservative think tank based in Washington, DC. But no one really knows the correct figure, because there hasn't been a census for thirty years.

On most Sundays in the Saddam era, I would worship at the white-stoned St. Mary's Chaldean Church in Shorja district. Sitting with people meditating and singing quietly in an ancient language was a respite for me from the madness of prewar Iraq and from my dank hotel room in the Al Rasheed, where everything was watched and recorded. Everywhere I went, there were the Mukhabarat in their leather jackets and furry mustaches. They always looked the same, shamelessly conspicuous. Journalists and diplomats all feared the compromising films, often of a sexual nature, that were said to be taken of visitors. After the war, a British security official found an entire building of such films—the Mukhabarat had kept them in storage in the event they needed to blackmail someone. On nights when Saddam's crazed sons, Qusay and Uday, visited my hotel, everyone spoke in a whisper. I would stay locked in my room.

After Mass, my Palestinian driver and I would have lunch at a Christian restaurant, Saj Al Reef. They served delicious chicken sandwiches on toasted *saj*, dough placed on a hot griddle and baked over a wood fire, something like an Iraqi pizza. I frequented a Christian grocery store that sold alcohol and other rare and pricey provisions. When I could get permission from Iraqi officials, I would drive north to Mosul and Nineveh to meet with Christian communities. Staying in people's homes, I would get to celebrate holidays and talk to the priests and bishops.

"In five years, we will be no more," one priest told me in 2003. Seventeen years later, I think back on what he said. He was not entirely correct—Christians still exist in Iraq. But their numbers dwindle with each passing year, and their position is precarious. At the time, his prediction seemed alarmist. But he was not far off.

After the US invasion, insurgency groups launched a series of bombings targeting churches. On October 31, 2010, six ISIS jihadists wearing suicide vests entered the Church of Our Lady of Salvation in Baghdad during the evening Mass. They killed fifty-eight people, including priests, worshippers, and police officers. Some were murdered by sprays of gunfire, others by grenades. The brutal attack was an act of retaliation against a Florida evangelical minister who had threatened to burn the Quran. In a later message, ISIS called the church "the dirty den of idolatry."

A few days before Christmas in 2002, we knelt with terrified Christians celebrating Mass in Mosul as the congregation prayed for the war to end. A few months later, on Ash Wednesday, we sat with a group of Chaldean Christians—descendants of some of the oldest Christians in the world. This sect, the Chaldean Catholic Church, had grown from a faction of the Assyrian Church of the East during a schism in the sixteenth century. The church we visited, St. Mary's, on Palestine Street in Baghdad, would be blown up by a bomb in 2009 as worshippers were leaving.

It was a jarring time, surreal and strange, poised, waiting for the apocalypse to start. On the trip around the country, I did seek out monasteries, universities, libraries, archaeological sites, and hospitals, in search of documents and books, but mostly I spent my time talking to people. I asked them about their standing in society and how secure they felt—or didn't feel—in their communities. I listened to their stories of the biblical Abraham, of Assyrian kings, and of Nineveh, city of great sin. I traced maps of Mesopotamia, the ancient land that also included parts of what are now Kuwait, Syria, and Turkey. We stopped driving when it got dark and slept in eerie, empty hotels with only the omnipresent Mukhabarat for company.

In a kind of fever of those last days of peacetime, I collected as many names and phone numbers of ordinary Iraqis as I could. I wanted to be able to return after the war and track how many of them were still living, and find out how radically their lives had changed.

I never really left Iraq. After a brief period when my son was born in 2004, I thought I would not go again for many years. But Iraq has a pull, and I returned when Luca was only six months old. After that, I would visit as often as I could, sometimes several times a year.

I would pull out the old notebooks from time to time, trying to find places or people. But so many of the people in my notebook were gone: emigrated, dead, or simply vanished. And some of the places had been overrun or were too dangerous even for me to access. It was as though the country that had existed before the flood of war descended had disappeared.

One sunny morning in Baghdad, Munzer and I talked our way into the Iraq Museum. It would be looted in April 2003, when, over the course of two days, thousands of artifacts were removed. Many of them are still lost, though the museum reopened a little over a decade later. Another time, Munzer got us into an obscure Baghdad museum devoted to gifts and tributes to Saddam: a testament to his egomania, like the towering bronze statues and gaudy portraits of him everywhere.

But what stands out most in the haze of memory was our trip to the place that had come to be known as the remains of the mythical Hanging Gardens of Babylon. Reem and I spent a gloomy day wandering through the gardens, which were in disarray—a sad fate for one of the Seven Wonders of the Ancient World (if in fact they were not just a creation for the Travel Channel). There were no green meadows arranged by Nebuchadnezzar II for his queen, Amytis; nor was there a Tower of Babel in the background. It was empty except for one lone family wandering through the ruins and a darkened gift shop selling key chains.

Saddam often compared himself to Nebuchadnezzar II, king of Chaldea, the country that existed between the late ninth and mid-sixth centuries BCE in the marshy southeastern corner of Mesopotamia. Many people know how that story ended: the king conquered Jerusalem and destroyed the First Temple, exiling many Jews to Babylon. But according to the Book of Daniel in the Old Testament—written in the second century BCE and combining a prophetic history with a cruel vision of the end times—God humbled the great conqueror. The king went mad, succumbing to bouts of shrieking insanity and living in the wilderness—eating grass like the cattle—for seven years.

Reem was silent after this stop, sitting in the back seat with an oversized black plastic handbag at her feet. The Hanging Gardens of Babylon had disturbed her. They seemed to symbolize fallen empires and worlds disappearing.

I knew she felt waves of endless anxiety about what lay ahead for her, for her family, and for her country. "Our country will vanish," she repeated like a lament. Her studies had been halted, as had any plans for marriage. "There's no future for anyone right now," she said without a hint of self-pity.

She stared out of the car window, taking in the endless rows of swaying date trees along the highway. Ali had told me once that the trees represented the soul of the Iraqis, their profound connection to their country and their sacred land. The memory of those dreamy, plentiful trees haunted me after the invasion. The Iraqi soul had been lost.

The people we visited in those strange, dark days were mostly in a panic. The Christian worshippers at the church in Mosul sat in tears on cold pews, begging God to spare them from another war. They prayed in Aramaic, the language Jesus spoke. I found it to be achingly beautiful. Nazareth and Capernaum, near the Sea of Galilee, where Jesus did much of his preaching, were Aramaic-speaking communities in his day.

Shortly before Christmas in 2002, the relics of St. Thérèse of Lisieux arrived in Mosul. Thérèse, a French saint known as "the little flower of Jesus," had died from tuberculosis in 1897 at the age of twenty-four. This was but one stop on the long tour the relics made around the world—they visited everywhere from Ireland and the United States to the Philippines.[*]

In the unheated church in Mosul, I sat with an older woman, blue eyed and fair skinned, who bent over her rosary beads as the priest carried the box of relics through the church. She reminded me of my mother in her devotion and her courage. When we spoke, she whispered in broken English and French. She shook slightly, perhaps from the cold.

She said she would not flee Iraq when the war started. "Where will we go?" she whispered. "The archbishop has begged the Christians not to leave. This is our home, our ancient land. If we go, we are deserting what is also ours."

When it was our turn, we joined the snaking line that led to St. Thérèse's relics. As we approached, people bent in reverence to kiss the glass that shielded the bones, as if the dead saint were a kind of talisman for protection from the darkness ahead. It reminded me of Good Friday services from my childhood: the cross being unrobed of its purple cloth bit by bit and people kneeling to kiss it.

We reached the front of the line and knelt before the relics. Some people didn't kneel but simply laid their cold palms on the glass beseechingly, looking inside.

The more I talked to Iraqis in those days, especially to Christians and other minorities, the more I realized that most of them had no plan for when "zero hour," the American invasion, actually came. It's always hard to really believe that war is coming to your doorstep.

I learned about what it's like when war is coming from the many refugees I had interviewed over the years. In a panic, with

danger near, what do you take with you? Photos, marriage cer-
tificates, pets, food, your favorite article of clothing? Or perhaps
you have time for nothing at all, just time enough to run out the
door, forever leaving your old life behind.

There is always a sense of denial in the buildup to war, a
vague hope that someone—some diplomat, some world leader,
God—will stop it.

It was in Mosul that I first realized, while talking to the
members of a Christian family who had begun some simple
preparations—storing water in their cupboards and hoarding
candles—that all of these ancient people were in grave danger
of disappearing, of being swallowed up like Jonah inside the
whale. Chaldeans, Babylonians, Sumerians, Akkadians, these
intricate branches of ancient Christianity, were all threatened
with extinction.

In Bashiqa, a village northeast of Mosul in the al-Hamdaniya
district, I met a small community of Yazidi people who welcomed me into their family life. I spent part of a week there,
attending a wedding and then a funeral. This was long before the Yazidi genocide. In these times, the Saddam days, the
Yazidi were isolated, but they lived their lives in the same manner to which they had been accustomed for hundreds of years.
We stayed with a family with five children and ate with the
local mayor. The women remained in the kitchen, preparing
vast quantities of incense-scented rice, lamb, flat bread, and
honey, passing their plump babies back and forth as they got up
to tend to other children. Aside from a few rusted Chevrolets
parked outside their simple homes, the Yazidis' traditions had
changed relatively little in more than two millennia.

One of the elders sat on the floor and explained their faith to
me. He spoke of how they were often wrongly accused of being
devil-worshippers and described the injustices they had suffered
because of it. They worship Melek Taus, the "Peacock Angel,"

whom they also equate with Satan. But in a break from traditional Christian theology elsewhere, they believe that this archangel repented. Their bible, which tells his story, is called the *Black Book*.

There was something simple and humble about the Yazidis' dignity and isolation, as well as the fact that they were great survivors. They had been gravely persecuted through the ages, most of all—at least until ISIS arrived as their ultimate tormentors—by Saddam.

Twelve years later, in the summer of 2014, ISIS raced through Iraq swallowing up entire Yazidi and Christian villages, killing or displacing anyone who did not embrace their strict Salafist ways. The Yazidis were once again driven out, forced to seek refuge on a bare mountainside near Sinjar, where they faced scorching temperatures and a lack of water, food, and medical care. They were eventually rescued and brought to refugee camps, but ISIS maintained control over the Yazidi homeland for several years. The Yazidis became refugees and wanderers, just as they had feared.

My son was only a few months old in August 2004, when I returned to a new Baghdad. It was not the same city I had left behind a month after Saddam fell, in April 2003. My room at the Al Hamra Hotel had not changed much—there were threadbare sheets, chipped sinks—but we no longer lived under the same paranoia as we had under Saddam. When I turned on the television, I saw, in fact, images of a grizzled Saddam Hussein in custody. He looked like a feral animal. Six months earlier, on December 13, 2003, he had been pulled—"like a rat," as President George W. Bush put it—from his hiding place in a spider hole near Tikrit, the same city where Reem and I had watched proud Nebuchadnezzar-style military parades. Most of his Ba'athist cronies who had terrorized me and my colleagues at the Ministry of Information were either on the run or in hiding.

"Ladies and gentlemen, we got him," announced a jubilant Paul Bremer, the man appointed by the Americans to run Iraq, at a press conference later that day (his formal title was director of the Coalition Provisional Authority). But it was no triumph. I was no fan of Saddam's, but I sensed that a gigantic scab had been picked, leaving a raw and bloody wound with no ability to heal.

Everyone I knew had left Baghdad. Reem was in Dubai, Ali had gone into hiding, and Munzer had run away. The country was being ripped apart at the seams; Munzer's prediction that they would fight was perhaps even more accurate than he had anticipated. Everyone was fighting. The Sunni insurgents had risen up and were battling the US-led coalition. Later, they would go after local collaborators who worked with the new Iraqi security forces.

REPUBLIC OF FEAR

In August 2011, a car bomb exploded outside the Holy Family Church in the oil-rich southern city of Kirkuk, killing twenty people. The year before, in the worst massacre since the 2003 war, around one hundred worshippers at Our Lady of Salvation Church attending a 6:00 p.m. Mass had been herded into the center of the church, and gunmen from an al-Qaeda-affiliated group had showered them with bullets. Fifty-eight people died.

"We've lost part of our soul now," said Rudy Khalid, a sixteen-year-old Christian who lived near the church, speaking to the *New York Times*. "Our destiny, no one knows what to say of it." "They came to kill Iraq, not Iraqis," Bassam Sami, a survivor of the Our Lady of Salvation attack, told the *Times*. As the reporter explained, Bassam Sami had "huddled in a room for four hours before security forces managed to free him." Bassam Sami said, "They came to kill the spirit of Iraq. They came to kill the reason to live, every dream that you want to make true."[5]

The mélange that had made Iraq diverse—the religions, the traditions, the fables, the prophets, the ceremonies—was being eradicated. It wasn't only the Christians. Nearly the entire Jewish community had fled. I remembered how a friend and colleague of mine, the writer Tim Judah, whose ancestors had come from Iraq, had, just as Saddam fell, been asked by their families abroad to find the last Jews of Baghdad.

In the spring of 2003, Judah toured the city, showing up unannounced to the homes of these stunned and terrified people, and then handed them his phone so they could tell their families they were alive. Buildings were on fire, and there was looting of Saddam's ministries and palaces. In the past, Iraq's Jews would make a pilgrimage to the Prophet Ezekiel's shrine in the town of Al Kifl on Passover. As it was, coincidently, Passover, Judah and a family he had found left to make the pilgrimage—for them for the last time before they fled Iraq forever.

"Until World War II, roughly a quarter of Baghdad's population was Jewish," Judah later wrote in *Granta* magazine. "In June 1941, following a Nazi-inspired coup, 179 Jews died and almost a thousand were wounded in a pogrom while the police and army stood by. Until 1948 there were still 150,000 Jews in Iraq but by 1951, after the Israeli government had organized airlifts, the vast majority of them had left. The government placed severe restrictions on those who stayed. Even so, a community of some six thousand lingered on. But now, according to those that remain, their numbers add up to the grand total of thirty-four people."[6]

It was as though all of Iraq were dying as the minorities were being driven out or killed. Judah's family could trace their lineage in Iraq back to the 1540s. In March 2021, with death of Dr.

Thafer Eliyahu, who had kept his Jewishness secret, there were believed to be only four Jews left. "Today it's hard to imagine that so many Jews lived here," Judah mused.

Shortly after the attack on Our Lady of Salvation, I went back to stay in Baghdad with the writer Tamara Chalabi, whose father, Ahmed Chalabi, was Iraq's deputy prime minister in 2005 and 2006. Before that, following the American invasion, Ahmed had been one of the most controversial figures in Iraq. He had served as an adviser to those in the Bush administration, all neoconservatives, or neocons, who had pushed for war; along with powerful lobbying groups, he had provided unreliable evidence that Saddam was in possession of weapons of mass destruction and had links to al-Qaeda, claims we now know were untrue.

After the invasion, Chalabi was in charge of "de-Ba'athification," the removal of senior officeholders judged to have been key supporters of the deposed Saddam. It was an attempt to dismantle a regime, but it was a crass mistake. I remember attending "classes" for those officers who were meant to be reeducated and thinking to myself how indiscriminate the policy was: the lack of due process, the unfair dismissals for those who were simply rank-and-file and had joined the party because it was the only path to career advancement. The Ministry of Education, which had been in charge of teaching propaganda to students, and other departments were dismantled entirely.

I had known Chalabi since the 1990s, when he was the leader of the Iraqi National Congress, an Iraqi national alliance in exile committed to overthrowing Saddam. His attempts to unite the Kurds in the north and the Marsh Arabs in the south with the help of the CIA had failed miserably when his Washington cronies let him down. Those who had believed in him eventually faded away, one by one, until he had no allies left. Eventually, Chalabi and the neoconservatives fell out. They pushed him aside, and the last time I saw him, at his Baghdad farm, he was aggrieved and angry. He died in 2015.

The Chalabis are an old, wealthy, and gracious Shia family. Tamara is a Harvard-educated historian with a PhD. She did her dissertation on the Shias of Lebanon, her mother's homeland. She was writing a memoir, the story of her father's political family, with recollections of a haughty and beautiful grandmother, grand palaces, and lost Ottoman traditions. She was also involved in other projects to bring Baghdad some semblance of normality: trying to work with archivists at the National Library, establishing a young historians' prize, and restoring the Chalabi farm near Kadhimiya.

The farm was an organic project intended to be replicable so that Iraqis could learn to care for the soil and benefit from good produce, which would save money and improve their health. The farmlands of Iraq had been largely ruined from the effects of the war, and Tamara said she wanted to "purify" the soil. As we walked through rows of vegetables, she described the earth as though she were describing the people, explaining that it had been so damaged by the pain and loss that it was unable to produce new life until it was once again treated with proper care.

Tamara was training local women to plant and sow. She taught them to use donkey manure and leaves as compost. I watched them work under the blistering sun, wearing large straw sun hats, methodically planting and pulling weeds. The American troops were supposed to be pulling out soon, and people wondered what life would be like after they were gone. One sticky afternoon, Tamara and I drove to the gravesite of Gertrude Bell, the British Arabist who had helped draw the map of modern Iraq in the wake of the breakup of the Ottoman Empire. Bell was one of the first women to graduate from Oxford with a degree in modern history (though she and the other female graduate in her year were not listed with the men of the class). I had been intrigued by Bell's life throughout my time living in Baghdad during the Saddam era.

It was a tragic story. Bell had been deeply in love with two men, both statesmen as strong and vibrant as she was. One was deemed unsuitable for marriage by her Victorian father's standards, and the other was already married and unable to leave his wife. The former died in Persia, and the latter fought and died in Gallipoli in 1915. So deep was her heartbreak that she took to the desert on horseback and began surveying and studying Arab tribes, seeking solace in her work. Her studies and mapmaking were brilliant, but her private life was empty. She died, not yet sixty years old, by her own hand in her Baghdad home. She was rumored to have died a virgin. She was a brave, strong, and inspirational woman who had loved Iraq with the kind of passion reserved for a first love.

During the Saddam years, I had often crept through a barbed-wire fence to visit the old, uninhabited British Embassy on the river, where Bell and her rival and friend Freya Stark used to stay in between long desert trips. I would sit on the riverbank and imagine the parties that went on inside it in the time before Saddam: the whispers, the diplomatic intrigue, the swish of Bell's stiff silk evening gowns, and the sight of her with a velvet ribbon around her neck, dressed for dinner after a day of mapmaking.

For many years during the Saddam era, Bell's grave had been untended, and Tamara had started a project to restore it. As Tamara and I bent in the hot sun to pull weeds, with our headscarves and our long abayas covering our bodies, I wondered what Bell would think of the hollow city now, and the destroyed country she had loved so much.

Tamara's armed guards hovered near us as we stood looking at the grave. We had driven to the farm silently in an armored car. Everyone was worried about the possibility of stalling in traffic and being trapped next to a car bomb.

In 2014, three years after we had visited Bell's grave, I returned. I had roamed the region before and during the Arab Spring, beginning in Tunisia in 2010, then Egypt in 2011, and west to Libya soon after, and finally moving to Syria, where I began recording atrocities against civilians. More Christians had fled Iraq during the years I had been away. Everything had changed. The little stability we had seen when we cleaned Gertrude Bell's grave was gone; Tamara's organic food project was on hold, as were most things. The American troops had pulled out two years earlier. The roads—aside from the ones in the International Zone, where the embassies and the United Nations headquarters were now located, utterly removed from the Iraqi population—were appallingly bad.

There seemed to be no easing up of the sorrow that had dogged the Iraqi people since the invasion. The car bombings were back. One exploded on the airport road the day before I arrived. ISIS was swallowing up entire swaths of countryside, farms, and villages.

On June 10, ISIS fighters drove into Mosul, Iraq's second-largest city, and raised their black flag. Then they moved to Tikrit, Saddam's birthplace, before their advance stalled about twenty miles from Baghdad. ISIS confiscated farm animals, grain supplies, oil, antiquities, and women. They kidnapped anyone they thought would bring them cash. The women were ordered to don headscarves.

Christians, terrorized, fled. ISIS wanted a return to Islam in its strictest seventh-century form, as they believed it was practiced by the Prophet Muhammad. Nothing else was tolerated. Those caught smoking were beaten and fined. A female dentist was beheaded for treating female patients. They chose Raqqa, in Syria, as their capital, installing strict Sharia law. They started beheading Western hostages, including two of my journalist colleagues, Steven Sotloff and James Foley. And they kept fighting to seize control of the whole of Iraq.

Soon there were reports that they were closer, in the so-called Baghdad belt surrounding the city. The fear was that, while ISIS was not poised to take the entire city, it could infiltrate it with sleeper cells and cause havoc with car and roadside bombs.

It was heartbreaking to see the tension in the city after the fall of Mosul. These people, who had lived through so much in the aftermath of the American invasion—sectarian killing sprees, roadside bombs that left headless corpses on the side of the road—were terrified once again. I returned several times in those years.

In the autumn of 2018, I went back to find those same Christians that I had known in the Saddam days, the ones I had prayed alongside in Mosul, or the Yazidis with whom I had attended weddings and funerals. So much had happened. These trips I now took to Iraq no longer meant terrifying overnight drives from Amman to Baghdad in pitch black, fraught with worries about bandits or checkpoints. Now I flew directly into Kurdistan from Istanbul's sophisticated airport. There were no more Saddam checkpoints, no mandatory blood tests for AIDS at the border—a strange requirement in the bad days, a futile exercise intended simply to humiliate foreigners. (For all the blood tests I was made to take in the middle of the night at the Iraqi border with Jordan, I never once saw the results, although I was always issued a paper stamped by Saddam's Ministry of Health.)

Now, Iraqi Airways brought me to Erbil, and from there I drove with ease to the Christian villages outside of Mosul. And although there was no Saddam and no Ministry of Information to hinder me and shadow my every move, there was something equally sinister in the air: a deep-rooted fear of extinction.

Those Christians who remained had survived another war, but just barely. Now they faced the prospect that their battle-hardened communities would cease to exist.

THE TIPPING POINT

Considered the oldest continuous Christian community on earth, Iraqi Christians have roots going back two thousand years. Yet this millennia-old connection may be coming to an end.

One man who had lived through the ISIS invasion and occupation spoke about these fears with me: "We're worried," he said. "Even with ISIS gone, there's another big threat: there is no work for us. Our enemy is emigration. People are leaving every day."

This is the tipping point, possibly the end of Christianity in the Middle East. Thousands are fleeing the birthplace of Christianity—the lands where the prophets wandered, where Jesus Christ walked and preached. And it's not only because of religious persecution, but also because of a bleak economic future. What does their fate mean to the West, and how can Christians fleeing the Middle East be understood in terms of the current migrant and refugee crisis?

In 2013 and 2014, I worked for the UN Refugee Agency in Lebanon, Iraq, Turkey, and Egypt, interviewing and gathering testimonies from Syrian refugees who had fled the war. Most of them knew they would never return to their homes in Hama or Homs; the question was where they would resettle. A majority told me they wanted to go to Sweden or Germany, but European countries were offering only a limited number of spaces. Most of them realized miserably that they would remain in the settlements or refugee camps for years, withering and rotting, until it was "safe enough" to return to Syria. Which it may never be.

Many of the Christians who had endured the ISIS years were intent on leaving Iraq for good. They knew that countries such as the United States and Canada would accept Christian refugees from the Middle East more readily than they would accept Muslims or those crossing the southern border from Latin America.

Evangelical Christians and religious groups worldwide were even pushing to allow Middle Eastern Christians to resettle. France, for instance, has a particularly strong movement to protect Christians from the Middle East. Former vice president Mike Pence, himself a born-again evangelical Catholic (he has described himself as "a pretty ordinary Christian"), was also a keen supporter of persecuted Christians. The unjust logic seemed to draw a distinction between the "good" Christian refugees and the "bad" Muslims, who were usually denied access to the United States. The drivers and staff who had protected and worked with me for years in Baghdad, who had risked their lives to help me document war crimes and the insurgency, were denied entrance to the United States simply because they were Muslim.

Back in Saddam Hussein's time, from 1979 to 2003, Christians in Iraq and throughout the region survived brutal dictatorships. Often they managed to live under Saddam, or the Assads or Hosni Mubarak, only through an exchange of loyalty. They gave their support in return for protection. Their generational attachment to the land gave them the resolve to live through periods of terror and insecurity. Yet, once Saddam fell, even before the rise of ISIS, they knew they would no longer be able to protect their communities.

Saddam's Iraq was ruled by the secular Ba'ath Party, which, like the secular regimes in Egypt, Syria, and Algeria, had long protected Christians in exchange for their support. Saddam belonged to a Sunni denomination that made up less than 30 percent of Iraq's population. Because his government was itself a minority government, other minorities, including Christians, enjoyed a degree of security. Many Iraqi Christians told me they felt much more protected under that regime than they did after it fell. "Life under Saddam was difficult," said Catherine, a nurse in Baghdad who worshipped at St. Mary's before it was bombed. "But most people will tell you it is better than what we have now. We felt safe."

It is hard to imagine benefiting from a regime as brutal as Saddam's. Yet during that time there existed a kind of social contract in Iraq between minorities and the regime. Adeed Dawisha, a professor at the University of Miami in Ohio, quoted in a summary of the issues affecting Christians in the region by *PBS NewsHour*, explained it like this: "Under Saddam, it was understood that if you don't interfere in politics, then you are provided with a good life. If the Christians supported Saddam, [it was] not because they loved what he was doing, it was in fear of the alternative."[7]

As a result, Christians prospered economically. They were "businessmen, doctors, lawyers, and engineers," the *NewsHour* article noted. They ran the shops, the markets, and the better hotels. A select few were part of the political elite—such as Tariq Aziz, a Chaldean who was foreign minister and deputy prime minister under Saddam. In the Saddam days, the Chaldeans, alongside other groups of Iraqi Christians, did well economically. Their families were provided for, and they had a secure foothold in society. According to Brian Katulis, a national security expert with the Center for American Progress, who also spoke with *PBS NewsHour*, all of this meant there was a "network of protection . . . [in] Saddam's inner circle [that] . . . trickled on down" to the Christian community. But despite the supposed secularism of Saddam's regime, ancient rifts endured.[8]

After the 2003 invasion, attacks against Christians became more pronounced, inspired by Osama bin Laden's radical interpretation of Islam. A Sunni Jordanian named Abu Musab al-Zarqawi planted the seeds of al-Qaeda in Iraq in 2004. His targets were Shiite Muslims (who are seen as inauthentic believers by extreme Sunnis) and Christians. At the same time, Jamaat Ansar al-Sunna, another jihadist group fighting against US troops and their allies, began to threaten Christian families in Iraq.[9] As the years went by, jihadist groups shifted their attention from the "far enemy" of the West to the "near enemy," local Christians and minorities together with the regimes that protected them.

Having been lulled into a false sense of security under Saddam, the Chaldeans found themselves mired in bloody chaos in his aftermath. There was a dramatic spike in brutal crimes against their community. Cardinals and priests were kidnapped, tortured, and murdered, along with anyone thought to have money, even if they did not. By the time ISIS came, the persecution of Chaldean Christians in Iraq was being called a genocide.

In August 2014, as ISIS was pushing farther into Christian territory in Iraq, a Chaldean community leader in San Diego, Mark Arabo, began to push for safety measures and humanitarian aid. He relayed a desperate message he had received from inside Iraq: "By the time you guys do everything you're doing, there will be no Christians left (in Iraq). We'll all be dead."

"This is our chance to act," Arabo said at the time. "My worst fear is that we'll look back three years from now and say we could have stopped this genocide."[10]

On June 10, 2014, when ISIS took Mosul, I was in a hotel room in Baghdad lying on a dirty coverlet. I was listening to the BBC. The hotel was owned by Christians—my driver had taken me there believing I would be safer from kidnapping in that hotel than in any of the others in the city. It was steaming hot outside. There was a pool, and even though it was dirty, I swam in it once in an attempt to calm my nerves after a long day of working. I waited until after dark because, even in a conservative one-piece bathing suit with a T-shirt over it, and even in a Christian hotel, I felt too exposed in the daytime. Still, men gathered to watch me do my laps. I crept out of the pool and donned a long robe and covered my head. The men snickered and stared. So I didn't go swimming in the pool again. But I wondered: If it was this bad in Baghdad, the most cosmopolitan and educated city of Iraq, how bad could it get with ISIS, whose members scorned women and wanted to push them back to the seventh century?

Earlier that same day, before I heard the BBC report about ISIS, the driver had rushed into my room in terror. He was hearing reports that ISIS was advancing on the capital. Everyone was stunned at how quickly the group had moved south, and my friends were talking about leaving the city. I couldn't help but think of the people still in Mosul. I was especially worried for the Christian and Yazidi families there who were now under ISIS control.

For days we had no news, and then the reports began to trickle in. Christians were told to leave or die. "In addition to forcing mass exodus from thousand-year-old villages," wrote Sajad Jiyad, a respected analyst from the Baghdad-based think tank Integrity and the Century Foundation, "ISIS militants destroyed churches, libraries, and monuments to wipe out any trace of these being Christian areas."

Shocked and worried for those inhabitants of Mosul, I drove across town to visit William Warda in his Baghdad home. Warda was the leader of political and military affairs for a party called the Assyrian Democratic Movement. Deeply rooted in his country, he was born in Mosul and had grown up in the city, graduating from the university there.

When I found him in his office, Warda was distraught. The news from Mosul was unreliable; no one quite knew what was going on. Warda was trying to reach relatives, but the phone lines were down. He kept picking up his cellphone, putting it down, and picking it up again, as if some kind of magic would restore the network.

"It's a cleansing of all Christians from the region," he said.

We sat silently drinking coffee in a dark room, and Warda shifted the small cup between his hands. His aides came in and out, speaking urgently to him in Arabic. Confused people— parishioners, friends—kept knocking at the door for advice. Should they stay in Iraq and risk extermination (the word they used in Arabic), or flee to relatives outside the country and risk living in permanent exile? Warda spoke softly to them and then returned to me.

"How can I tell them not to go?" he asked, his voice thick with emotion. "I know they have no future here. But if they go, we as Christians have no future here."

By the grace of God or sheer luck, Warda would survive ISIS's reign of terror in Iraq, though he would be irrevocably changed: How do you ever trust in life again if your world falls apart?

MAR MATTAI

On a warm autumn day, a few months after the final liberation of Mosul from ISIS in 2017, the photojournalist Nicole Tung and I were invited to lunch with some Christians. A group of neighbors and friends were gathering at Mar Mattai, or the Monastery of St. Matthew, one of the oldest Christian monasteries in the world. It had been founded in the fourth century by Matthew the Hermit, a noted healer and converter who practiced asceticism on the site, Mount Alfaf. The monastery seems to grow from the mountain's terrain. In the ninth century, more than seven thousand monks worshipped and communed amid the monastery's arched courtyards and corridors, which overlook stunning views of the surrounding countryside. By 2015, as ISIS came to the region, only five monks remained.

Lining the mountain's edge, the monastery is the same sandy color as the stone cliffs that jut out above and below. We arrived in the morning as the heat rose. I had walked up the hill to the monastery in the late morning light, and the priest and the gathering congregation greeted me with a kind of resigned wariness. I found a quiet spot by one of the walls and looked out at the dried-out landscape, imagining what it would have felt like to be there as ISIS was running wild. The monastery was twenty miles from Mosul, where more than one hundred thousand Christians had been displaced from their homes.

They had gone through so much, and a stranger, though welcomed, was another reminder of the trauma they had recently endured. One of the children led me to a wall at the edge of the monastery and pointed below to the brown dusty tracts of fields. From high above, I saw how close the villages were, and how exposed the road to Mosul was.

My hosts unloaded baskets of food and arranged themselves around a long table in the courtyard. A woman named Niser spread out a white tablecloth and laid out a plate of dolmas. "It's a way of celebrating that we still exist," she told me. More people were arriving—babies, children, grandparents, cousins, aunts, distant relations—all members of one of the oldest continuous Christian communities in the world. Many had not seen each other for three years, since the beginning of the ISIS brutality.

Their conversations, as they unpacked their food, centered on rebuilding: how to fix their charred homes and shattered churches, now pockmarked with shells and bullet holes. They wanted to restore their dwindling families. They wanted to find people who had been lost.

I sat quietly, talking to small groups of people and trying to record what had happened to them. I wanted details: How had they first received information that ISIS was closing in on Mosul? When did they decide to flee? What had they taken with them? In three decades of working with refugees, these are the questions I have always asked. In the days of the Bosnian War, when there were no cellphones, people passed information from village to village. In Syria, during the worst days of fighting, people got messages on WhatsApp. The Christians I spoke with at the monastery, who told their stories readily, reported that their families had been in close contact and made decisions together as to when they should flee, and when they went, they went en masse.

After the meal, when the heat became unbearable, people retreated to the cool shade of the small monk-like cells of the monastery. I went from room to room with my notebook, talking to each of them. The most anxious of the people I interviewed, it seemed, were the young. The older ones seemed resigned to a difficult life. "We are minorities, we have endured a lot already," one told me. But when I spoke to Sara Bahodij, a twenty-three-year-old from Mosul, she recounted the early days of ISIS with a shaky voice. She told me how the militants had raised the black flag and given Christians an ultimatum: convert to Islam or pay the *jizya*.

"How did they ask you?" I inquired gently, trying to soothe her.

"They came to our house," she replied. "They went door to door looking for Christians."

At first, she said, it wasn't too bad. Her family was able to remain in the city for a few months after the occupation because they paid.

"How much?" I asked.

She said there had been no set fee, but instead a sliding scale depending on a family's wealth.

"It could be $10,000, it could be $1,000, it was whatever they wanted to charge," Bahodij added bitterly. She told me that her father sold their gold—her mother's wedding gold, family gold—and in total paid the militants $800,000.

"It's all gone, our history," she said. Their land was confiscated. She described the feeling of having everything you had ever known suddenly slip away "between your fingers."

Even after paying off ISIS, her family did not feel safe. Christian women were used to adopting a more Western style: jeans, Turkish-made T-shirts, and knockoff handbags. The younger women often had long, flowing hair that came down past the waist. They looked less like Iraqis and more like Parisian schoolgirls, albeit not as wealthy. Now they had to cover up their hair and clothes with abayas and hijabs. Bahodij found shapeless garments, things she could use to cover her jeans. She felt ugly and angry.

The ISIS fighters had left, but then they came back. This time, they went from house to house, marking the doors with the letter N—an ancient reference to *Nazaria*, or Jesus of Nazareth. It was horribly reminiscent of the yellow stars that Jews were forced to wear during the Holocaust.

Daniel Williams, then an official with Human Rights Watch's Emergencies Team, recalled that the cleansing of Christians from Mosul and the surrounding area was highly organized. "A systematic campaign was underway," he wrote in 2016, describing how quickly the ethnic cleansing of Iraqi Christians had begun.[11]

After I spoke to Bahodij, she led me to Elham, a primary school teacher who looked much older than her fifty-nine years. She spoke of her childhood, of growing up in the Saddam days. It was not a bad life, she told me. She remembered that she "had many Muslim friends." But she always felt like an outsider in Iraq. "Even if we felt protected, we felt odd," she remembered.

"They still looked at us as if we were weird, because we were Christians and they were Muslims. I always felt they were looking at me as if I were wearing strange clothes."

In 2008, Elham told me, things began to unravel. Insurgency groups, the precursors to ISIS in Iraq, told her family to leave their simple home in Mosul. She was scared for her own life and for the lives of her family members. "They knocked on the door and said we would be safer if we left," she said. "They reminded me I had three sons."

It was not until the arrival of ISIS in August 2014 that she and her sons would finally flee. This time, they could not afford to ignore the jihadists' threats: ISIS rhetoric toward Christians had become more belligerent as the group's power increased across Iraq. In 2015, to spread more terror, ISIS released a video titled *A Message in Blood Written to the Nation of the Cross*, showing the execution of Ethiopian and Egyptian Christians. That October, the front page of one ISIS magazine featured a picture of St. Peter's Square in Rome with an ISIS flag superimposed over the obelisk that adorns the iconic center of Catholicism. The founder of ISIS, Abu Bakr al-Baghdadi, had promised to march "all the way to Rome" to "break the crosses" of the Christians and to "trade and sell their women."

Elham remembers the fear. She told the family to gather some of their things. They packed what they could in an hour and drove with a few Christian Orthodox families to Qaraqosh, an Assyrian Catholic town on the outskirts of Mosul, not far from the biblical cities of Nimrud and Nineveh.

Before ISIS, Qaraqosh, the country's largest Christian city, was one of the most prosperous towns in the region, with agricultural fields stretching for miles and successful leather and weaving industries. Elham was sure it would survive. It seemed incomprehensible to her that a thriving town could be overrun by jihadists no one had ever heard of. But it was. In August

2014, shortly after Elham and her family arrived, ISIS forces arrived from the south. Surrounding Christian towns were falling one by one. They burnt churches and smashed statues, toppled bell towers and destroyed icons. They broke crosses and left churches barren and naked, their roofs blown off, filled with scattered bullets from target practice or chemicals used to make bombs. Walking through the remnants of these battered churches two years later, I felt sickened and cold.

As ISIS advanced, people tried to move ahead of them, fleeing to the north. On August 6, 2014, Elham packed up her family up again, not sure where they would go. As they drove out of Qaraqosh, she saw the ISIS fighters arriving in the distance. This is what the future looks like, she thought, men in short pants with beards, waving guns. The family spent several months staying with friends or relatives, anyone who would host them. Other families ended up in teeming refugee camps outside of Erbil. Some went farther north, to Dohuk, and some slept for weeks on the ground below the chipped statue of Our Lady in Ain Kawa, a Christian suburb of Erbil, before finding temporary homes.

"We did not want to stay to welcome ISIS," Elham said, shuddering at the memory. They didn't unpack their bags. "I felt like we were frozen."

After such knowledge, what forgiveness? So asked T. S. Eliot in "Gerontion," his 1920 poem about history offering no redemption. Christianity is based on forgiveness and turning the other cheek. Yet how could these people ever recover? The level of abhorrence was startling. I remembered the sixteenth-century Ottoman bridge in Mostar, Stari Most, which had been commissioned by Suleiman the Magnificent, being blown up by Croatian paramilitary forces during the Bosnian War in 1993. That war was long, bitter, and rife with hatred. After the bridge—a symbol of coexistence between Muslims, Orthodox, and Catholics for centuries—came down, an old man, tears running down his face, said to me, "That bridge stood through so much: invasions, world wars. It took this much hatred to bring it down." I could only imagine the ISIS killing spree, the insanity of hatred that went into destroying the churches of Qaraqosh.

A man I met at Mar Mattai, Nazar Esa, also described fleeing Qaraqosh, which was his hometown.

That night, also in August 2014, "the streets were packed with cars, with people on foot, with everyone running away," he recalled. "It was 4 a.m.—utterly surreal." In the dark, their car packed with people and suitcases, his family went to Dohuk in the north. Qaraqosh became an urban battlefield, he told me, with suicide-vest-clad militants engaged in hand-to-hand combat against Iraqi Army soldiers in the streets.

In October 2016, the Iraqi Army liberated Qaraqosh after a two-year occupation, during which time the ISIS fighters lived in the townspeople's houses and stole their goods, their animals, their farms. When Nazar went back to help clear explosive devices, working alongside the Nineveh Plain Protection Units (NPU), a military organization formed largely by Assyrian Christians in late 2014 to fight ISIS, he was stunned by what he found.

As he walked through the destroyed town, he kept seeing things he thought he recognized, but it was hard to tell. Everything was ruined. There was the old school he had attended, destroyed. There was his aunt's house, a pile of rubble. But at least, Nazar told himself through tears, he was home.

"It was like a boyfriend separated from his girlfriend, and then we found each other again," he said, growing emotional.

"We have an old saying here: 'This village is ours.' We don't give it to anyone," he told me. "Mary and Joseph were here," he added, referring to an ancient legend that says that the parents of Jesus had passed through the town. The heartwarming Bible story did little to stop ISIS from destroying a thousand homes and partially burning another three thousand, according to Sabri Rafo Ibrahim, an NPU captain.

As Nazar and I were talking, a few dozen people gathered in a circle and began to play a dancing game. The men danced while the women clapped and sang. "Come," Nazar said, leading me to the group. He pointed out people and whispered brief comments about what had happened to them: this man had lost his daughter, that woman's husband had died, one family had been separated for two years.

These were families bound together by fear, dread, and survival. After all that had happened, they could hardly believe they were still alive. One woman took my arm and explained that she had lived in the monastery during the fighting. At the height of ISIS's expansion, sixty-five families had lived in Mar Mattai, the rooms swollen with ten or more people in each cell. They took shifts sleeping. The priests shared their food. Fortunately, ISIS never reached the ancient place.

"ISIS was as close as Bashiqa city," said Father Joseph Ibrahim, one of the Assyrian priests. He led me to the edge of the monastery and pointed to the town below, just beyond the walls. "If they wanted to occupy the monastery, they could have easily done it."

I asked him if he was afraid.

"No," he answered. Not of ISIS. Not of them coming back. But of the unknown.

Father Joseph's brother, an outspoken Christian leader brought up in Mosul, was killed in 2006 by Islamic jihadists during the first wave of anti-Christian violence. "The killers were not ISIS, but they had the same mentality," he said. "ISIS might be gone, but the sentiment is not."

A young mother shyly came up to Father Joseph holding her five-month-old daughter, who had been born at the end of the

ISIS reign. Rita al-Niser was twenty-four years old with long hair and a T-shirt that said, "Live in Paris. Love in Paris." She offered her infant to the priest, who blessed the baby.

Al-Niser is Elham's daughter-in-law. Her parents, a successful chemist and an engineer, are from Bartella, a town of fifteen thousand people a dozen miles east of Mosul. She grew up in an educated, sophisticated family. She assumed her life would continue the way her parents' lives had: that she would go to university, marry, and live in peace.

In 2014, she was in her last year of university, living with her family and studying English literature—"with three exams to go"—when ISIS came. The night they arrived, she had been studying before going to bed. She slept easily but was awakened at 3:00 a.m. when a relative in a nearby village called. He told them to leave immediately. She remembered her father rousing her and her siblings in tears. They had to pack their bags rapidly, taking only essentials. She remembered how her hands shook.

"ISIS were everywhere, so quickly," she said quietly. The family loaded their SUV and headed to Erbil, joining a community of some thirty thousand Christians there. The roads, she remembered, were full of cars, each one packed with families and whatever possessions they could grab. She went through a list of everything she had left behind: her books, her clothes, her photographs.

Erbil was meant to be temporary. "Originally we thought we would only stay there a few hours," al-Niser said. "That it would all be over in days." But the purge was more brutal than they could have imagined. ISIS cut a path through Christian territory, destroying houses and universities, burning books, even setting gardens alight. They stole first, then bombed or burned after, she told me. The university where she had almost graduated was completely destroyed.

It would not be for another three years, until June 2017, that her family would finally return to their home. The door to their house was open. They found broken furniture, smashed dishes, and torn curtains. It was as though the ISIS fighters had tried to erase any evidence that the family had ever existed.

Bahodij, who is al-Niser's cousin, walked over and sat with us. She listened to al-Niser, nodding. Life now, she said, is just as hard as living in exile.

"We just get promises. Promises for new homes, promises for jobs. Promises that ISIS will be gone forever. Promises that we will live in peace," she said.

The alternative is to emigrate to the United States. But she didn't think this was the solution. "In a few years," she said, echoing a sentiment I heard constantly, "everyone will be gone."

Whether emigration is the true enemy of Christians in the Middle East remains to be seen. While Donald Trump's 2016 election meant a dramatic dialing back of US human rights diplomacy, Mike Pence's presence as a conservative evangelical held out the potential that there could be some effort to protect persecuted Christians around the globe.

In the autumn of 2017, I had an off-the-record meeting with senior White House officials to discuss Pence's strategy for Christians in the Middle East. This was not long after Trump had signed his third version of the Muslim travel ban, and the officials clearly wanted to signal that Christians would still be welcomed to the United States with open arms. I remember leaving the meeting feeling deeply conflicted. On the one hand, I was relieved that my Christian friends in Iraq, Syria, Lebanon, and throughout the Middle East could find refuge in America, but on the other, I was deeply concerned about the greater political implications of the policies preferred by far-right evangelicals who had embraced their cause.

That fall, Pence spoke at a solidarity dinner for the advocacy group In Defense of Christians, where he declared, "Christianity now faces an exodus in the Middle East unrivaled since the days of Moses." He went on to pledge that the United States would "work hand in hand from this day forward with faith-based groups and private organizations to help those who are persecuted in their faith." Pence even floated the idea of a Middle East visit specifically to highlight Christians' plight in the region.[12]

But following Trump's December 2017 announcement that he would recognize Jerusalem as Israel's capital and move the US Embassy there, many Christian leaders in the region, including the Coptic pope, refused to meet with the vice president. During Pence's visit to the Middle East in January 2018, he addressed the Knesset, Israel's parliament, where he announced an accelerated timeline for the embassy move, sparking protests from Arab lawmakers. He also discussed spending $110 million to assist Christians and other religious minorities in the Middle East.[13]

The proportion of refugees admitted to the United States who were Christian had risen to 63 percent by the spring of 2016, up from 47 percent the year before—mostly because the total number of refugees admitted to the United States had plummeted. The latter number continued to decline during the Trump years, largely because the president's zero-tolerance border policy meant that many refugees were turned away before being allowed to apply for asylum. There is little doubt that Trump's immigration policies hurt the prospects of those escaping violence in their homelands from a variety of regions around the world. Yet Middle Eastern Christians appeared to be the exception. For many in this group, the administration's policies were a boon.

In 2019, the reporter Emma Green, writing in *The Atlantic*, noted the strange union between Middle East Christians and the Trump administration:

Since Trump took office, the Nineveh Plain has received significant amounts of investment from the U.S. government. In part, this foreign-policy position is grounded in domestic politics. The conservative voters who helped elect Trump care deeply about oppressed Christians, and they convey their concern through an exceptionally effective lobbying machine in Washington, D.C. But the plight of Christians in the region is also a natural cause for an administration that views foreign policy as a struggle to maintain the West's global clout. For Trump, Christianity can be a bulwark of Western values in a region full of perceived enemies.[14]

It's hard to imagine that any foreign policy strategy could do much in the face of the widespread crisis facing Christians in the Middle East; in fact, any policy friendly to the Christians of the region could exacerbate the situation by driving resentment against them from other groups that covet American aid. Over the past two millennia, Christians in the Middle East have lived through periods of quiet tolerance interrupted by bursts of brutal persecution. World War I and the subsequent fall of the Ottoman Empire contributed to the first such wave of anti-Christian violence in modern history. The American invasion of Iraq in 2003 presaged another. The chaos sown in the aftermath of that conflict has compromised the safety of countless Christian communities beyond Iraq, including those in Egypt, Syria, and perhaps even Lebanon. In each of those places, conflict has made the already complicated and dangerous position of Christians even more precarious.

In Erbil in 2015, with ISIS still in power, I met Aziz Emmanuel al-Zabari, a Chaldean Catholic professor from Salahaddin University. Al-Zabari had fled Mosul in 2006, when he felt that rising tensions were already making it unsafe for Iraqi Christians to stay there. He told me that more than one hundred thousand Christians from the Nineveh Plain and Mosul had fled the ISIS advance in June. One by one, he listed the names of the Christian villages that had been purged: Qaraqosh, Karemlash, Bartella, Bashiqa, Tel Keppe, Batnaya, Tesqopa, Alqosh, Sharafiya. "For the last nine months, the church bells have gone silent and there is not a single Christian in those villages and the city of Mosul," he said.

He told me how to find the houses where Christians were camped out with relatives in Ain Kawa, as well as in refugee camps on the roads leading out of the city. Wandering through the camps, I stopped in tent after tent to talk to people who had recently fled ISIS. "Are they trying to kill us all?" one woman asked me. "Are we ever going to be able to go home?" It's hard to offer any kind of consolation to people who have not only been deprived of their homes, but also of the ability to practice their faith. They could no longer meet with fellow believers and take Communion, or if they did meet as a congregation, they did so, with grave fear, in broken-down churches.

Monsignor Nicodemus Sharaf, the archbishop of the Syriac Orthodox Church in Mosul, was the last priest to leave the city. His family had lived there for generations, and he was adamant that he would not abandon a place that meant so much to Christian history. He tried to stay in Mosul as a symbol of defiance. When he finally left, he carried a five-hundred-year-old Aramaic manuscript under his arm. I met him a few weeks after Mosul was liberated in 2017. He was still mourning the loss of the relics and the texts he had left behind, which ISIS had burned. "But," he said firmly, "they cannot take God from us." They have taken everything else, he repeated. "But not God."

The monsignor did not believe that ISIS was finished. The mentality would continue. The war against Christians, he said, had started when Saddam Hussein fell from power, and it would only grow.

A few days after my long afternoon in Mar Mattai, I drove to Qaraqosh, where most of the former streets were piles of rubble. Teenagers associated with the NPU guarded the town at make-shift checkpoints. They seemed more interested in taking selfies than in protecting the villagers. On the main drag, only a few kebab shops were open, as well as a barbershop.

The town looked almost abandoned, and I wondered if people were home inside, hiding, or just escaping the heat of the day. I was with Nicole Tung, the photographer, and we stopped for some food. I bought some roasted chicken—remarkably, a butcher was open and selling meat—and we ate outside, sitting on some abandoned folding chairs on the sidewalk. There were a few men drinking tea on benches outside the shop, and some Shia women, dressed in full abayas, walking with their children and speaking Farsi. Our driver told us the Shias had been brought to the town by militias that had come to fight ISIS. I didn't feel entirely se-cure, but I wanted to wait and go to Mass on Saturday night in the bombed-out church, St. Mary's al-Tahira, one of the largest churches in Iraq. Its altar was now blackened with fire, and its relics and crosses had been destroyed and broken by ISIS.

Around dusk, after the heat abated, a huge crowd gathered: men holding newborn babies, families taking up entire pews. I stood quietly in the back, then wandered through the destroyed courtyard, stepping over shattered glass and broken concrete. I came across a group of elderly women who were sitting in one of the back rooms, listening to the Mass in a cooler place. They looked elegant in their flowered cotton dresses and straw hats, and they were wearing lipstick. They all wanted to talk to me, to tell me what had happened to them: how their possessions had been stolen, how teenage ISIS fighters had threatened them with violence or rape. I sat on a rickety plastic chair and listened.

When the Mass ended, people walked to the one ice cream shop that remained open. If you ignored the destruction around us, it could have been a Mediterranean seaside village with families doing the *passeggiata*, the traditional evening walk after a long, hot summer day.

A few days later, we drove to the Monastery of the Virgin Mary near the village of Alqosh, about twenty miles north of Mar Mattai. It had been built at the request of the nineteenth-century Chaldean Patriarch Joseph VI Audo, who had needed a place to house the monks of the Rabban Hormizd Monastery—also Chaldean, built in the year 650—in a more modern and secure location.

The Monastery of the Virgin Mary is beautiful: sand-colored, with a square courtyard full of trees, green grass, an intricately carved gate featuring text and florals—the iconographic language of the area. There is also a promenade where families peacefully gather around a golden sculpture of the Virgin. There, I met Father Andrew Toma, who told me that over the centuries, the Christians in Iraq had adapted to being outsiders. "An eagle will live here," he said, "with all these pigeons." One of his fears for Christians in the region was the uncertainty about their economic future.

"In the 1980s, Christian families left because they did not want their sons to fight in the Iran-Iraq war," Father Toma explained, recalling a bloody and bitter conflict that went on for eight years and left nearly a million dead. "Now they are leaving because there is no life for them. How can I tell them to stay? How can I save them?"

The priest sat down wearily on an ancient wall outside his home. "I can't even save myself," he sighed. I kept encountering this kind of despair, a sense that the past was important and faith needed to be preserved above all, but that there was an insurmountable oppression bearing down on the Christians. I kept thinking of all the Christian tattoos I had seen among the young waiters in Ankawa, outside of Erbil: the large crucifix tattoos etched on their skin, the rough drawings of saints and prophets, the garish ink depicting a permanence that was belied by their current predicament. I talked to them about their insecurity: how they had been separated from family during the ISIS invasion, how they feared the future, how they were saving their wages so they would be able to pay illegal smugglers to get them out of Iraq. But once out, where would they go? Would life in Istanbul be any better? Many wanted to go to Canada, ultimately. Most of them had family there, or had heard that life would be easier there than in Erbil. As indeed it would, if they could get there.

And yet, despite the yearning for a fresh new life, they were canny and streetwise enough to know that even beyond the borders of Iraq or Turkey lay the wandering life of a refugee, another job waitering but in a foreign country, a language not their own, without the comfort—however slim—of traditions and roots and family and community that had lived on this land for centuries. "It is a terrible gamble," one waiter told me on a hot August day in Erbil. "A miserable choice."

Down the road, Sharafiya was a ghost town, an abandoned village destroyed by ISIS, until families slowly began returning in 2016. There appeared to be no one in the village except in the house where the local priest lived. I knocked, and Father Asad interrupted his family lunch, pushed aside one of his children's bicycles, and came outside to talk. His children watched from the windows.

Father Asad told me his parish was originally a community of four hundred families, most of whom had fled. "People left their animals and their houses, took their gold and left quickly," he said. He remembers the lines of villagers in panic, rows of cars stuffed with people and possessions. We walked through the hills of the town. Doors were closed and locked; people had fled in a hurry. On the hillside were a few abandoned sheep.

But people were determined to restart their lives, and by January 2018 thirteen babies had been baptized in Sharafiya's restored Church of St. George. Six months before, when I had first met Father Asad and attended an evening Mass, there had only been a handful of worshippers in the pews. The newborn babies, he told me, were a sign that the Christians would prevail, no matter how difficult the situation.

Still, he added, local politics would continue to haunt the Christians. The Kurds were preparing for a referendum in September 2017 to officially separate from Iraq, and while he was doubtful it would happen, he wondered if the Christians would be caught in the middle of the Iraqi-Kurdish feud.[15]

"It's not about me convincing people to stay," he said. "We have no problem with Kurds and Arabs. But if the Kurds and Arabs continue to fight, we will be the victims in this game."

Iraq's Christians have a complicated relationship with their Kurdish neighbors. On the one hand, they find solidarity in their joint identity as often oppressed minority communities. Many Christians see Kurdish Muslims as more tolerant of their faith than their Arab Sunni coreligionists, and they appreciate the services and stability that the Kurdish Regional Government usually provides. Nevertheless, the worry remains that tension between Erbil and Baghdad could erupt into a new spate of violence.

It was eerie to pass through streets of tiny villages that had been deserted after the ISIS occupation. In some, such as the Assyrian village of Sharafiya, there was virtually no sound but for the bleating of goats. From far away, I heard a distant horn blowing. Fields were overgrown. Houses were empty, with doors open as though people had left just for a moment, expecting to return quickly.

On my last day in Nineveh, as the sun was setting, Nicole and I climbed a hill to the Chaldean Rabban Hormizd Monastery, which looks like a sandy ancient castle nestled in the cliffs. I could have been taking those steps in the seventh century. The monastery was empty, lit by a few flickering candles. The sky was drawing down for night. But we faintly heard otherworldly singing, chanting. I followed the cool stone passages, laying my hands on the ancient rock.

Far in the back, in an almost hidden room, we found the source of the singing. A man and a woman had their backs to me. The woman had long, flowing hair that fell below her waist and was wearing a simple dress. The man, a priest, was wearing robes. The woman turned, saw me, and smiled widely. They continued singing in Aramaic in front of an altar with a single lit candle.

I knelt, growing emotional at the sound of their voices, harmonized in an ancient prayer—an evening vigil. Afterward, the priest approached me, extending his hand. He was an Iraqi-Australian, Father Isaac Royel. With his wife, he had come in the wake of the fall of ISIS to visit his elderly mother in the nearby village of Alqosh.

Father Isaac had been an Orthodox priest (and thus allowed to marry) since the age of twenty.

"I wanted to live a spiritual life. I was dying in the real world," he said. "I wanted a connection to spirituality that I could only get through fasting, vigils, and prayers."

We found a place to sit on a wall outside, looking down at the expanse below the monastery. We spoke as the sky grew dark, eventually taking out our cellphones for light. Faith is diminishing in every way, he told me, even in this ancient place.

"This country is our root," he said, stressing the need to preserve Christianity in Iraq. He used himself as an example: moving to Australia had been more than just crossing borders. His Iraqi culture was diminished, and he fought to maintain it.

"For people moving from the East to the West, it is very difficult, because they will assimilate, and we will disappear forever,"

he said. "The West is technology, knowledge. The East is something more traditional. If something is demolished, it can never
again be rebuilt."

He motioned to the road below us, now darkened, and told
us it was time to go because the descent was difficult. He was
staying inside the monastery for the night, a monk with just his
wife, his prayers, and his faith.

2

GAZA

2019

SHORTLY AFTER ARRIVING IN GAZA ON A BLISTERING JULY DAY IN 2019, I settled into a simple hotel, only half-built. At the front, facing the main road, was a cavernous wedding hall, occasionally used by those Gazans who could afford to get married. The music and the sound of the pounding feet of the dancers—segregated men and women—would go on until late in the night. My room faced the back, with large windows opening onto a long, spectacular, crescent-shaped beach.

I chose the hotel because of its location and its name: Gloria, my middle name. The beach was empty during the searing heat of the day, but when the sun went down, it transformed into a colorful circus of people: families setting up elaborate picnics with grills and kebabs, teenage acrobats doing backflips in the sand, two solemn sisters in long dark robes lounging in chairs at the edge of the water. Children built sandcastles and screeched as the Mediterranean rolled in and soaked their legs. Before dawn, Nicole Tung, who was working with me, would rise the next day and go to the beach to see the fishermen leaving in their boats in the darkness.

This was where I had begun my career as a reporter more than three decades earlier. When I first started working in Gaza, I had much hope for what could happen in the future to improve the situation for the people. I had never gotten used to the smell of trash in Gaza; nor had I forgotten my first sight of the dusty roads, or the number of people packed into such a small space, or the sense of desperation, helplessness, misery, and injustice. And in thirty years, not much had changed. Gaza seems to have been forever left behind.

I remembered a trip from a long-ago warm spring day in 1991, three years into the first intifada, the uprising of the Palestinian people against the Israeli occupation of the West Bank and Gaza. I stood at the edge of the shore on a deserted Gazan beach, staring at an endless view of the Mediterranean. My Palestinian friend Ali was with me. Ali was an activist who had recently been released from an Israeli prison in the desert, a notorious place called Ansar III (also known in Hebrew as Ktzi'ot Prison). He had endured torture, physical and psychological, at the hands of the Israeli security forces known as the Shin Bet. His treatment had been so harsh that if you came up behind him without warning, he would leap up like a frightened cat. I didn't know a lot about post-traumatic stress disorder in those days. Now I understand something of what Ali must have suffered.

We stood looking out at one of the most beautiful vistas I had ever seen: golden sand, a vast red horizon, and shards of light scattered across the water. The border blurred between the water and the endless sky, us and the heavens.

But the beach was littered with trash, and it was empty. This was two years before the 1993 Oslo Accords, a set of agreements between the Palestine Liberation Organization (PLO) and Israel that created a path toward a peace treaty. The accords broke down when the second intifada—which was far deadlier than the first—erupted in 2000. But for a few years, there had been something akin to hope in the air. Yasser Arafat, the chairman of the PLO, returned to Gaza after signing the accords to face jubilant crowds who believed he had delivered a self-ruled Palestine free from oppression.

"Someday we'll stand on this beach together and there will be peace here," I said. "There'll be a Palestinian state, and you'll be free." Ali looked skeptical, but he managed to smile. "*Inshallah*," he answered. God willing.

In the summer of 2019, I stood on that same beach, where Palestinian fishermen were not allowed to take their boats far out to sea. I was alone. Gaza was in the worst state I had ever seen. I passed the abandoned airport, which was meant to be a symbol of Gaza opening to the world. It was now an overgrown field of weeds, an abandoned skeleton of what was supposed to be a terminal. Despite all my efforts, I couldn't find Ali. He had vanished into the Palestinian diaspora, or worse, down the rabbit hole of despair.

At the beginning of the millennium, in the early 2000s, I had come back to Gaza to try to find children I had met earlier, in the late 1990s. As usual, I drove to the Erez checkpoint in an overcrowded taxi, this time with the gifted American photographer Judah Passow. We went to various refugee camps, searching for the children we had encountered and documented years before. We came armed with their photographs. At that time, they had been small, confused children sitting on the floor drawing pictures in crayon of soldiers, guns, helicopters dropping bombs. A decade later, only two remained in the camps. They were teenagers now, hardened by war, by deprivation, by misery.

FAULT LINES

On my first Sunday back in Gaza in July 2019, Nicole and I left the Gloria Hotel to go to Mass at the Church of the Holy Family after enjoying an enormous Palestinian breakfast on the terrace

overlooking the sea. The waiters told me they were lucky to
have jobs, and they loved their work. They smiled and brought
too much food: watermelon juice, baskets of bread, honey, hum-
mus, and pickles. I sat drinking Arabic coffee scented with car-
damom and watched the fishermen pull out their boats in the
milky light.

The heat was already unbearable. The temperature in Gaza
always seems several degrees higher than the thermometer read-
ings because of the density, both of buildings and of people—
almost two million of them living in an area twenty-five miles
long and seven miles wide, nearly four times the population of
Atlanta, which is just a little larger in terms of square miles.
And with each passing year, the Palestinian territory becomes
smaller and more claustrophobic. Ali once explained to me that
under the Oslo Accords, the fishermen were meant to be able to
take their boats twenty nautical miles out to fish and earn their
livelihood. But Israeli restrictions over the years have shortened
their limits: they can now go out less than half that distance, or
they might receive a large fine and have their boats and equip-
ment confiscated. So the beauty of the Mediterranean and its
vast horizon taunt the fisherman, who are bound to the shore.
Somehow, the magnificence of it all makes the hardship of the
siege—because that is what it is like to live in Gaza, surrounded
by the humiliation of checkpoints, inspections, and barricades—
seem even more desperate.

In the early days of my reporting in Gaza, I often went to the
Christian churches, which seemed removed and distant from
the violence on the streets and in the camps. In the darkness,
the quiet, amid the heavy smell of incense, the reminder of faith
in something better beyond this life, I could think and I could
breathe.

The Church of the Holy Family is a simple white stone building in a compound on Zeitoun Street attended by about some

five hundred congregants, not all of them Catholic. In addition to the church, there is a community center where people gather after Mass to drink tea and mingle with their fellow parishioners. Arriving slightly late, I took a seat in a pew near the back, first dipping my finger in a bowl of holy water and making the sign of the cross on my forehead, a motion I had been taught from the time I could walk.

Despite the heat, the Mass was full: there were families, small and noisy children, women in cotton dresses, their long hair uncovered. Western nuns from the order of Mother Theresa, part of the Holy Family religious community, were there as well, dressed in bleached white robes. When I tried to talk to them, they were kind but firm: they could not discuss the difficulty of the situation for Christians in Gaza unless I spoke with their spiritual head in India.

The Mass was in Arabic, but I followed the order that unites Catholics throughout the world: liturgy, homily, Transfiguration, Communion. There was a slight commotion as people pushed forward to receive the host, an anxiousness to receive a Holy Sacrament to protect them from the terrible trials of life outside the church.

After Mass, I stood in the courtyard while people filed out. An elderly woman with a wide-brimmed straw hat approached me. Deeply tanned and speaking rapid English, she thrust her hand into mine and said her name was Elham Fara. Tiny, energetic, and slightly bossy, she told me she had family in Maryland and New York and that she was a music teacher in Gaza.

"I specialize in piano," she said. "But I'm the only one who can play the organ at Mass, so I do that, too."

As the parishioners gathered in the courtyard outside the church, Elham vented about the impossibility of life in Gaza. "We are prisoners here," she said. "That's the best way to put it." She asked us for a ride home, then climbed into the front seat to

direct us to her house. She asked my driver if he was Muslim.
He was.

We passed people headed to the market, donkeys carrying
overloaded wicker baskets of fruit, rickety stands with vendors
selling fresh juice. Elham recounted stories of life in her tiny
community. "It is difficult for all Christians in Palestine," she
said. "But Gaza is—well, Gaza is impossible. But we stay. It is
my home."

Palestinian Christians date back to the original followers of
Christ. Of the nearly 47,000 Palestinian Christians still resid-
ing in Palestine, 98 percent live in the West Bank.[1] A tiny frac-
tion of the Christian community, between 800 and 1,100 people,
lives in the besieged Gaza Strip, the poorest part of Palestine.
Of all the communities I visited, their situation is the most
precarious.

As their numbers continue to decline, Palestinian Christians
face immense discrimination. According to the *Jerusalem Post*,
at least three major instances of violence against Palestinian
Christians occurred in 2019 alone, including a mob that targeted
a Christian village in the West Bank, terrifying the townspeople and damaging property, and the vandalism of two churches,
one in Bethlehem and the other in Ramallah. Elias al-Jalda, the
religious relations manager for the Greek Orthodox Church in
the Gaza Strip, criticized Hamas for making border crossing increasingly difficult for Christians through invasive searches and
for pressuring Christians in interfaith marriages with Muslims
to convert to Islam.[2]

Beyond the threat of violence, restrictions on movement make
the lives of all Palestinians extremely difficult. Since 1993, Palestinians living in the West Bank and Gaza have not been able
to enter East Jerusalem without a permit, which is nearly impossible to obtain. This means Palestinian Christians are prevented
from accessing some of the most sacred sites in Christianity.

They cannot visit the wondrous and deeply moving Church of the Holy Sepulchre, built on the spot where Christ is said to have been crucified and buried. Its gargantuan cerulean dome seems to reflect the blue skies overhead; the cracking arches welcome you inside to gaze in wonder at the brilliant golds and ruby reds that cover the space, all celebrating the life of Jesus. Nor can Palestinian Christians walk along the Via Dolorosa's Stations of the Cross, where legions of tourists follow priests reciting the Rosary in countless languages, tracing the points of the crucifixion where Jesus fell, having been whipped and humiliated. Nor can they experience Gethsemane, a lush garden at the foot of the Mount of Olives where, according to the New Testament, Jesus prayed in agony before Judas betrayed him.

I had spent many hours in all of those places, both as a Christian and as a reporter, and I had witnessed the politics of Israel bringing direct repercussions to these holy places. During the first intifada in the late 1980s, when I was on my very first reporting assignment overseas, the Old City was usually under lockdown and heavily guarded. It was too dangerous for me to wander alone there with notebook in hand. Even within the sacred walls of the Holy Sepulchre, the religions that presided over the place—Greek Orthodox, Roman Catholic, Armenian Apostolic, and to a lesser degree Coptic Orthodox, Syriac Orthodox, and Ethiopian Orthodox—tended to squabble among themselves about the rituals or who held a more important role. But the fact that Palestinian Christians are caught in the web of political conflict, making it harder for them to practice their faith, seemed especially painful.

Even Bethlehem, the small town in the West Bank where many Gazan Christians have relatives, is difficult for them to visit. The town, which in 1947 was 85 percent Christian, is now dominated by Palestinian Muslims, part of a larger demographic change in Palestine explained by a lower birthrate among Christians compared to Muslims and an increased rate of Christian emigration.

Yet it is not just Christians who are leaving Palestine for good. Nor are discriminatory Israeli policies the only factor driving emigration. In Gaza, the problems have been compounded by the rigid government of Hamas, the Sunni Islamist group elected in 2006, as well as by years of poverty, an infrastructure battered by four wars, and continued political infighting between Palestinian political parties. Since 2007, there has been a political rift between the Palestinian Authority (PA), based in Ramallah in the West Bank, and Hamas. The division has fomented violence in the region and diminished hopes for a future independent Palestinian state. The people of Gaza are the ones who suffer the fallout.

The United Nations predicted that Gaza would be unlivable by 2020. While the many Gazans still tenaciously clinging to their homeland make that prediction seem overly pessimistic, conditions show that it was not a baseless claim. There have been three wars in Gaza since the 2007 Battle of Gaza. If there was a winner in any of them, it's not really clear what the benefits of victory were; what is certain is the cost of losing. The last war took a horrific toll on the infrastructure of Gaza. The physical damage affected the delivery of electricity and has led to frequent power cuts (on average, Gazans receive four hours of electricity per day). Freshwater supplies are also limited: only 5 percent of the water is drinkable.

Since Hamas's takeover in 2006 and the start of the ensuing blockade, poverty and unemployment have skyrocketed. Gazans have been punished from two sides: by the Israelis, who continue to subjugate, humiliate, and dominate the lives of Gazans even after pulling out their troops and evicting the Israeli settlers who lived there, and by the Egyptians, who regard the Hamas government with deep suspicion and treat Gazans like the plague. Palestinians living in the Gaza Strip are alienated from their own seat of government in Ramallah because the PA and Hamas are at odds and because the blockade prevents Gazans from easily entering the West Bank. Caught in the middle of a political mess, Gazans have taken the hit. The restrictions on movement for Palestinians have intensified since 2007, and despite some recent political reforms, Gazans are stuck on their shrinking piece of land, denied access to the rest of their territory and the rest of the world.

The Fatah political party, founded by Yasser Arafat and with deep roots in the revolutionary struggle for Palestinian liberation, dominated Palestinian legislative elections until 2006, when Hamas won a majority. The two parties then formed an uneasy coalition government.

For years, the secular Fatah movement aimed to build a Palestinian state based upon the territories that Israel occupied in 1967. Fatah recognizes Israel and believes that negotiation with Israel is necessary to achieve Palestinian statehood. In direct contrast to Fatah's nonreligious identity, Hamas is an Islamist radical party. Hamas does not recognize Israel and believes that Palestinians should employ armed resistance against it, rather than negotiation, to achieve a Palestinian state based on the pre-1967 borders.[3]

In 2006, people in Gaza were fed up with the corruption and distance of the Fatah-led PA. It is no coincidence that Gaza, which suffers the most violence from Western-backed Israel, would vote for the less Western party. They wanted a change. Hamas, like Hezbollah in Lebanon, promised so much: social programs, education, health care, freedom, and a new life. Many of the people voted for them not out of fear, but out of a desire for a new path out of the drudgery of everyday life in Gaza.

The differences in ideology and methods between Hamas and Fatah, as well as personal grudges, led to a quick

unraveling of the unity government. By 2007, the two parties had had a violent falling-out. Hamas grabbed sole control
of Gaza, while the PA, now free of Hamas and led again by
Fatah, kept hold of the West Bank. The Ramallah-based PA
considers itself the sole representative of Palestine in the international community, and this tends to be reciprocated by
Western countries, many of which regard Hamas as a terrorist
organization.

Hamas, led by former PA prime minister Ismail Haniya, is an
authoritarian government. It doesn't rule with the same degree
of repression as Saddam's Iraq, Muammar Gaddafi's Libya, or
the Assads' Syria, but nothing happens in Gaza without Hamas
approving it. It has not left power in Gaza since 2007, yet it has
failed to accomplish what its leaders set out to do. That's not
entirely their fault—the Israeli and Egyptian blockades have
prevented Gaza from thriving economically—but they haven't
helped the situation much either. Once seen as incorruptible by
the local population, because of its Sunni religious principles,
Hamas is now increasingly viewed as being as compromised as
the PA. "They're becoming like the people they ran against," as
one student put it to me.

Hamas has proven to be corrupt in a variety of ways, notably
by profiting from illegal medical transfers out of the country. A
journalist named Hajar Harb who tried to expose the corruption faced violent threats and was sentenced to six months in
prison before finally being freed on appeal.[4] An Amnesty International official told me that Harb was punished by Hamas
simply for doing her job as a human rights researcher.

The suffering of Palestinians, already great owing to the
weight of the Israeli occupation, has been exacerbated by the
political divisions pitting them against one another. Like many
people, I believe the split between Hamas and Fatah is a gift
to the Israelis, who want to see the Palestinians' political base

divided. Yet a former Israeli military commander in Gaza that I met in Jerusalem, Grisha Yakubovich, disagreed with me.

"The split between Palestinian powers does not benefit Israel," he insisted. "Both the left wing and the right wing [Israeli parties] are suffering because of it."

What saves Gaza from complete internal destruction is Palestinian emotional solidarity, which is as strong as their family units. Gazans are tremendously resourceful, and even in the most congested refugee camps, despite immense suffering, families gather for meals, to commiserate, and to dream. The collective Gazan spirit yearns for freedom, Christians and Muslims, radicals and moderates alike. They all share a common thread: they are under siege.

THE PURGE

In the birthplace of Christ, in the land where he was raised, where he was baptized and where he died, his remaining followers affectionately refer to themselves as "living stones." The term is a reference to 1 Peter 2:5: "You yourselves like living stones are being built up as a spiritual house, to be a holy priesthood, to offer spiritual sacrifices acceptable to God through Jesus Christ" (ESV). Today, the term reflects the fact that the Christians of Israel and Palestine are living artifacts from the days of Jesus, proof of a two-thousand-year-old Christian history in the Holy Land that continues to this day. From the night when Mary birthed a child in Bethlehem, Palestine and Christianity would be forever intertwined. The first Christians in Palestine were the original disciples of Christ; the first man to preach in what is now the Gaza Strip was the Apostle Philip, student of Paul the Apostle.

Philip, who may have had Greek origins, was believed to have been born in Bethsaida, where he might have encountered Peter and Andrew. He was present at the wedding of Cana—when, according to the Gospel of St. John, Jesus turned water into wine, his first miracle—and he may have been present when John the Baptist proclaimed Christ "the lamb of God." It was the Apostle Philip whom Jesus challenged with a question about how to feed five thousand people: "Before the miraculous feeding of the multitude, Christ turns towards Philip with the question: 'Whence shall we buy bread, that these may eat?' to which the Apostle answers: 'Two hundred penny-worth of bread is not sufficient for them, that every one may take a little.'"[5] Later, the religion would continue its spread in the region among Messianic Jews, Romans, and Greeks.

Though Bethlehem had a special status as the birthplace of the Christian faith, it would not be a true center of Christianity for another three hundred years. The Byzantine Empire, led by the newly converted Constantine, would legalize the religion and establish Syria-Palaestina as a Christian province in the early fourth century. After that, Christianity grew and flourished in Palestine until the arrival of Islam in the region in the seventh century. The Christians who remained in the land were a mix of the descendants of the earliest Messianic Jews, converted Romans, and Muslim invaders. After 1095, the Christian crusaders who arrived tried but failed to wrest Palestine from Muslim control. In this way, the Christian inhabitants who remained, "living stones" indeed, held the key to Christianity's earliest history in their traditions and their family lines.

Today fewer than 1,100 Christians remain in Gaza, and that number is decreasing rapidly, down from 4,500 in 2014. In 2015, according to the Institute for Middle East Understanding, Palestinian Christians made up approximately 1 to 2.5 percent of the population of the West Bank, and less than 1 percent in the Gaza Strip.[6]

League of Nation records from the time of the British Mandate show that Palestine's Christian population constituted 9.5

percent of the total in 1922 and 7.9 percent in 1946.[7] The decline has been long, but it has now entered the stage where it feels like an extinction.

～

Driving toward Rafah one afternoon, at the far end of Gaza near the Egyptian border, we stopped to see the ruins of an ancient monastery. Established in the early fifth century when most of Gaza was Christian, it had been headed by St. Porphyrius, the bishop of Gaza who led the conversion of the pagans living in the region at that time—as well as their subsequent persecutions. His tomb now lies in the northeastern corner of the Church of St. Porphyrius in Gaza City, a golden brick church with deep blue ceilings and hanging glass chandeliers. It is packed with the remaining worshippers in Gaza even in the heat of summer.

I took sanctuary in the church's cool, dark rectory with Kemal Ayyad, an unofficial spokesperson for the congregation. He told me the life of Porphyrius according to the writings of Mark the Deacon, a fifth-century monk.

In the year 395, when Porphyrius came to Gaza from Salonica, the old city was surrounded by eight gates. He was already in the middle of his life, nearly forty-five years old, and ahead of him lay a colossal task. Apart from a handful of Christian families, some of whom had suffered martyrdom, the majority of the population was pagan.

The tradition of the pagans was to pray to the relentless sun to ask for rain, and Porphyrius had arrived in the middle of a drought. He convinced them to pray to the Christian God instead, and the rain duly arrived. After that, they brought their sick to him to be healed, and he founded a budding community of Gazan Christians. His next step in establishing Christianity in Gaza was to destroy the temples and build a church. But first, Porphyrius needed money.

He sent his deacon, Mark, to Constantinople, the seat of the empire, to request help in destroying the pagan temples. Later, in 401, Porphyrius himself made the long journey, and he asked the Empress Eudoxia for help. He succeeded. The legend says that Eudoxia had suffered two stillbirths. Porphyrius prayed with her, and she eventually had five children. She rewarded him with money and soldiers.

In May 402, the burning of the temples and the idols in Gaza began. Porphyrius started with the great temple Marneion, which had been built under the Emperor Hadrian to honor Zeus Marnas, the god of agriculture. Pitch, sulfur, and fat were used to set it alight. Other temples burned alongside it. Soldiers went from door to door, seizing books and private "idolatries." The Christian church, then named after the Empress Eudoxia, was built in 407 on the ruins of the Roman temple. Paganism officially ceased to exist in Gaza; Christianity won out.

Ayyad continued the tale. "In 640 CE, during the Roman Empire, Persian soldiers destroyed the church. In the seventh century, Islam came," he said. By the early 1950s, Ayyad reckoned, there were some forty-six thousand Christians still living in Gaza, making up about 20 percent of the population. Then began the period of emigration.

"I remember my uncle left for Kuwait, then Australia," Ayyad told me. "He died there, never got back to Gaza."

Ayyad said that under Yasser Arafat, who became the symbolic president of Palestine in 1988, Christians were protected. There was a Religious Affairs Administration that tended to their needs. "Things were changing in Gaza," he recalled. "There was an airport opening. There was a core of a state. People were going to stay and build a future."

Many of the Christians who were able, however, took Egyptian citizenship as protection. When Arafat died in 2004, the political climate changed. Hamas was elected two years later.

The brutal wars came, and those Christians who could leave did. Like everyone else I asked in Gaza for an estimate of how many Christians remained, Ayyad was uncertain. "A little over a thousand?" he speculated.

That night, I tried to read a French document that Father Mario, a priest at the Church of the Holy Family, had given me. It was written by a priest who had served before him, detailing the vast rise and decline of the Christians: "Christianity in Gaza is a history that began over two thousand years ago and continues today with the descendants of the first converted Christians. This is the story of the first Christians persecuted by the Romans. It is also the story of the first anchorites, the mystical Christians separated from the rest of the world, the famous 'Fathers of the desert' living in cabins built on the ruins of the first Palestinian monasteries." The priest wrote of the monasteries founded in the fifth and sixth centuries and how, even under various Muslim rulers, the Christian community had always had a priest. Some Muslims even prayed in the Christian churches.

A famous English bishop and explorer, St. Willibald, visited Gaza for three years beginning in 723, becoming one of the first Englishmen to step foot in the Holy Land.[8] He mentioned a beautiful "cathedral mosque," where he thought Christians and Muslims might have been combining their religions in some shape or form. Even while the crusaders were destroying Jerusalem in 1099 during the First Crusade, Gaza was a refuge. The document went on to say that friendship between the two communities, Christian and Muslim, was sincere; nobody worried about the religion of his or her neighbor. "The only thing missing," he noted, "was inter-religious marriage, but that is to be understood, given that people did not get married for love but because of their family's decision." Ramadan and Easter were celebrated alike.

The desert monks who arrived in Palestine between the fourth and sixth centuries wrote of a life that was hard but spiritually fulfilling. Despite enormous challenges, they thrived. The descendants of those ancient Christians follow in their footsteps, pressing on through the hardships of life in Gaza.

In the modern day, the purging of the Christian community is partly the result of the economy and the siege, but it is undeniably made worse by life under Hamas. One year after Hamas was elected, in 2007, the last Christian bookstore in central Gaza, known as The Teacher's Bookshop, was firebombed twice. It was only one of a spate of similar bombings that occurred in Gaza at the time. The bookshop, a haven of sorts, with an Internet café and educational services, had been established by the Gaza Baptist Church ten years earlier. Its Christian owner, Rami Ayyad, a deeply religious and kindly man, was kidnapped, tortured, and murdered by extremists. He had received death threats from jihadists for years but had refused to close his shop. Hamas condemned the murder and vowed to protect the remaining Christians, but the assailants were never found.

I had passed the bookshop numerous times on my many trips and remember when it opened in 1998—a time when we could drink beer in Gaza and sit outside in cafés at the beach. When I returned in 2019, people seemed frightened to talk to me about Rami Ayyad's death or the bombings, even though they had occurred years before. Instead, a woman piling books in the bookstore that took the old one's place directed me to the fifth floor of the building, where an evening church service was taking place. "You are just in time!" she said excitedly, hustling me out of the bookstore and up a flight of steps.

The service did not have the trappings of a Catholic or Orthodox Mass but instead showed what I assumed were the Baptist roots of the organization behind the bookstore on the ground floor. The setting reminded me of some of the makeshift Latinx churches on the Lower East Side of Manhattan, that look as though they have been set up overnight but have passionate worshippers. In Gaza on a Sunday afternoon, a tiny crowd sat on worn brown velvet chairs while their children played in the back of the room. It looked more like someone's living room or a play group than a church. There were paintings on the wall of birds flying against a deep sunset, and unsettling electronic music played above the shouts of the children.

The pastor stood next to a young girl who was wearing high-waisted jeans and a cold shoulder T-shirt, an iPhone shoved in her back pocket. They stood side by side at the pulpit, taking turns reading from the Bible in Arabic. The girl sang in a rich melodic voice, raising her arms for the congregation to join in.

I was unsure what role the Baptist Church played in Gaza, and many people were wary of talking about it. Finally, Dr. Attalah Tarazi, who runs the Gaza Center of Light and Culture, another Baptist organization, met me in his office. The Tarazis are an old, revered Christian family in Gaza, full of doctors, lawyers, professors, and landowners, with many branches and dozens of cousins twice and three times removed. Attalah was born in Gaza near the Orthodox Church right after the 1948 Nakbah—from a word meaning the "catastrophe" in Arabic—when Israel won its War of Independence and started the mass displacement of Palestinians from their ancestral homes.

"Israel was born and we lost Palestine," he said simply.

Gaza in 1948 was a different world. The streets were miles and miles of sand. The Tarazis were a powerful clan in the region. Attalah's father, a wealthy jeweler, had been born in 1906 when it was still the Ottoman Empire; his memories were of an old Middle East that no longer exists. The family consisted of eight sisters and four brothers. One brother was killed by a British soldier during the Mandate, the quarter-century-long period of British control over what is now Israel and Palestine.

The Tarazi family home was a large villa covered in brightly colored flowers. As his wealth grew, Attalah's father acquired more and more land, which he eventually passed on to his children. Attalah was due to take his university exams in 1967, but they were canceled because of the war. He crossed the border to study in Egypt, where he received his medical degree in 1973, just as another war was starting. For many years he worked as a surgeon at the Baptist Hospital, where one of his cousins is now the administrator. He now operates at Al-Shifa, the overcrowded, underfunded government hospital.

Attalah told me that Christians in Gaza are generally in better health than other Palestinians, but he doesn't treat only Christians. "We are not that far apart," he said. "We have good relations with Hamas. They are my patients." He paused and added, "They heal the same as everyone else."

Another Sunday, Elham Fara, the organist I had met at the church the previous Sunday, took me to tea with a family who lived in her building. Like most of the people in the building, they were Christians. We parked and climbed over piles of trash—the amount of rubbish in Gaza never ceases to amaze me—and came to an unlovely gray concrete high-rise in the midst of a wasteland.

The electricity was out, which meant a long hike up stairs and awkwardly using the flashlight on our telephones when the door finally opened. "For Christians or Muslims, this is intolerable," Boolus, a twenty-one-year-old dentistry student, said in greeting, pointing up at the fans that were not working.

"No electricity. We are on the seventh floor. My father has a heart condition and has to climb the stairs every day. We have no clean water. The thing is, we are Christians, we suffer. But all of us, all Gazans, suffer the same deprivation."

There were wool tapestries depicting the Last Supper and the Good Shepherd on the walls. There was a small electric organ, and as we drank tea and ate watermelon, Elham sat down uninvited and began to play "Old Black Joe," a melancholy parlor song written by Stephen Foster in 1860. In one corner of the room were instruments, music stands, and a speaker. Boolus and his brother played cello and trumpet, while their father, Maher, joined them on the piano. "We are all Christians," Boolus shrugged when I asked him about the specific branches of Christianity in Gaza. "It's the same God." Boolus was named after St. Paul. He is an Orthodox Christian but prays at the Catholic church. As a child he went to a Catholic school, so he never noticed any discrimination. He described himself as being "in a Christian bubble." When he got to Al-Azhar University in Gaza at the age of eighteen, he suddenly felt like a minority. "The first thing people ask you—teachers, students—is, 'Are you Christian?'"

Every Christmas and Easter, the family applies for permits to go to Bethlehem. Usually, not all members of the family get one, which means they are separated on their most important holidays. The previous Christmas, Boolus got one, but his father didn't.

Elham, as if on cue, began to play "Jingle Bells" on the organ.

Boolus wanted to leave Gaza to find a better job, but he couldn't stand the thought of leaving his close-knit family. Studying is a futile endeavor, he said, because he knows there is no reward, no job at the end.

He also yearned for stability. Boolus said his father had lived through the war of 1967 and the many uprisings and crackdowns since then, "and he deserves some peace and freedom from worrying." His parents, both government workers, had been receiving only half their salaries since the most recent political falling-out between Hamas and the PA in 2017.

"So we are being punished by our own people," Boolus said glumly.

He took a slice of watermelon and handed me a plate. "This is what happens to normal people. You should study, then you should work. But in Gaza, you study and then stay at home. When I graduate, I will be the three-thousandth dentistry graduate. Maybe five hundred are actually going to get a job."

Boolus said he most likely would eventually leave Gaza and get a master's degree, then return.

"It's my people," he said. "They need dentists. And doctors. And lawyers. If all the professional people leave for a better life, who will represent us?"

FATHER MARIO

When I met Father Mario, the priest who had given me the French document detailing Christian history, he was preparing to leave Gaza. Originally from Brazil, he was the pastor of the Church of the Holy Family and spoke quietly in accented English. He welcomed me into a quiet and sparse office, painted white against the heat, and poured me a glass of water. He looked tired. He had ambivalent feelings about leaving Gaza.

Father Mario had spent seven years at the Church of the Holy Family. When he arrived in 2012, he spoke no Arabic. It was just after the second Gaza war, and there was utter desolation. The tunnels, Gaza's lifeline, were closed a few months later. The infrastructure was broken. "Everything was destroyed," he said.

He had come from a long service at the Vatican, and he was unsure about spending years in Gaza. He prayed for God to guide him. He asked for happiness. He said to God, "Take everything from me, but give me happiness."

"I felt so bad," he said of the early days. "As a priest, I asked for consolation. I prayed for Gaza to get better every year. But every year it gets worse."

Father Mario stood before his people each Sunday at Mass and tried to encourage them to keep their faith, but he was unsure of how to do this. He was concerned about the pressure that the Hamas leadership would put on his congregation. Most of all, he had no idea how to lead his constantly shrinking flock.

"We are now 117 Latin [Roman] Catholics in my Church," he said. "Fifteen years ago, there were four thousand Catholic and Orthodox Christians."

His parishioners were largely from warm-hearted, close-knit families. They welcomed him, but they were deeply troubled about their situation. Still, Father Mario was moved: by the closeness of the Palestinian communities, by the profound bonds between family members. Despite what seemed to him to be absolute misery, there was a connection to their Christian roots, stretching back centuries, that they clung to.

"It was a beautiful community," he said. "But we lost 70 percent of them. People ask if it is Hamas. But I can tell you the main reason."

Father Mario stared at his hands. "It's too difficult to live here. Difficult for people without income. Difficult to live without freedom. Christians can't visit their families in Jerusalem. They can't work in Tel Aviv. There is no future."

Among the Christian youth, many of whom were graduating that week, there was 70 percent unemployment. But it was not only the Christians who were suffering, he added. In 2018 alone, he said, thirty thousand Muslims left Gaza.

Two years after he arrived, another war with Israel started, even more brutal than the previous one in 2008: the ferocious bombing, the bodies trapped inside concrete, inside steel. The overcrowded hospital with the bloody, the battered, the broken. No electricity, no water, just punitive bombing for weeks. The wreckage, when the war finally ended, was monumental. Father Mario stayed in Gaza throughout. He tried to pray. He could find no reason, no logic for the suffering around him.

Two years later, in 2016, there was a moment of hope for the Christian people during a brief respite between Fatah and

Hamas. Then Father Mario allowed himself to believe, briefly, that his prayers had been answered.

"We thought we would have electricity for twenty-four hours!" he said. "That we could travel. It was a wedding of Palestine!" He was referring to a hope that the two main political factions, Hamas and Fatah, were at last uniting.

But the rapprochement did not last. Soon, he said, Palestinian president Mahmoud Abbas began punishing Gaza. The Israelis stepped up their security measures, making the borders impossible to cross, even for Christians.

That year, families in the congregation asked for six hundred permits for Bethlehem or Beit Sahour; they got three hundred. Half the people who wanted to celebrate Christmas with their families could not. Families were divided. They came to Father Mario pleading for advice.

He felt a great anguish. People told him they had chances to leave, to go to Canada or America, to join family.

"What can I say if they are looking for a better life?" he asked me in a pained voice. "How can I stop them from leaving?" It was the same anguished response I heard from priests in Iraq, in Syria, and in Egypt when their parishioners were facing the choice of whether to emigrate or remain in their ancestral land.

"In Gaza, we are looking at how our community is dying," he said. The Christian leadership in Gaza—the doctors, the government workers, the engineers—left when Hamas came in. And they took with them their sons and daughters. "The people who are left are old," Father Mario added.

The relationship between Christians and Muslims in Gaza, he said, is deteriorating. No one will admit it, no one wants to talk about it. He told me that his parishioners spoke of times in the past when their relations were better. But Hamas changed that.

Father Mario had some good days in Gaza, when he baptized a newborn or officiated at a confirmation. When he saw new life. But other days were less positive. "I'm working for God," he said. "I do what he's asking me. I stop to think why he's doing this, but I often don't understand."

As I got ready to leave, Father Mario told me, "I'm giving my life trying to keep Christians here. But the reality is, it is not in my hands."

He revealed that the prospect of departing Gaza left him desolate. "Yesterday I was thinking about leaving, and I cried," he said. "I am saddened to leave . . . but this year was the hardest of my life. People came to me every day to solve problems. 'Father, can you pay for my electricity?' 'Father, can you help get my son a job?' And you can't help everyone. If you give to one, you get everyone upset. These are not bad people. These are desperate people."

He told me that if he were a real father, he would suffer if his children did not have food. This was what it was like, he said, being the father of a church where people were suffering.

Just before I left, I asked him what he asked for when he prayed.

"When I pray," he said simply, affirming his early comments about his hopes, "I ask for happiness."

At his last Mass, he said goodbye to his people. Again, he cried. He said he was disheartened to leave, but he was not leaving them alone. God would always be with them, the people of Gaza. He told them they were not alone in their suffering.

Then, he closed the door of the church and drove to the crossing and into Israel. He went through the checkpoints. In 2020, as COVID-19 restrictions eased in the summer, I wondered where Father Mario was and how he was managing. I wrote to him and he responded quickly. He was in Brazil, his home country. He missed his challenging mission in Gaza, but he was also reflecting on the long-term effects of the never-ending lock-down in Gaza: "It was a good experience for me but it was also a difficult time," he wrote. "I think the situation in Gaza touches our psychological side. It is impossible to live there and not be affected by the problems we have there. It was my reality, even if I lived there for only seven and a half years. We cannot imagine what the problems are like for the people who have been living there for all of their lives."

THE GREAT MARCH

The plight of Christians in Gaza should be seen as part of the wider struggles faced by all of the inhabitants of this narrow strip of land boxed in by Israel, Egypt, and the Mediterranean. On a sweltering summer day in July 2019, when the air was so thick it was hard to breathe, I met Ahmed Abu Artema. In January 2018, Artema, who was then thirty-one, had written a Facebook post prompting a protest movement called the Great March of Return. It was a crucial moment in modern Gazan history.

The Great March started as a peaceful demonstration, and Artema, a poet and former journalist who had studied Dr. Martin Luther King Jr.'s civil rights protests, led the heaving and cheering crowds toward Gaza's border fence with Israel. His goal was to bring the world's attention to the plight of the Gaza Strip: three wars in less than a decade, broken infrastructure, young people hindered by unemployment and Israeli subjugation. But the main goal was to demonstrate their collective desire to return to the homes that were taken from them during the creation of Israel, when 750,000 Palestinians were dislocated.

The protesters saw it as their "Gandhi moment," explained Matthias Schmale, the head of the United Nations Relief and Works Agency for Palestine Refugees in the Near East

(UNRWA), the UN's refugee agency in Gaza. Every Friday, Palestinians gathered at the border. They called for an end to the Israeli and Egyptian blockade, which has become a symbol of deliberate, unjust violence between actors on an uneven playing field.

The Israelis on the other side of the fence saw the Great March in an entirely different light: as a nuisance that must be put down. Grisha Yakubovich, a former colonel of the Israeli Defense Forces (IDF) and an expert on Israeli-Palestinian relations, pointed to the cause of the 2014 war between Gaza and Israel, Operation Protective Edge, to understand Israel's violent reaction to the Great March. Following the kidnapping and murder of three Israeli teenagers by Hamas members, Israel and Gaza traded air strikes and rocket attacks. The conflict finally ended after a ground invasion by Israeli forces, with over 2,000 people dying in the process. Of the dead, 1,462 were Palestinian civilians and 638 were Palestinian soldiers, while 7 were Israeli civilians and 66 were Israeli soldiers.[9] The conditions in Gaza, already difficult before the war, deteriorated even further, and the reconstruction promised by the international community failed to materialize. "The terrible reality in Gaza created the conditions for another war," Yakubovich said.

The Israeli military was still psychologically present in Gaza during my 2019 visit, even though it had officially pulled out of the area. This was most noticeable during the Friday protests. As the protesters moved closer to the fence, the Israelis on the other side would mow them down with live ammunition. By mid-2020, 214 Palestinians had died and 36,000 had been wounded in the Great March protests.[10] More than 100 people had had limbs amputated, because the IDF fired at ankles and knees, deliberately aiming to cripple.

Although Yakubovich told me the IDF believed they were firing at "terrorists," there had been calls from global human rights groups (including B'Tselem, the remarkably brave Israeli watchdog for human rights) for war crimes prosecutions for IDF actions as more people were killed. The Israeli Army said it opened fire only as a last resort and considered firing at the lower limbs an act of restraint. It blamed Hamas for orchestrating the march.

Yakubovich said, "There are too many casualties on both sides, but I acknowledge that there were a lot of Palestinians. Even one death is too many. From the perspective of the IDF, however, the snipers are instructed not to kill anyone. They are aiming not to kill. Unfortunately, we cannot know who wants to cross the border. This is why we must shoot as a safety precaution."

It is a brutal and heartless form of restraint, one that will leave its mark on amputees and victims in Gaza for decades. The Israeli military, for its part, demonizes the Palestinians and sinks into a systemic "us vs. them" mindset. This mindset shows up in all aspects of Israeli culture, from politics to media. In the popular Netflix series *Fauda*, which examines the inner lives of an elite Israeli commando unit that infiltrates Arab lives and villages—causing a great amount of destruction—not once are the Palestinians shown as human beings trapped in a terrible set of circumstances, held down by oppressors. Instead, the series most often depicts them as cold-blooded killers.

I went to the Great March of Return one Friday, and I saw young men and women rush to the fence singing protest songs, knowing they could be shot down by the Israeli soldiers perched in secure mud-colored shelters several hundred feet away from them. A beautiful young girl carried a Palestinian flag. There was the whir of ambulances carrying the wounded and, strangely, the aura of a party. Farther back from the wall, people were bused in from camps and sat listening to a play put on by Hamas officials. The women embroidered and ate salted nuts that they passed around.

But not everyone was in a festive mood. Schmale of the UNRWA told me that, in a sense, going to the fence was a form of suicide for some. The suicide rate had risen drastically in Gaza despite the immense shame it brings on the families of the deceased, partly because suicide is forbidden in Islam. "I guess the thought is, 'Before I jump off a house and bring shame to my family, I'd rather go to the fence and die a hero,'" he said.

In a clinic run by Doctors Without Borders in Gaza, specifically set up in the wake of the march in order to deal with the massive influx of orthopedic emergencies, a staffer showed me X-rays and described how the Israelis were clearly aiming at joints to cripple and inflict as much pain as possible.

The victims I met had all been unarmed when they were shot. They ranged from a thirty-something mother who had been seriously wounded, and was at the clinic with her two children, to damaged teenagers and middle-aged men. All had ungainly metal pins on the outside of their bones, which Jacob Burns, a Doctors Without Borders staffer, described to me: "That kind of debilitating bone pain is hard to imagine," he said. "Then they run a huge risk of infection, and we're just not equipped to operate." He grimaced. "You have no idea how much they suffer." Burns explained that many would be disabled for life.

When I asked one protester, thirty-one-year-old Ahmed, a laborer who had lost the lower part of his leg, why he'd gone to the fence knowing he might be shot, he replied, "I went to the fence to be patriotic. If I'm not there, who will be?"

Then I saw Reda al-Banna, a forty-five-year-old mother of five huddled in a corner. She smiled and hobbled over on crutches to join the conversation. She was one of the volunteers treating the wounded near the fence when she was shot. She had just had her third operation after sustaining horrible bone infections and narrowly escaping amputation. "I have not slept since the day I was shot. The pain is huge," she told me. She sat in a chair and showed me her damaged leg. Metal pins were soldered into her bone and jutted out through her skin. She winced as she lifted her leg to show where the pins went deep into her flesh.

Most of the Christians I spoke to did not go to the Great March, largely because of their desire to keep their heads down politically and to remain more or less anonymous, but it affects them: their daily life, their security, their anxiety level. Even though young people of every religion are affected by the misery of Gaza, the protests were driven primarily by Muslim youth, who railed against widespread unhappiness and stagnation. Since the Great March began, it had become common to see young people on crutches limping through the streets of Gaza. Mahmoud Abu Zer, a young protester, told me, "There is no such thing as a future for young people here. I'd give both of my legs to make things better for my family."

"Gaza offers nothing," agreed Dr. Caitlin Procter, a Harvard political scientist working in Gaza and studying migration patterns. "When they go, they go. Leaving with no thoughts of return."

I had met Procter in a mostly empty fish restaurant overlooking the sea. She led us inside where it was dark and cool. Procter, an Arabist, conversed fluently with the waiters, then went to the fish tank alone and selected a perfect sea bass, scales glistening.

She sat and ordered a fresh juice. Picking up where she left off, she told me that leaving is not easy for most Gazans. "They take crazy risks to leave," she said. "In early 2019, it cost between five and seven thousand dollars to get from Gaza to Egypt."

Procter added, "There are only a few buses. You have to put your name on a list and pay to move up the list. Belgium used to give asylum to between thirty and seventy thousand applicants from Gaza per year, but there is no real data available." And all this was before the COVID-19 pandemic began in early 2020, which made border crossing even more difficult.

Making Gaza unlivable plays into the "settler colonialism" mindset, the goals of which, Procter explained, are to "make Palestine fade away. . . . If it ceases to exist, you kill it politically and economically."

This is why many East Jerusalem Palestinians apply for Israeli citizenship, Procter told me. They are giving up their identity in many ways, but it makes their lives bearable. Because it is easier. Gaza offers nothing, she told me miserably—because Procter is an academic who loves her work, who cares deeply for the people and the place, and who has spent years studying migration patterns in the hope of making Gaza a place worth staying in.

She stared down at her hands, still a little dusty from the street.

"Palestine offers nothing," she said finally.

DIGNITY

For the foreseeable future, for the youth in Gaza, Christian and Muslim alike, life is stifling. Their memories, especially for those under twenty, are of little more than the three wars, of aerial bombardment. Every family lost someone or knows someone who was killed. For those slightly older, it is the memory of the Israeli occupation here, and of profound injustice. They remember when soldiers would come into the camps, taking parents or siblings away in the middle of the night.

Why do they emigrate? "When you put a man in a locked room without food, he will knock on the door to get food. If there is no solution, he will break the door," explained Artema.

"Every human being wants to live in dignity," he added.

Dignity is the word I heard the most when I was in Gaza. Not freedom, not wealth, not poverty, but dignity.

Dignity includes the ability to be financially independent, yet the economy, according to Mahmoud Sabra from Al-Azhar University in Gaza, is hindered because of the "two governments, Hamas and the PA," as well as by the Israeli/Egyptian blockade.

The PA stopped making capital improvements when Hamas took power back in 2006, and the infrastructure—roads, schools, health care, the water supply—has suffered drastically as a result. International organizations donate fewer resources because of Hamas's presence. The Trump administration, which openly despised the Palestinians, cut all of its funding for the UNRWA, ending the United States' role as the refugee organization's largest individual donor.[11] This news came two days after Trump announced a $200 million cut to the United States Agency for International Development (USAID), which had led programs helping thousands in Gaza. Hamas has also had to cut pay for its employees. Sabra estimated a 53 percent poverty rate.

Sabra also highlighted Gazans' difficulty in procuring necessary supplies from abroad. "Protected imports can't get into Gaza because of the blockade," he pointed out. Remittances are declining. These used to help families in Gaza with education and health care, but more and more Palestinian expats are severing their ties to their homeland, laying down fresh roots in their new lands, where they consider themselves to be permanent immigrants rather than temporary arrivals.

Despite this, Sabra said, there is a huge potential for the Palestinian economy in terms of growth and human capital. "We have cheap labor skills," he said, "and a highly productive workforce." Judging by the number of brilliant young graduates I met, the level of education is extremely high, as are language skills. Palestine has a literacy rate of more than 96 percent, well above the regional average. Women, Sabra told me, have made the greatest strides, jumping from a 78.6 percent literacy rate in 1995 to 94.1 percent today.[12]

What could change the desperate economy and high unemployment? In addition to using all of that brain power, Sabra said, the answer is government restructuring, as well as expanding the infrastructure and the seaport. "If the Israelis saw the Palestinians as equal trade partners—and we don't see them as occupiers, but partners—it would greatly benefit both of them," he said.

Even then, Gaza might be pulled out of the depths economically, but the long-lasting effects of trauma would remain.

The pain in Gaza is as much psychological as physical. "Conditions are getting worse and worse. They are going backwards," said Dr. Yasser Abu-Jamei, who runs a Gaza Community Health Program. Even after the war ended in 2014, the trauma did not cease. He sees high levels of PTSD and depression in Gaza. "For recovery to take place, we need peace. For the mind to have recovery, to recover from tragedy."

This sentiment is echoed across Gaza. "A big issue is the state of the people's mental health after three big wars," said Schmale from UNRWA, which runs 274 schools and 22 health centers in Gaza and is responsible for feeding 1 million people. "There is a persistent, slow social decay. It's not like people are starving to death and falling dead in the streets from lack of food."

In response to the World Bank prediction of 2020 being Doomsday in Gaza, Schmale shrugged. "It's already unlivable now. What's livable about being unemployed? What's livable if you depend on the UN for food? What's livable if you don't have safe drinking water? Or your dignity?" That was in the summer of 2019, a good nine months before COVID struck Gaza. Social distancing was that much harder for Gazans, especially those living in close quarters and using the beach as a way of escaping confinement.

Gaza is a manmade disaster, a deprived community. People should not be facing hunger. When I went to the Friday market, the stalls were full—there were pyramids of peppers, cucumbers, and eggplants, as well as mounds of grapes and peaches. I saw crate after crate of chickens waiting to be beheaded and plucked for the Friday lunch after prayers. There were piles of cellphones. Fresh sugarcane juice was available, and stacks of clothes for sale from Turkey or China. But few Gazans had the money to buy any of it.

I sensed collective claustrophobia, a constant state of repression, heaviness, and weighted tension. For even the extremely well educated, for determined, focused youth, graduating from university brings no promise of success—there is nowhere to go. Khaled al-Nairab, a twenty-two-year-old from Gaza City, called Gaza "a cemetery of talent."[13]

There are no jobs available, and even if they find something abroad, Gazans can't get visas or the permits to leave. Taxi drivers I met had completed numerous college degrees. One, a sociologist by training whose thesis was on poverty, told me he cleared twenty dollars a day after renting his car and paying for gas and fees. Still, he felt lucky for that small income. Gaza, despite its economic stagnation, is also populating quickly. The median age is 17.4.[14] Each woman has, on average, about four children. Two-thirds of the population is under the age of twenty-four. So what do these young people do when their world denies them wings to fly?

OMAR AND THE SKY GEEKS

One afternoon in 2019, I met Omar Al Khatib, a young journalist who worked as a project manager for a collective called #wearenotnumbers.[15] The collective had been set up in 2015 "to tell the human stories behind the numbers in the news" in Gaza, to explain how people lived without reducing them to politics and statistics. They wanted to move beyond numbers, which were "numbing." They did not want to simply convey how many people died, how many Christians were disappearing, how many were unemployed, and so on. What they wanted to write about was the daily lives of Palestinians on the streets and in the refugee camps: "the struggles and triumphs, the tears and laughter, the aspirations that are so universal," as their Facebook description put it.[16]

Omar, a tall, shy twenty-five-year-old, told me his story. He had suffered through a family tragedy. His brother, Abdel, was at a friend's house, enjoying jello with whipped cream, in 2014 during the war when the house was struck by an Israeli F-16 rocket.[17] Abdel, only twenty-three, was blown out of the house and killed.

Five of Omar's friends were also in the house that day. They had been buried alive in the rubble, unable to escape. During eight days of targeted attacks, no one could dig through the debris to find them. By the time the attacks ended, they had all suffocated or been crushed. Omar went into a deep depression, but he decided to transform his misery into writing.

A few months before I met him, Omar had attended a conference in Egypt, thrilled to leave Gaza and meet people from the outside. He had traveled the usual way, via the Rafah crossing at the southern point of Gaza, which leads to Egyptian territory. Somehow, he had received a valid Palestinian passport, issued by the PA, and permission to travel to Egypt.

One day he was picked up by an Egyptian policeman when he tried to renew his residence permit. Egyptian security forces are notorious for their brutality: in 2015 alone, 267 people were killed by the Egyptian police, there were 1,250 forced disappearances, and over 40,000 people were taken as political prisoners.[18] The police officer roughed him up and accused him of forging his passport. The officer told Omar that he knew he had

done nothing wrong, but spat at him, "I hate dirty Palestinians."
He refused to let Omar go.

Omar was taken in front of a judge who ruled that he should
be released on bail for 20,000 Egyptian pounds. Unable to call
his parents or even a lawyer, he was desperate, so he paid. He
was nevertheless then jailed for an entire month, and for half of
that time, forced into solitary confinement. Finally Omar was
deported back to Gaza, but he'd been stripped of his passport
and all of his other travel documents.

Omar asked me to come teach a journalism class to the "word
artists" at the Gaza Sky Geeks (GSG) center, a tech incubator
founded by Google and Mercy Corps. So one afternoon in late
July 2019, I went to Gaza City for a visit. The Sky Geeks were
founded by Google and Mercy Corps, but other tech companies
and foundations have since added their support to the program.
GSG hosts a coding academy, provides grants for start-ups, and
runs mentoring programs to help people succeed in a variety of
freelance businesses in different fields. It emphasizes diversity
and inclusion, with 50 percent female participation in its programs, and claims to have "helped thousands of young people
collectively earn millions of dollars in life-sustaining income."[19]

When I arrived at GSG's nondescript building, I asked about
the name—why "Sky Geeks"?—and a staffer cheerfully told me,
"We call it that because the sky's the limit." However unlikely
that seemed in Gaza, I had to admit that upon entering I felt
like I could have been in Silicon Valley. The spirit of the place
was astounding. Rooms were named after foreign cities that the
employees will likely never see: Berlin, New York, Tokyo. In
each room, participants gathered and worked on projects that,
without the Sky Geeks mentorship, might have never seen the
light of day, simply because of Gaza's isolation.

All of the "Geeks" speak perfect English. GSG is based on
the idea that high-speed fiber-optic Internet can uplift young

communities. Maybe in the modern world, the sky can be reached digitally.

I spoke with several staffers and participants. Zada explained to me how the coding academy worked, then showed me the rooms and projects. He talked about how confining the wars were for young people especially, how it killed their innovative spirit. Brain drain is a death knell, he said, but it's also the only alternative for many. "How long can we endure?" he asked. "But on the other hand, no one wants to leave their home."

Iyad, a computer scientist, laid out the options for me. "Basically, when you graduate, you can work for an NGO if you are lucky, or you work as a government official for Hamas for a couple of hundred dollars every few months."

Schmale told me that Gazans were the most innovative and gutsiest people he had ever known. He had a lifetime of experience working in conflict zones. "But until people take the boot off their neck," he said—referring to Hamas, the United States, Israel, Egypt, and the PA—the Gazans would not be able to thrive.

Once Omar had returned to Gaza, stunned and confused by his ordeal, he had found out that he had won a Chevening Scholarship, a prestigious academic grant that would allow him to pursue a master's degree in the United Kingdom. A few weeks later, he was notified that he had also received a Fulbright Scholarship to study conflict resolution in the United States. This is when the real nightmare started.

When Omar applied for a new passport in Ramallah, PA officials told him he would not be getting one, because he "was from Gaza, and therefore Hamas." When he turned to Hamas officials for help, they shrugged. The British organization that had awarded the scholarship was powerless to help Omar regain his passport or obtain permission to leave. For months, he wrote letters, made phone calls, and knocked on office doors.

By July 2019, when I met him, Omar was desperate. He had a chance to leave Gaza, study, then come back and bring his knowledge home, yet he was being punished by his own people. "All my life, I did the right thing," he said, not in a self-pitying way, but out of bewilderment. "I never broke rules. I did what I was told. Now I'm being punished by Palestinians because I am Palestinian?"

In early September, he sent me an emoji with a teardrop, writing, "All the other Chevening Scholars have arrived at the university." I activated my own contacts to try to help, writing letters to chief negotiators, aides of President Mahmoud Abbas, diplomats, senior UN human rights officials, anyone who I thought might be able to help. There was a deafening silence from Ramallah.

I went to Omar's home to make sure there was nothing suspicious, in case they were holding back his passport because they suspected his family had close ties to Hamas. Instead, I met parents who had raised nine children with love against horrendous odds, including the murder of one of their beloved sons. There was no radicalism or extremism. These were just hardworking, kind people. Over vast servings of delicious *madfouna* (a flatbread stuffed, in this case, with heavily spiced chicken with rice), trays of bursting fruit, and honeyed sweets, Omar's parents spoke of how proud they were of their children.

It seemed Omar was the victim of collective punishment. The PA refused to reissue his passport as a sign to all Gazans that they had elected the enemy. The cruelty of withholding Omar's shot at a new life was staggering.

The second week of September, when classes were beginning, a European diplomat wrote to the PA in Ramallah in a fury. He said that if they did not reissue the passport within twenty-four hours, he would go public with their corruption and with the story that they were thwarting a young scholar's chance at a dream.

Whether due to that letter or for some other reason, the passport arrived. Omar was forced to travel through Egypt, then on to Jordan, to get a flight to the United Kingdom. He texted me from Amman. He is now studying international journalism. His dream had come to fruition, but it had taken a huge amount of outside help, both from me and from a cadre of diplomats and high-level sources. What if he had been alone, in a refugee camp, with no help and no voice to guide him out of Gaza? An entire chance at a new life would have been lost.

Now I wonder if he will ever go back to Gaza. I think back on the dinner I had with his family, how much love they shared between them: his mother serving huge plates of chicken, his brother teasing him, his cousins dropping by for coffee after dinner, people calling out to each other from the windows. I remember a strange feeling of envy wash over me. Western lives, so much more materialistic and disconnected from family, sometimes seem less joyful.

I thought, and so hoped, that Omar's story would be a happy one. But when I reached out to Omar in the summer of 2020, the terrible summer of COVID, I was overwhelmed by his heartbreaking response.

He wrote, "When I first arrived in the UK and joined my class, I was out of this world! The moment I took my first steps in London, I forgot all the pain in my life. I was very happy." He believes now, however, that "a Palestinian is not destined to be happy." The past several months had slowly and dreadfully eroded his spirit. His painful ordeal in Egypt had resurfaced, with officials issuing an arrest warrant for him. Then, in the early days of the pandemic, Omar's sister called to inform him that his mother was ill: "Doctors said that we will lose our mother in a few days." His mother's dying wish was to see her son. Omar could not return home for fear of being arrested in

Egypt. His mother passed away, without her beloved son by her side.

Omar's words haunt me: "My mother died, and part of my heart died with her. I still cry as I write this to you. I will graduate in a month from now. And then my visa to stay in the UK will expire. I can't stay in the UK and I can't go back to Gaza because the Egyptians will arrest me. I feel stranded and trapped. And I have no idea what to do."

As of this writing, Omar is still in the United Kingdom studying, caught between two worlds. He misses his family in Gaza. He was in the process of applying for asylum as a political refugee, but he felt ashamed of this. He was grateful to the country that had taken him in, and the kindness of many strangers. But he was worried that his identity would be erased. He had spent his entire life in Gaza. Now he was not sure he would ever be able to return.

THE LIVING AND THE DEAD

For decades, I have witnessed and watched some of the most horrific scenes imaginable: ethnic cleansing, genocide, systematic rape. My concerns always lay with the survivors and the way that some societies managed to return to, if not normalcy, at least some semblance of regular life. How do you recover, how do you move forward with life when the unthinkable happens?

So Gaza has always bewildered me. For such a deeply wounded place, people survive, including the tiny, outnumbered, and vulnerable Christian community. During my trip there in 2019, I went to the beach most nights after sunset, when families gathered with picnics and beach chairs, enjoying a respite from the heat and claustrophobia of the camps. I sat and talked with them. One night there were two beautiful sisters, one a dentist and the other still a student. Another night I encountered a famous blind imam. Then there was a new mother with her infant and an extended family who insisted on serving me tea in tiny china cups they had carried onto the beach. Despite their joy in being together, the message was always the same: we are living, but we are dying.

There is a constant sense of injustice. Schmale told me a story of one of his colleagues, a fifty-three-year-old woman with cancer who needed chemotherapy to prolong her life. She died after the Israelis denied her request for a permit to travel to the West Bank. "There are hundreds of stories like that," he said.

Dr. Jihad El-Hissi, a Gazan from the Catholic charity Caritas, also expressed his worries about the toxic environment on the Strip, which causes grave damage not just to mental health but also to physical well-being. He recited a catalog of illnesses in Gaza: chronic stress, diabetes, hypertension, cancer at an unnaturally high rate. But of all these, his gravest concern was environmental illness. "There are hundreds of pounds of solid waste on the beaches. The sea is polluted. There are no treatment plants. Marine life is threatened, but this is where the children swim," he said. "We see eye and skin infections. Then there is air pollution from burning plastic. There is no control over pesticides for agriculture, which leads to long-term illnesses."

El-Hissi said he was convinced Gaza had a higher rate of breast cancer than other regions because of the pollution. "We are seeing girls of nineteen with breast cancer," he told me. "This is surely environmental pollution." Radiation treatment is not available anywhere in Gaza, he added, and often the clinics lacked the chemotherapy drugs necessary to complete treatment programs.

Yet despite the tide of misery, there was also a tremendous resilience. There were people who somehow carried on with their lives, invented projects, were creative, produced original ideas and concepts. I met poets and organic farmers. I went to the YMCA to see teenage girls playing basketball with gusto.

In the midst of this chaos, Hamas, according to spokesman Hassim Qasser, is "rebranding." He insisted they were developing a kinder, gentler face, with a new manifesto recognizing the state of Israel. "We don't deny it," he said. "We are changing, adapting. Even our relations with other Palestinian parties: we are accepting of communists, the PFLP [the Popular Front for the Liberation of Palestine, a hard-line secular party in the PLO], other parties."

More interesting was my conversation over tea with Dr. Ahmed Yousef, a former deputy foreign minister and senior adviser to Prime Minister Ismail Haniya. The author of forty books, Yousef had been educated in the United States and had a staff of mainly women whom he treated as equals, something unheard of in Hamas's former manifestation.

Yousef believed that when Hamas was first elected, it did not have the political awareness to run Gaza. It was made up of religious people, he said, suspicious people who had never left Gaza. But they have changed radically, he claimed. "Now, they are in the universe," he said, although he admitted they were still struggling.

Like everyone else I talked to, he agreed that the only solution was stronger leadership: "We need a great man—or woman— to lead the struggle. We need to keep the Great March going, to remind people around the world there is still an occupation." But, he added, smiling, "We don't know what to do, to be honest with you. If you put someone in a cage, they'll start moving in all directions. He doesn't know what to do. He's hungry. He's thirsty. He wants to get out." He paused and sipped his tea. "We need to get out. We need to get out of this siege."

SISTERS

Before I left, two Christian sisters I had met at the Orthodox Church invited me to their home. I had noticed them both on their way into Mass. Dressed in chic linen suits with hats, they reminded me of my own mother and her sister Rosemary, devout Catholics who always went to church dressed as if they were on a fashion runway.

These women seemed to me to be part of an old world that was vanishing: a time when Gaza was elegant, when wealthy families lived in huge villas with servants, when tea was served on silver trays, the English and French were taught by nannies, and trains went to Cairo and Beirut for summer holidays.

Their home was a respite from the relenting heat, the sand, the pollution outside their door. I arrived sweaty, leaving my dusty shoes in the hallway, embarrassed at how grimy my feet were, although I had already showered twice that day.

Margaret was wearing a silk dress, and her hair was beautifully arranged. She had been a teacher in UNRWA schools for many years and had never married. Helen, who was quieter and seemed shy, possessed the same elegance. She had married a man from Jaffa, a former refugee who had come to Gaza in 1948. Her daughter lived in Kuwait.

The women lived not far from the Gloria Hotel in an elegant high-rise. From their window overlooking the Mediterranean, the view rivaled one you might see in Miami or Los Angeles. Even the elevator worked, at least on the day I visited.

The sisters' lives were a world apart from those in the refugee camps. Each had her own apartment, Helen living across the hall with her husband, but with a communal room in between. Margaret's living room overlooked the vast expanse of the Mediterranean. It was air-conditioned, elaborate, and tastefully decorated with statues of Our Lady, wooden crucifixes, and sofas. A housekeeper brought coffee, Arabic sweets, and chocolates on a silver tray with cubes of sugar. They described themselves as "old Gazans," meaning their family had arrived and settled before the refugees came from Israel in 1948. They remember whitewashed villas, grand parties, swimming pools, gardens of bright flowers. "It was paradise," Margaret says. "There was space."

Their father came from Jaffa, the port city north of Gaza in Israel proper, and had been appointed by the British as the supervisor of the railroad that went from Gaza to Egypt, an eight-hour trip. It was a gentleman's job, and he was chosen because he spoke perfect English. The family was brought up to speak English and Arabic, and they traveled throughout the region, to Syria and Lebanon. Their father died at the age of thirty-nine, when Margaret was only two, and their eldest brother stepped into his role. Their mother sold their large house in Jaffa and bought a villa in Gaza.

Margaret never married, receiving a degree in Arabic literature in Lebanon in 1979 and returning to Gaza to teach. "They took anyone who knew how to teach," she said, reaching for a sugar cube. She said that when she began teaching, the children, many of them refugees, were so poor that their lunch was a slice of bread with red pepper.

The sisters said their Christian faith is important to them. They are culturally and religiously tied to it; it is a part of their identity and the basis of their sense of community. They are aware that their world is shrinking around them, but they won't leave. Like everyone else, they try to get permits to go to Bethlehem for Christmas. They go to the YWCA complex with the other Christians in the community and play bingo or watch the children play basketball.

Will there ever be peace in Gaza? Margaret laughed lightly. "We are not optimistic or pessimistic," she said. "We just want a small state of our own. We are still waiting."

Before I left in Gaza, I did a favor for an Australian friend. Her great-uncle had been wounded while fighting in North Africa during World War II and was brought to Gaza, where he died. He was buried in the Commonwealth War Cemetery, a place I had never been in all my years working nearby. During their occupation, the British built Anglican churches and hospitals, mainly at the end of the nineteenth century, which have mostly disappeared. But still there was this strange, lonely cemetery where forgotten soldiers, defenders of the old British Empire, were buried.

Nicole Tung, the photojournalist, and I arrived in the morning, before the unbearable heat had risen. Not far from the Erez crossing into Israel, I found his grave. Someone had been looking after it; it was clean and neat. There were trees nearby, shading row upon row of graves of foreigners who had died in Gaza. It was quiet and still. Then a Palestinian family came out and joined me, looking at the graves. They were the caretakers. The children had brought the family cat.

We stood silently in front of the gray stone that marked the grave of Sapper J. G. Eckford, who died aged twenty-eight in October 1942 from his wounds, so very far from home. I laid some red flowers. It was a poignant moment, full of all the sadness of so many wars and so many tragedies. "To live in hearts we leave behind is not to die," read his epitaph.

I took photos for his relatives in Australia and left, slightly tearful. I thought of all the people I had met in Gaza, from farmers near Erez to families clinging to the hope of getting out from Rafah, where you can see Egypt across a fence. I thought about all the children I have interviewed over the years, when they were small during the first intifada and sat on the floor with me drawing tanks and Israeli soldiers and automatic weapons. I thought of how I had tried to find some of them a decade later, then two, and how many of them were dead, or just gone. Vanished.

There has been so much catastrophe here. Gaza is a flattened place. It makes survival, let alone any kind of hope or any dream of improvement, all the more incredible. Perhaps the next generation has a vision that their parents did not. There is, despite the misery, so much brilliance. So much potential.

Besides, Gaza has a tradition of stoic endurance, of solitary waiting for a transformational moment. I reflected on this at Tell Umm El-'Amr, which holds the ruins of the Byzantine-era monastery of St. Hilarion, an ascetic monk who lived in Gaza in the third and fourth centuries and spent most of his life in prayer in the quiet and solitude of the desert.

The monastery lies south of Gaza City, on the road to Rafah. I had passed it countless times on my many trips to Gaza over the years, but I had never before stopped, or wondered about the people who had worshipped there so long ago. The remains at the site actually span more than four centuries, from the late Roman Empire to the Umayyad period. Once, five churches stood here, as well as baths, a crypt, and a sanctuary. Today it is a pile of scorched rocks.

The monastery was abandoned after an earthquake in the seventh century and was only rediscovered by archaeologists in 1999, shortly before the second intifada erupted. It is in dire need of preservation and was added to the World Monuments Fund's watchlist in 2010.

I stopped there briefly on a hot day with Nicole, along with a Gazan friend from an old farming family. The heat from the low sun was unbearable. I was disappointed by how unimpressive the ruins were. They were disappearing into the sand.

I contemplated St. Hilarion, wondering what his life must have been like in the desert, and thought about the gentle, elegant sisters, Margaret and Helen, who had given me presents before I left to take to my own mother. Packed in my bag when I crossed over the border from Gaza to Israel were rosary beads, a statue of Our Lady, and a small bottle of holy water.

One of my earlier visits to Gaza had been to Marna House, where I had stayed during my very first reporting assignment. During the first intifada, this had been just about the only place to stay in the Gaza Strip. It was an old hotel run by the Shawras, an old, well-known Gazan family.

Back in 1991 I stayed at Marna House for several months, working on a book. A caretaker, Radwan, doubled as my waiter and cook. In those days, he must have been in his forties or even early fifties, with a huge shock of dyed black hair that he wore in a pompadour. I would sit at the long, wooden dining-room table alone night after night, eating my Gazan fish, and because I was so young, Radwan treated me like a daughter. I used to sit on the porch each night transcribing my scribbled notes and reading *The Histories* by Herodotus, but mostly being lonely and scared. Older reporters came and went, and I felt shy about having so little knowledge.

Back then, Radwan and Marna House's owner, Alya Shawra, were kind to me. They gave me the nicest room with a cool window overlooking the garden, brought me coffee and sugared tea, and took care of me when I became sick after a long day working in the refugee camps.

Years later, back at Marna House for the first time since, my request for Radwan yielded an old man, smaller than I remembered but with the same tremendous shock of hair (though now gray). He remembered everything: friends of ours who had been killed or died, the old dining room—the hotel had been remodeled entirely—and the early hopes of the first intifada.

I sat in his garden for an hour, drinking a lukewarm Pepsi, remembering, seeing my younger self, trying to recall how I had first seen Gaza, through fresh eyes. When it came time to leave, I hugged Radwan goodbye. He stood in the garden waving. My throat closed with emotion. So much time had passed.

And in Gaza, when you say goodbye to someone, you cannot know if you will ever see them again.

It took me about three hours to get through the security checks to enter Israel, even though I had a press card, a foreign passport, and the privilege to be able to voice my disgust at the arrogance of the Israeli guards, and my anger when they tore through my suitcase, ripping through notebooks and bottles of aspirin, unscrewing my tubes of toothpaste and face cream. I saw their disdain for Gaza. It is a wound, a sore.

I always leave with relief. I want to take a good shower, I want to sleep in a good bed, I want to breathe air that is not thick with pollution, and wake without the smell of trash. But there is also guilt, shame, and the fear that maybe life there will never change.

Pray for us, Margaret and Helen had requested of me when they said goodbye. More than money, they told me, what people need here is prayer.

3

SYRIA

2011–2020

IN FEBRUARY 1995, SEVEN MONTHS BEFORE MY FATHER DIED AND JUST TWO before he was diagnosed with incurable cancer, Joan Osborne released a song called "One of Us."

It played continually on the radio in London, where I lived that year, throughout the summer and into the autumn. The song would make me cry unexpectedly when I would hear it in a supermarket while buying eggs and milk, on my headphones while I was running in Hyde Park, or on plane trips back and forth between Africa, the Balkans, and Israel, where I was frantically working at the time.

> *What if God was one of us?*
> *Just a slob like one of us*
> *Just a stranger on the bus*
> *Tryin' to make his way home?*
> *If God had a face, what would it look like?*
> *And would you want to see if seeing meant*

That you would have to believe in things like heaven
And in Jesus and the saints, and all the prophets?

It reminded me also, for some reason, of a time in London when a homeless man approached my car and rapped loudly on the window, asking for money. My father was with me. The man startled me, and I told him no, to go away, perhaps too harshly. It was raining, and we were waiting in the car for something—I can no longer remember what—when my father suddenly said, "Wait a moment." He left the car and was gone for twenty minutes or more while I sat listening to the radio and the steady thump of the windshield wipers. Finally my father reappeared, soaking wet, and said nothing. He got into the passenger seat and I drove home.

Later, he told my mother that he had gone to look for the man I had turned away so abruptly, not out of cruelty but out of indifference and perhaps cynicism.

But he had been unable to find him.

I have often thought back on the shame I felt at my inaction then and the pride that my father's search, though futile, inspired in me. Now, the world is doing to Syria what I did to the homeless man. We have turned our backs on a population struggling to weather the most terrible storm.

Once COVID hit in the spring of 2020, countries around the world retreated into their own respective bubbles. Even as clashes continued in Idlib, the last holdout of the rebels fighting against President Bashar al-Assad's regime, the country faded from the global consciousness.

By 2020, the war in Syria was in its ninth miserable year. The United Nations had gone through four special envoys, each in his own way unique, each desperately trying to broker an end to the war, each failing. Peacemaking had shifted into the hands of the Russians, who aided and abetted Assad's war crimes in the air and on the ground. The Turks and the Russians had become the power brokers. Jihadi groups had infiltrated what had once been a revolutionary resistance against an authoritarian regime. Historic cities like Homs, Aleppo, and Idlib were in ruins. Ancient landmarks, such as Palmyra's Temple of Baal, nearly two millennia old and one of the most important historic sites in the country, had vanished into sand.

Syria was ripped apart at the seams, half of its people dead or displaced. It was one of the worst humanitarian crises in history, certainly the worst I had witnessed in thirty years of fieldwork. There were nearly six million refugees outside the country, another six million internally displaced, and an estimated twelve million more in dire need of assistance. As for the dead, no one had an exact number. The UN had stopped counting in 2016, no longer able to verify its sources on the ground. The best estimates were close to seven hundred thousand, but whatever the true figure, it was staggering. The lack of a definite death count symbolized the indifference of the international community. We did not even know how many people had died in this senseless war, where they were buried, or where their remains lay.

Dr. Omar Muhammed, an Egyptian neurosurgeon friend of mine who lived in Idlib for six years, operated during that time in an underground basement, largely on children who had shrapnel embedded in their brains. Russian-led bombing campaigns buried civilians under rubble, bones broken, skulls crushed.

Omar would send pleading texts, desperate to awaken a public that simply did not care. He would post images on Twitter of children's brain scans and try to make the public see his patients' humanity. These were people, kids, attacked in their homes, in the wrong place at the wrong time—collateral damage, so to speak. He tried to contain his anger at each needless death. Eventually, after years of hard work, even he left Syria.

It is hard to reconcile living a comfortable life while you know that people elsewhere, people you care about, are in agony. I found it hard to believe that I had started working in Syria in 2011, and that nine years later I was still receiving reports of villages being bombed and women and children fleeing from incessant violence.

Human rights abuses by the regime were far-reaching. In Assad's prisons, operatives carry out mind-numbingly cruel torture against any and all people who threaten the power of the regime. Human rights defenders and activists have disappeared, never to be seen again. Syrian and Russian forces in Aleppo and Idlib deliberately targeted civilian areas, relentlessly dropping barrel bombs into heavily populated areas. Hospitals were a favorite target. Doctors and nurses were slaughtered in droves. Humanitarian workers, such as members of the White Helmets, effectively first responders who dug civilians out of the rubble, were not only targeted as they were working, but also became the victims of a Russian-led propaganda campaign implying they were terrorists. Much of the public believed these claims.[1] But having worked alongside them and their founder, the late James Le Mesurier, I can attest to the fact that they were simply men and women trying to save lives.

The day Aleppo fell to regime forces in December 2016, I felt a deep and profound sorrow. I grieved for all those who were lost, but I especially feared for the Christians who lived across Syria and who were left vulnerable as the chaos escalated.

Although the war began as a battle between protesters and the Assad regime, Syrian Christians quickly became targets of violence. ISIS and other extremist groups began their campaigns against the region's religious minorities in late 2012, when Human Rights Watch reported the destruction of two churches in Ghasaniyeh and Jdeideh near the northern port city of Latakia.[2] A few months later, opposition forces looted and destroyed minority religious sites in towns near the Turkish border.[3] By March 2013, many Christian communities in the country's north and east had fallen to ISIS or Jabhat al-Nusra, a rebel group with ties to al-Qaeda.[4] The approximately five thousand Christian inhabitants of Raqqa on the shores of the Euphrates River in northern Syria were given less than a day to make a heartbreaking decision: convert to Islam or abandon the city with nothing but the clothes on their backs.[5]

The group's campaign against Christians intensified in 2015 and 2016. In February 2015, ISIS fighters attacked several Christian towns in northeastern Syria and took hundreds of people hostage. Three were executed, and the rest were eventually ransomed. Later that year, ISIS attacks on villages in the far northeast corner of the country led to the burning of centuries-old churches and the kidnapping of hundreds of Assyrian Christians, many of whom were tortured.[6] ISIS fighters bought and sold kidnapped Christian women and girls as slaves in Hassake's bazaar. As a result, virtually all Christians in the northeast of the country left, taking with them a rich cultural tradition that dates to the earliest days of the faith.

The conflict has had ripple effects even on Lebanon's well-established Christian community, as Syrian refugees poured into the neighboring country. Once 1.5 million Syrian refugees, the overwhelming majority of them Sunni Muslim, arrived there, the demographic balance between Christians and Muslims—the basis for a long-standing power-sharing agreement—began to tilt. The shift threatened the stability of the Lebanese Christian population, one of the largest groups of Christians in the Middle East. Worse, when I worked in Lebanon on refugee issues for the UN, I found two disturbing trends. One was the recruitment and radicalization of young refugee men who were left to rot in "settlements" in Lebanon, without schooling, activities, or any hope for a future. The second was a disturbing rise in xenophobia in

Lebanon and a growing tendency to blame refugees for everything, from electricity cuts to local violence.[7]

BROKEN PROMISES

In 2012, when I was still allowed to travel to regime-held territory, I saw what was only the beginning of a great uncertainty about the future for Syrian Christians that would shadow them throughout the war. In the early days of the fighting, especially in Damascus, I went to Sunday Masses across the city and spoke to the priests or parishioners—those who were not too frightened to talk. What they expressed was an underlying confidence that Assad, or the state, would protect them.

"Christians believe in law, believe in the state," explained Riad Adoumie, a Greek Catholic vascular surgeon, originally from Aleppo. He now lives in Southern California in a home built on a cliff with a sprawling terraced garden full of lush trees that remind him of his homeland. Dr. Adoumie left Syria for Lebanon when he was young, yet his heart "still rests in those terraced hills."

Dr. Adoumie explained that through the years, Christians in Syria wanted to be integrated, productive, successful components of society. They worked hard to achieve social standing, and the Ba'ath Party, which has ruled the country since 1967, gave them the platform to do so.

For most activists, and for journalists like myself, the Ba'ath Party is synonymous with thuggish politics, with Saddam Hussein, with the Assads. But to Adoumie, the party "really presents a framework of modern society or a vision where minorities could essentially be integrated into a secular society." There are not many models of that in the Middle East, he added, and without such a secular model, "most Christians and minorities are treated as second-class citizens." As a Christian, he personally remembered feeling safe in Syria, living without discrimination.

Perhaps not everyone seemed as accepting of Christians, but "the law was behind your back," as he put it.

When looking to Syria's future, Dr. Adoumie still held on to hope that some kind of peace could be achieved that would allow the country to remain united. He imagined a tolerant government, where he and other Christians would be treated as equal citizens. Yet he expressed his resentment toward outside influences in the Middle East that continue to tear countries apart, fragmenting society. "Our present is a failure, but our past is glorious," he said. "We are faced with such defeating, crushing irrelevance on the world scene and such miserable existence on the local scene. You see us humiliated, diminished, as international law is violated over and over again with careless disregard for any minimum level of fairness." If this treatment continues, he warned with melancholy, "there will not be a future, not just for the Christians."

The Christians in exile I spoke to always expressed a similar sentiment: a yearning, a nostalgia to return, and yet a pragmatic and resigned understanding that conditions were not likely to permit that in the years remaining to them. Still, many retain a flicker of hope. Although the United States is now a permanent home for Dr. Adoumie, he dreamed of one day taking his children to visit Syria. He has always promised them that he would. "If you give us the chance to rebuild," he declared, "we will rebuild."

I often wonder about how Syria will be rebuilt, once the war ends. Entire parts of Aleppo, Idlib, and Homs were reduced to rubble by the airstrikes ordered by Assad and, since 2015, Vladimir Putin. In Homs, a city brutalized by war, I remember sheltering during a street fight with a Christian family that lived opposite a church that had been splintered into dust and rubble. It was the first summer of the war, and the Syrian regime in Damascus was still willing to provide me with a visa.

I was allowed to travel to government-controlled areas, though always with minders who were supposed to keep me in line. It was clear that they wanted to give me their version of the war and theirs alone. I could not see, hear from, or talk to the opposition.

On this occasion, the Ministry of Information, which controlled the movements of foreign (in other words, enemy) journalists, had placed me with a pro-Assad unit of soldiers who were going into Homs to eliminate opposition snipers. We left Damascus in the early morning, abandoning a still thriving urban scene. There were pool parties, opera events, rooftop dinners, and champagne cocktail parties on elegant terraces. It seemed all of Damascus was in denial of the war that was swiftly approaching.

In contrast, Homs was a broken skeleton of a city. We dropped our bags in a dark regime-run hotel where we were the only guests, aside from the secret police and some higher-ranking soldiers. It felt creepy, unsettling, dangerous. There was no electricity, and the cavernous restaurant was closed except for a few Mukhabarat, who sat smoking and drinking acrid-looking orange juice. We met our unit at midday—just kids, basically, with precious little military training—and the soldiers mostly ignored us as they continued their house-to-house operations, taking shots at opposition forces from behind concrete walls. It was strange for me to travel with Bashar al-Assad's forces, though I had the sense that these young men wore their uniforms less out of profound loyalty to the regime and more through chance and bad luck.

As we ran from home to shattered home, ducking through "tunnels" built into the walls of houses to shield ourselves from sniper fire, stumbling over broken walls, broken lives, broken histories, I wondered if this city, once the third largest in Syria and renowned for its vast industry, could ever be repaired.

Certainly the fabric of it, its colorful religious and ethnic mixture, was irrevocably damaged.

The soldiers I accompanied were mainly Alawite, the offshoot of Shia Islam to which the Assad family adheres, but there were a few Christians as well. At one point, one of them led me to a family hiding in their gutted house in Homs's old Christian neighborhood. Upon entering the home, I saw small children cowering in fear from all the shelling. Their mother was exhausted, with deep, dark circles ringing her eyes. Her husband was off fighting somewhere. She struggled to feed the kids on the remaining tins of food she had left and to keep them entertained inside while bombs fell around the house. I scooped up one of the smaller ones, a tiny boy who planted wet kisses all over my cheeks. He seemed oddly undamaged by the mayhem around him.

When the bombing quieted down, I walked with the soldiers across the street to the bombed-out church. We picked our way through pieces of a statue of the Virgin Mary and blocks of wood that had once been pews where parishioners sat. The regime soldiers told me the Islamists had bombed the church, though I doubted they knew whether that was true or if it had been struck by a regime rocket.

The children followed us, kicking pieces of stone and rubble. The altar had been destroyed, the windows shattered. A priest sat outside with me on a bench. The church had been deliberately targeted, he said. As we observed the wreckage of a holy place, he said Christians needed Assad's protection against what could come next.

This was a year before the first sightings of ISIS. Before the Free Syrian Army, the opposition fighting to topple Assad, would fracture into a million little pieces.

I asked the priest what he feared losing the most in all the destruction.

"History," he replied.

ON THE ROAD TO DAMASCUS

The history of Christians in Syria is as old as the religion itself. Hundreds of churches, shrines, and monasteries in northern Syria and southern Turkey remain from the earliest days of
Christianity. In one of the greatest of all biblical stories, St. Paul
the Apostle (also called Saul, his Hebrew name) was converted
on the road to the current Syrian capital, Damascus, while he
was en route to the ancient city. The dramatic conversion took
place when he had a vision of the risen Christ, who spoke to him
amid a light so bright that it literally blinded Paul:

> As he neared Damascus on his journey, suddenly a light from
> heaven flashed around him. He fell to the ground and heard a
> voice say to him, "Saul, Saul, why do you persecute me?"
>
> "Who are you, Lord?" Saul asked.
>
> "I am Jesus, whom you are persecuting," he replied. "Now get
> up and go into the city, and you will be told what you must do."
>
> The men traveling with Saul stood there speechless; they
> heard the sound but did not see anyone. Paul got up from the
> ground, but when he opened his eyes he could see nothing. So
> they led him by the hand into Damascus. For three days he was
> blind, and did not eat or drink anything . . .
>
> Then Ananias went to the house and entered it. Placing his
> hands on Saul, he said, "Brother Saul, the Lord—Jesus, who ap-
> peared to you on the road as you were coming here—has sent
> me so that you may see again and be filled with the Holy Spirit."
>
> Immediately, something like scales fell from Saul's eyes, and
> he could see again. He got up and was baptized, and after tak-
> ing some food, he regained his strength.[8]

Damascus, the city Paul was traveling to, is now the seat
of power for the Assad family and the center of its war machine. It was already an ancient city in Paul's time. Indeed,

some Christians in Syria trace their lineages back to the pre-Christian days of the Aramean and Assyrian civilizations. The town of Maaloula in the mountains of southern Syria remains one of the only places in the world where the inhabitants still speak Aramaic, the language Jesus spoke.[9]

THE NUNS

When I reached Maaloula for the first time in the late spring of 2012, Syria was a country clouded by conflict, where neighbors and families were separated by sectarian divisions. But the war had not become a reality yet. My life in Damascus until then had been shadowed by compulsive denial. No one wanted to accept that a war was coming, no matter how obvious it seemed.

Before leaving in the early morning to drive to Homs or Daraya or Douma, opposition-held places where the war was very real and heavy fighting was taking place, I would see the remnants of yesterday's parties, dinners, and elaborate functions in my hotel, the Dama Rose. It was as though a line had already been drawn across Damascus separating the regime-held territory from the opposition, between those who would live in peace and those who would soon be bombed, gassed, and subjugated. I have always wondered why it took people so long to realize that even the capital was not an exception, that even Damascus would be scarred by the violence. While standing on the balcony of my room, I could hear bombing and see the dark smoke curling ominously from the suburbs of Douma. But beneath my window, children and their nannies were still splashing in the pool as though it were an ordinary summer day.

When I visited Christian friends in their lovely apartments, they would put their children in their rooms, make coffee, and sit with me, discussing what might happen next. They recognized that the country was in trouble. But still, most of them refused to leave. First, they could not conceive of themselves as refugees: most of them were middle class, well educated, and firmly rooted in Damascene society. Second, they had an almost unwavering faith that Assad would protect them. It would not be until the last minute that these people would gather together their families and their possessions and flee before full-blown war struck.

One early weekend morning, I drove to Maaloula with a Syrian friend who accompanied me everywhere (she must remain unnamed, however, for her own security). She had spoken often of Maaloula and had urged me to visit. In addition to its beauty and its aura of calm, Maaloula had long been an oasis of political tolerance. My friend had told me about the nuns living alongside Muslims and about how the town worked in harmony, everyone melding together. But the war had arrived, and one weekend we decided to go and see if one town could somehow barricade itself from the outside forces pushing tolerance to the brink.

As far back as 2011, when the demonstrations against Assad first started, the townspeople had gotten together and made a pledge. Residents of the ancient and predominantly Christian town vowed at the beginning of the conflict not to succumb to sectarianism and be dragged into the chaos.

Maaloula's determination to remain as neutral as Switzerland was all the more remarkable given the town's prominent location, on the main road from the battered city of Homs to the increasingly embattled capital, Damascus. But the vow also reflected Maaloula's own bitter history.[10]

Maaloula, which is being considered as a UNESCO World Heritage site, was besieged during the Great Syrian Revolt in 1925, when rebel Druze, Christians, and Muslims tried to throw off the colonial yoke of France. The sting of that insurrection lingers. Many older residents were weaned on stories of women and children hiding in the caves of the three mountains that surround the town to escape atrocities.

The five thousand Christians there are largely Greek Catholic and Antiochian Orthodox, praying in seventeen different churches across the town, while the Muslims are Sunnis. But most people are loath to classify themselves by religion, preferring to simply say, "I am from Maaloula." When I asked them their faith, even the nuns, they preferred not to answer. It reminded me of the civil war in the former Yugoslavia, when even close friends of mine refused to tell me their ethnic lineage: it was not "I am half-Croat, half-Serb," or "I am half-Muslim, half-Catholic," but "I am a Yugoslavian." There was something proudly and determinedly defiant about remaining separate from religion. It did not define who they were.

After a bit of coaxing and knocking on his door, I got Mahmoud Diab, the Sunni imam of the town, to agree to talk to me. We sat on a shaded bench outside, escaping the scorching sun, while his wife brought sugared coffee. He was adamant that war would not reach the town; Maaloula, he said, would somehow remain untouched by conflict.

"But you are not sealed off from the rest of the world," I argued. "How are you going to manage this?"

"Early on in this war, I met with the main religious leaders in the community, the bishop and the mother superior of the main convent," he said. "We decided that even if the mountains around us were exploding with fighting, we would not go to war."

Born and raised in Maaloula, Diab was also at that time serving in Syria's parliament. We were sitting in the courtyard of his mosque, shadowed by olive and poplar trees, where there was a fading poster of Syria's president, Bashar al-Assad, on the wall. Diab firmly supported Assad. He shrugged off my stories of unarmed protesters being shot in the first demonstrations

in Da'ara in March 2011, and he seemed unmoved by the interviews I described with victims tortured in Assad's prisons.

"It's a sectarian war, it's politics," he said with a wave of his
hand, brushing the war off as a topic for people somewhere else,
far from Maaloula's borders. "The fact is, there is no war here in
Maaloula. Here, we all know each other."

Earlier, explaining the history of Maaloula, Diab told me that
tolerance had been a tradition since St. Thecla, a follower of the
Apostle Paul, had fled to these mountains in the first century.
She was escaping soldiers sent by her father, who was threaten-
ing to kill her for her religious beliefs. Legend has it that, exhausted, and finding her way blocked by the sharp, rocky sides
of a nearby mountain, Thecla had fallen on her knees in desperate prayer, whereupon the mountains parted. Hence, the area
was named "Maaloula," meaning "entrance" in Aramaic. The
Convent of St. Thecla was built at the site in 1935.

"Here in these mountains there are all different people, different religions," Diab said. "But we decided adamantly that
Maaloula would not be destroyed."

That, at least, was the intention. But war does not always abide
by visions of how things should be. Violence has a way of arriving
like a fierce sandstorm, devouring everything in its path.

We didn't know then, as we sat on the bench in his garden
sipping our coffee, that one year later, fighters from Jabhat al-
Nusra would hide in caves above the town and shoot down at
citizens with Russian rifles, right into the area around Diab's
garden where the ancient olive trees grew. There would be no
more prayers, no more unity. The church bells would cease to
ring. The vow the town made would be worth nothing.

I thought back to the morning of my first visit to Maaloula
earlier that year. Climbing the hills to reach the Convent of St.
Thecla in the early morning, I found the nuns laying out tiny
apricots on trays to dry under the sun. One nun was arranging

the fruit, fresh picked from their trees, in neat and orderly rows. Another was arranging clean glass jars. They were making jam to be stored for the winter.

Like Diab, the Christian nuns were supporters of the Assad government. They lived isolated, quiet lives, devoted to God and country. In truth, they didn't care who was in power, so long as they could maintain their ancient way of life. They passed their days working, praying, and tending to the needs of the sick, sleeping in small, spotless chambers at night. The convent was silent in the morning except for birdsong and the sound of the nuns scurrying up and down marble stairs with large glass jars of apricot jam.

They gave me a tour of the convent. The sun was blinding. I remember climbing down a small passage of stairs and finding a cell-like room bathed in pure white light. It held just a desk and a bed with a white cotton spread draped over it. There was a view of the mountains. Alone in the room, I sat down on the chair, looking out on the panorama. I remember thinking, *This would be a good place to hide if the war came here. But the war will never come here.*

One of the sisters told me the convent was one of forty holy sites in Maaloula. Before the war, Muslims and Christians alike came here to pray for cures for infertility and other ailments, drinking water from the crack in the rock that was said to have parted for St. Thecla. The nun explained to me, with great patience, how the water purged one from sin. I saw couples climbing the stairs to the place where the water flowed from the spring. There, they would kneel and pray to St. Thecla, perhaps for a child. I remember a lone woman with a long braid down the back of her floral dress bent over an altar, her hands knotted in prayer.

The lives of the nuns were so straightforward, so contained. I envied them for their simplicity. They rose at dawn and spent the day in prayer and contemplation, welcoming the sick. They also ran a small orphanage, tending to children of any faith who had already been orphaned or abandoned in war.

Back in the courtyard where the nuns continued their work with the apricots, blinded again by the sunlight, a smaller nun came and led me into a darkened room to see the mother superior. A Greek Catholic, she had lived in the convent for thirty years. She told me the spirit of St. Thecla was not about religion. It was, she said quietly, about faith. About goodness. About compassion.

"We had an Iraqi Muslim man who was badly wounded who came here to be healed," Mother Sayaf said. They did not look at people by their religion, she stressed, but by their humanity. In their eyes, a Muslim, whether adult or child, who was injured had the same worth as a Christian. At first, she avoided talking about Assad entirely, changing the subject and directing me toward icons on the wall to explain various saints and traditions. The last thing I ever wanted to do was push people to speak about a dictator in a country where the security apparatus was so powerful and could punish them with horrible consequences.

In the 1970s, Mother Sayaf said, doctors would send their patients to Maaloula to recuperate: it was a kind of Middle Eastern version of Thomas Mann's Magic Mountain, filled not with snowbound invalids but pilgrims seeking miracles. By the time I met her, the war was twenty-one months old. People were fleeing embattled Homs, Damascus, and Aleppo to seek refuge with relatives overseas or in parts of Syria not at war. People were also returning to Maaloula. "For the calm," she explained. "It is safe here."

I walked down the hill to find a small café that was still open and ordered a black tea. A dark-haired woman in her late thirties with a downturned mouth served me, returning with a small pitcher of milk. She spoke English and was eager to talk. She sat down.

"This is my country," she said stoically, as a way of introduction. Her name was Antonella, she said, and she was a Syrian American who had left Los Angeles and Miami three years earlier to return to her birthplace and start the café.

I told her it might have been bad timing to come home to Syria.

Antonella shrugged. She'd had a chance to leave when the war started and fighting was close to Maaloula, she said, but she refused.

"I want to be here," she said, though the situation had undoubtedly deteriorated since her arrival. Her main concern was the economy, not her own safety.

"There were fifty tour buses a day here when I first came back," she said wistfully, looking around her empty café, where she served American-style food: fries, omelets, sandwiches. For a while, she convinced herself things would get better. But in the winter of 2012, when there was fighting and people were dying across the mountain in the town of Yabrud, Antonella finally realized that her country was at war.

"I fell into a depression," she admitted. It was the uncertainty that troubled her the most. "The truth is, even if Maaloula is quiet, no one knows where this is going." She said her allegiance was largely with Assad, whom she referred to obediently as "Mr. Assad."

Everything was the fault of the opposition, she told me. They were Sunni radicals. "The rebels have destroyed our country."

Nature was to blame as well. A drought had plagued the country, which, combined with the mismanagement of water resources, had resulted in water shortages in the agricultural regions. Farmers fled to the cities. Because of sanctions against Syria, and the fact that transit had been halted across borders, trucks with supplies were stranded in Lebanon and food costs were skyrocketing. Foreign tourists stopped coming. People bought only what was necessary. Small businesses like Antonella's were dying.

"This is the beginning of World War III," predicted her brother Adnan, also a returnee, who came out of the back room where he had been cooking. "It is starting in Syria, but it will engulf the region. This is a proxy war."

It was a common refrain in Syria, that the country was being used because of its geopolitical significance. Most people in Maaloula and other small Christian and Alawite villages believed the war would spread beyond the country's borders. It was "foreign forces" that were causing the war, they argued. For the opposition or activists, these foreign forces were the Russians or Iranians who would come to the aid of Assad, or the Chinese who blocked any humanitarian vote in the UN Security Council. But to Antonella and her brother, foreign forces were the Turks, the Gulf States, and, to a smaller extent, the Americans, who were supplying arms to the opposition. They were the ones keeping the war going by fueling "Salafist extremists" who opposed Christianity.

It was a grim conversation. I stared into my empty teacup, which Antonella promptly refilled. Maaloula would survive, she and her brother insisted several times, but without much conviction. I had a question, but I wanted to be sensitive, and I wasn't sure how to ask it: Can a town famous for its tolerance resist the centrifugal pressures of a vicious, sectarian civil war?

"Everyone is a Christian and everyone is Muslim," Mahmoud Diab, the imam, had cryptically told me earlier when I asked him the same question. He had refused to break down the percentage of Muslims in the town. "The situation here will not deteriorate; it's the opposite," he said. "People support each other." While Diab was reluctant to take sides—far less so than Mother Sayaf, who had finally, after some time explaining her faith and the Orthodox saints, admitted to me that she "loves" Mr. Assad—he nevertheless stressed, "I am with the law. I just want the country to be legally run."

"If we become Salafist," he said, referring to the fundamentalist strain of Islam that has taken on new prominence since the Arab Spring, "we lose all of this ethnic mix, and that is tragic. Everyone has to be like them. There is no room for anyone else."

Just one hour from Damascus, Maaloula was untouched that morning when I spoke to Diab. But during a drive down the mountain, and as I got onto the highway and drove into the capital again, reality crept back into view. At more than a dozen checkpoints, grim-faced soldiers inspected documents and car trunks, searching for weapons and rebels. Another car bomb had exploded in Damascus, and the gray, acrid smoke plumes curled in the air, a warning sign of darker days to come.

Later that year, I returned to Maaloula. The Christian shopkeepers, restaurant owners, taxi drivers, and families who had spoken to me about the harmony of the city were all gone. Fearful of what was to come, they had finally packed up their belongings and left. I tried to keep in touch with people, but as time went by, it became more and more difficult to find them. Telephone numbers no longer worked; emails bounced back. "Nothing will happen to Maaloula," Diab had told me, but he was wrong.

Not even two years after we met, the Battle of Maaloula began. The small town had the misfortune of being located in the strategic Qalamoun area in the mountains along the Lebanese frontier, making it the target of a government offensive in late 2013 that aimed to shut down the influx of fighters and weapons from across the border.[11] On September 4, a

Jordanian suicide bomber drove his truck to a Syrian army checkpoint at the edge of Maaloula, where it exploded and gave the signal for attack. By the end of the day, rebel forces from groups including Jabhat al-Nusra, Ahrar al-Sham, and the Qalamoun Liberation Front controlled much of Maaloula as the government launched air raids.[12]

In November, Islamic rebels attacked the St. Thecla convent and kidnapped a group of thirteen nuns, whom they later traded for government-held prisoners.[13] For clerics and historians, the most lasting damage was to the Church of Saints Sergius and Bacchus—a medieval structure, home to priceless religious icons and other works of art, destroyed during the battle.

The Assad government saw retaking the town as vital to bolstering the regime's claim that it could protect Syria's religious minorities from Islamist militants in the opposition forces. Control of the town swung back and forth between the militants and the government several times before the latter secured it in April 2014.

The battle dealt a heavy blow to both Maaloula's inhabitants and its religious sites. I wondered what had happened to the friends I had met over my several visits, especially the nuns. I kept thinking back to the clear glass jars of apricots, to the quiet white room I had found, hollowed out of a rock, which seemed such a safe place to take refuge.

By 2019, when the war was entirely in Assad's favor, Christmas trees and services returned to Maaloula. Russian TV—the Russians had joined the battle in 2015—filmed a service at St. Elias Church. People came back to light candles, to pray. No one mentioned the war that was still ongoing.

I tried to contact Diab again, and I tried to find out what had happened to the nuns, and to Antonella at the café, and to others I had met before the storm engulfed Maaloula. Emails, phone calls, and text messages were worthless. I could not find them.

They had, like so many others, vanished.

HISTORICAL SHIFTS

There are nearly a dozen factions of Christianity in Syria, many of them intertwined, some separated by esoteric religious dogma or tradition. Several centuries after the birth of Christianity, ecclesiastical divisions, stemming from the fourth- and fifth-century Christological debates—disagreements over the precise divinity and nature of Jesus Christ—began to emerge among the region's Christians. Over time, these theological differences culminated in cultural, ethnic, and political divergences among various Christian communities. The main split is between the Byzantine and Greek branches, on the one hand, and the Syriac communities, on the other.

The unique Christian traditions in modern Syria include the Greek Orthodox of Antioch, Greek Melkite Catholic, Syriac Orthodox of Antioch, Armenian Orthodox, Maronite, Armenian Catholic, Syrian Catholic, Latin Catholic, Chaldean Catholic, Arab Evangelical (Presbyterian), and Union of Armenian Evangelical. Although most denominations have their roots in Syria's early Christian history, some were established later by Catholic and Protestant missionaries, similar to the Baptists I met in Gaza or the evangelical Christians in Egypt.[14]

Then there are those Christians who say they were raised in one tradition but practice another. Dr. Adoumie, for instance, the vascular surgeon who emigrated from Aleppo to California via Lebanon, calls himself Greek Catholic but adds that his family is "intertwined with Greek Orthodox." "Fundamentally," he told me, "we are Eastern Christians." His father was educated in Catholic schools in Aleppo because he had lived under French colonial rule.

Now in California, he attends a Maronite church, which he describes as "vibrant" and the best way to introduce his Levantine culture to his kids.

"I shopped around for churches," he said. "I'm not a diehard about specific things about religion, but I wanted to give the cultural value to my kids so we could connect with the past and to my culture. I found the one that reminded me most of my school in Lebanon, after I left Aleppo."

In addition to differences in their traditions and rites, Syria's Christian denominations diverge in their leadership structures. The Greek Orthodox of Antioch, the Syriac Orthodox of Antioch, and the Catholic Melkite of Antioch communities all have their patriarchates in Damascus. Denominations like the Armenian Orthodox and Chaldeans have leadership hierarchies in neighboring countries such as Iraq and Lebanon.[15]

The history of these groups is long, winding, and often bloody. I have sat in churches for hours with priests and bishops, pen and paper in hand, asking them to methodically draw out the splits and divisions of the church. We ended up with flow charts, reams of paper scribbled in notes, and explanations of obscure doctrinal disputes. Often, the priests threw up their hands in exasperation, unable to pinpoint exactly where or why the sects divided. At the end, they would all sigh and choose to discuss the current situation rather than the past.

"So much has happened to us," a Greek Catholic priest told me after a stirring Mass on Mount Lebanon in 2017. "Wars shifted societies, societies shifted religions."

The Muslim Arab conquest of the region in the seventh century proved a major turning point for Syria's Christians, who until that point had made up the majority of the region's population.[16] Different communities held opposing attitudes toward the invading Muslims.

Many Syriac and Nestorian Christians, who had resented the authority of their erstwhile rulers, the Greek Byzantine Empire, regarded the invaders as saviors who would liberate them from the Greeks. Greek-speaking Christians, however, viewed the Muslims as dangerous foreigners, in the same way that many modern-day Syrian Christians regard the Sunni opposition as a threat to their security.[17] Overall, the invading Arab forces faced little active military resistance in Syria, especially because most of the Christian communities there, largely made up of traders and merchants, had no military class. They were quickly overrun.

The new Muslim rulers soon began to introduce Islam, Arabic, and an array of new laws regarding religious coexistence. Muslims regarded the new Christian subjects as *Ahl al-Kitab*, or "People of the Book," because they relied on a monotheistic sacred text. As a result, Christians had a right to continue to practice their faith, and would enjoy protection as long as they paid a special tax on religious minorities, called the *jizya*—exactly what ISIS had demanded from Sara Bahodij's family a millennium and a half later in Mosul.

Syrian Christians adapted to Muslim rule. Some held administrative posts in government, while others translated manuscripts from the Greek and Syriac languages into Arabic. Arabic became the primary language under the caliphate of Al-Walid ibn Abd al-Malik from 705 to 715, and Syrian Christians were forced to adopt Arabic in their daily lives and in their liturgies and prayers.[18]

For Christians who had spoken the language of Jesus Christ, I imagine this change must have been especially wrenching. In 2014, while living in South Sudan, the world's youngest country, I studied how the new government was attempting to enforce English as the official national language. The street Arabic and tribal languages of the country's people were stigmatized and thrown aside. Naturally, the new South Sudanese resisted the loss of something so basic and intrinsic to their way of life as their language.

In ancient Syria, this new way of living, Arabization, forced Christians to come to terms with their new status as a minority under Muslim rule. It had a direct effect on their standing in society. Syrian Christians began to scorn the word "minority" and instead referred to themselves as a "component" of society. Razek Siriani from the Center for Arabic Culture attributes this word choice to three sources: "First, to emphasise the authentic presence of Christians in the region prior to Islam; secondly, to contest the claim of extremist Muslims that Christians are affiliated with the Western world; and thirdly, to maintain the situation of state protection of their presence and identity as citizens of Syria."[19]

In the sixteenth century, after passing through the hands of a number of Arab dynasties, followed by the Mongols and then the Mamluks, Syria came under the control of the Ottoman Empire. Like other Muslim rulers before them, the Ottomans treated Christians as *Ahl al-Kitab* and granted them a great deal of autonomy, including the establishment of separate courts for different religious communities.

Christians also had their own schools, which for centuries were regarded as elite centers of learning, and they tended to have higher levels of education than most of their Muslim peers. When the Tanzimat reforms in 1839 made Christians equal to Muslims in the eyes of the law, Christians took advantage of their newfound opportunities to enter the civil service, engage in economic ventures, and build new churches and even more schools. A separate Christian school system, teaching French, geography, history, and a more cosmopolitan view of the world, continued up until the 1960s, when the newly empowered Ba'ath Party began to control Christian schools' curricula. Many people I knew said that in the mid-twentieth century Christians could ensure a better education for their children because they tended to have more money than Muslims.

Back in the nineteenth century, the Tanzimat reforms, and the subsequent improvement in Christians' social status, naturally prompted resentment among many Ottoman Muslims, who were unsettled by rising Christian prosperity and influence. A wave of Muslim attacks against the Christian population followed. Aleppo, home to much of Syria's Christian community, endured violent riots in 1850. Looting, fires, and house-to-house fighting culminated in the murder of approximately twenty Christians.[20] These riots, known euphemistically as "The Events"—*al-hawādith* in Arabic—were the beginning of a religious divide that would only widen in subsequent years. A decade later, another, much worse spate of violence and arson claimed the lives of five thousand to ten thousand Christians in Damascus.[21] Historians came to see the tensions created by the Tanzimat reforms as the beginning of a series of disturbances that pitted Muslims against Christians in the Middle East.

European powers harbored orientalist visions of Syria as "a timeless biblical land" and therefore felt a duty to protect the region's Christians.[22] This sentiment was especially strong in France, a Catholic country with strong regional ties. Angry against perceived Ottoman inaction, the French sent six thousand troops, along with naval forces from several European allies, to quell the violence.[23] Nevertheless, attacks against Ottoman Christians continued. As tensions escalated, Syria's Christians began to trade less with their Muslim counterparts and instead sought new trading routes with the West, particularly Europe. France became a haven for Syrian Christians. Today, an entire Syrian Christian diaspora, including relatives and close friends of the Assad family, resides in Paris and the south of France. Many Catholic churches in France still take up contributions for Christians in Syria.

The relationship between the two nations has deep historical roots. After the defeat of the Ottoman Empire in World War I,

France took over Syria and Lebanon as mandates. The mandate system was a new form of colonialism dressed up as paternalistic protection, the idea that the Syrians would be better off having France watching over them.

The French then adopted a policy of divide and rule, attempting to split Syrians along ethnic and religious lines, supporting minority groups, and promoting decentralization in order to undermine growing Arab nationalism.[24] At first, the French intended to split the territory under their control into three states—Muslim, Christian, and Druze—but instead they divided the region into Christian-majority Lebanon and Muslim-majority Syria, a move that would contribute to the unraveling of the latter so many years later.[25]

Under French rule, some Syrian Christians received preferential treatment, and many Christian missionaries, mostly French, arrived from Europe to build schools, hospitals, and churches.[26] The spreading of the French language was one way of keeping the population docile by encouraging loyalty to France.

Yet despite their privileged position under the French mandate, Syrian Christians played an active role in the struggle for Syria's independence. One of the first post-mandate prime ministers, Fares al-Khoury, was born to a Greek Orthodox family that later converted to Presbyterianism. By 1944, when he began his first term as prime minister, he was an ardent Syrian nationalist, and he is considered by many to be the godfather of secular political thought in Syria today. A graduate of the American University of Beirut, al-Khoury was staunchly opposed to pan-Arabism and the later union between Syria and Egypt.

Along with several other Christian leaders, al-Khoury contributed to the struggle for autonomy that succeeded in establishing an independent Syria in 1946. He went on to represent Syria at the United Nations Security Council in 1947 and 1948 and served again as prime minister in the 1950s, the highest position ever held by a Syrian Christian.[27]

Unlike Lebanese Christians, who formed their own political parties, Syrian Christians tended to participate in Muslim-dominated social and political movements. In exchange for their full participation in society and their loyalty to the state, Christians expected to be treated as full citizens on par with their Muslim peers.

The Syrian constitution written during the time of the French mandate guaranteed equal rights for all citizens, which for Christians meant a shift in status from a *dhimmi* community, meaning protected but second-class, to a group with the same rights, privileges, and duties of other Syrians. As a result, Christians in post-independence Syria were actively involved in the military, government, civil society, education, health care, and the private sector.[28]

To defend their status as equal citizens, many Syrian Christians supported Arab nationalist movements, including that of the Ba'athists, who drew heavily upon the thinking of Michel Aflaq, a Greek Orthodox Christian from Damascus and a philosopher trained at the elite Sorbonne in Paris. Aflaq believed that the Arab world needed to be united under one secular Arab nation in order to achieve economic and cultural greatness.

Initially, Christian cultural organizations made great contributions to this Arabic renaissance. By advocating a secular political philosophy that emphasized regional unity while downplaying religious and cultural differences, they hoped to end the bloodshed that had plagued Christian communities in the region. Syrian churches followed suit. In the early 1960s, the ecumenical movement urged greater dialogue between Muslims and Christians. Nonetheless, the mid-twentieth century was a time of great insecurity and uncertainty for Syrian Christians. Their birthrates were drastically lower than those of

Muslims, and a series of coups and internal violence from 1946 to 1971, including the rise of Hafez al-Assad, father of current president Bashar, led many Christians to flee the country. There was a major increase in migration to French-speaking cities, including Montreal. Since many Syrian Christians were better educated under the French schools and had more money than their Arab neighbors, leaving during times of unrest seemed a reasonable option. But it also meant abandoning centuries-old roots in Syria, even if they were fleeing to the extended communities of the diaspora where Syrian Christians gathered.

In the 1980s, Hafez al-Assad launched a bloody attack on the Muslim Brotherhood, a movement founded at the end of World War II. Banned in 1963 by the Ba'ath Party, the Brotherhood practiced in secret, playing a major role in anti-Ba'athist dissent. For a decade, Hafez had been leading a bloody purge against them, killing thousands and breaking their control. His offensive culminated in February 1982, when he sent in troops to quell a Brotherhood-led revolt in Hama. No one knows how many people were killed: government figures suggest around one thousand, while some journalists put the figure as high as twenty thousand. What is known, however, is that the Hama massacre instilled deep fear into the Syrian population. Hafez brandished the raw power of the state, and in doing so showed he would stop at nothing to crush dissidents.

The Brotherhood has since operated in exile, but many I spoke to remember well their uncles, fathers, brothers, and cousins being hauled to prison as suspects even when they were innocent. Some never came home. One man in Homs, whose family I stayed with, had been imprisoned while a student in Hama during the 1982 massacre. He walked with a limp from the ferocious beatings he had suffered in government custody. When he left the room, his mother told me he had emerged from his prison sentence a different man.

In his magisterial novel *In Praise of Hatred*, the great Syrian author Khalid Khalifa wrote of this time, "Bodies on both sides fell like ripened berries; the atmosphere was oppressive, saturated with the fear of nameless chaos." Set in Syria in the early 1980s, Khalid's work highlights the terror of the regime's crackdown on political opposition. It largely takes place in Aleppo, as seen through the eyes of a young woman confined to her grandparents' secluded home during the rise of the Muslim Brotherhood and the government's bloody campaign against them. The book, published in 2006, was banned in Syria but widely read anyway, particularly in France.

It resonated with a Syrian population that for decades had been forced to look on, unable to act, while their government restricted their freedoms and murdered their countrymen. The Assads, like Saddam, like Egypt's Mubarak and Libya's Gaddafi, like so many Arab leaders, controlled through fear and through coercion. At the center of this, forced to take a stand and a side, were the Christians.

EVOLVING IDENTITIES

The beginning of the war in 2011 led to a rise in political Islam that not only makes life more dangerous for Syria's Christians, but for some, particularly in the country's northeast, threatens to make them extinct.

This was the case for many of the Aleppo Armenians I spoke with, who are now in their late thirties or early forties and who fled either before or during the most recent war. Their memories center around a time when their education, which had been conducted in Armenian with French, and then Arabic taught in addition, abruptly changed after the Ba'athists began installing their high-level officials as administrators in private Christian schools. Although the schools had always been open to Muslim students who could afford the tuition and who wanted to go, the

Christian curriculum was independent and varied significantly from that of the Muslim school system. This suddenly changed when the Ba'athists took power. Now, all studies were to adhere strictly to the party line.

Thomas Bedrossian, born in Aleppo to the children of Armenian genocide survivors, left Syria when he was twenty-seven.[29] Now a lawyer in the United States, he recalls the rise of the Muslim Brotherhood in Syria as a time when political Islam also turned on Christians. Although he was too young to have witnessed the insurrection himself, he spoke about its history: "There were a lot of anti-Armenian protests, chants that shook the streets with people saying, 'We're going to butcher you.'" The famous Muslim Brotherhood slogan in Arabic was "Arman mskeen tahht el skkeen," which literally translates to "Poor Armenians, we'll put them under the knife."

Remembering this time, most Syrian Christians supported the regime when the uprising began in 2011, though many sympathized with the demands of the protesters, too. Yet the protests, which started with a universal call for respect for human rights and dignity, quickly became suffused with religion, particularly as jihadists arrived from abroad. As a result, Christians found themselves in the crosshairs of an increasingly violent conflict. "There were signs of Islamic infiltration within the revolutionary movement," said Bedrossian. He remembered Christians taking the brunt of the blame for their support of Assad, while Sunni supporters of the president were largely forgiven for their stance. The fixation on Christians and Armenians, he said, was not coincidental: "It quickly turned them collectively and individually into targets of hate crimes, killings, and kidnappings." The tight-knit community of Armenians, in particular, was highly sensitive to the increased intolerance, having escaped a twentieth-century genocide that left their parents and grandparents permanently scarred.

Sarkis Balkhian, who left Syria in 2005 to attend an American university—and had also grown up in Armenian neighborhoods in Aleppo, largely centered around the government-controlled areas of Aziziye, Suleymaniye, Villat, and Midan—remembers a time of vibrant community when Armenian and other Christian families knew and helped each other. They spoke their ancestral languages and kept their customs alive with food, holidays, and rituals.

"These were largely Christian neighborhoods, but heavily populated by Armenians," Balkhian said. He returned to Syria in 2009, and today he lives in Yerevan, Armenia's capital, and works with refugees—predominantly Armenian—who have fled Syria. He doubted they would ever return home to Aleppo.

Looking back on his childhood and adolescence, Balkhian remembered a time of self-imposed segregation in Aleppo. "We lived with very few Muslims," he recalled. "In those days, Christians wouldn't sell property to Muslims. These days, it's fair game." He recalled getting in taxis driven by Muslim cab drivers, who would make derogatory comments about unveiled women and girls while driving through the Christian neighborhoods of Aleppo. "There were always anti-Christian comments and catcalling," he said.

He described his childhood neighborhood as a "ghettoized, secular community," even if his relatives, he added, would balk at the term. Identity was important: most people, he said, would call themselves Armenian Christians first, Syrians second. This was largely because he, like so many other Armenians around the world, grew up with stories of his grandparents being driven out of their homes in Turkey, leaving everything behind, fleeing the Ottoman onslaught, and seeking refuge in Aleppo, or farther on, in Deir ez-Zor (the largest city in eastern Syria) and into the desert.

Like so many Armenians who survived the genocide, when Balkhian's ancestors arrived in Aleppo, they settled into what they felt would be a secure home. "The first thing Armenians do anywhere is build a church," he said. He pointed out that the oldest one still standing in Aleppo today, the Forty Martyrs Cathedral, is six centuries old.

Khalil Jouayed, a Melkite Greek Catholic who fled Aleppo in 2018, described the Christian community there as rich and varied, secular but not completely detached from their Muslim neighbors.

"In the 1970s, the Christian community was flourishing, they were doing well in all senses: business, socially. They had no problems at all with anybody. They were wheeling and dealing with everybody," Jouayed said. "We had a big Christian presence in Aleppo. I would say almost 10 or 12 percent of the city was Christian, and you could see it in the churches, the monuments. There were no objections to building churches or holding religious ceremonies, like on Easter. But even so, most of the vendors selling Easter bread were Muslims. So Christian communities, they didn't have any problems."

Now, things have changed for Christians in Aleppo and throughout Syria. Balkhian estimated that of his original Armenian community in Aleppo, nearly 75 percent have left. After leaving his position as an associate at Human Rights Watch in Washington, DC, he served as the director of the Aleppo Compatriotic Charitable Organization in Yerevan, where he conducted a survey first in 2018, and again in 2019, on labor rights violations against refugee workers. As part of the survey, he asked Armenians in exile whether they would return to Syria once the war ended. Around 94 percent said they would not. Balkhian blames this dismal statistic not only on the ongoing violence, but also on the corruption of the state and the economy.

"Not just for Christians, but for everyone," Balkhian said, explaining how expensive life is in Syria. "Officially, it is five hundred Syrian pounds to a dollar. Realistically, it's about three thousand." Buying a loaf of bread requires taking a sack of money.

Beyond money, there were many other reasons why the Christians would not come back, Balkhian told me. "More than any destruction of infrastructure or even the killing and murder of hundreds of thousands, it is the dissolution of the social fabric, caused by ethno-sectarian violence, that is the greatest tragedy of the ongoing Syrian conflict," he said. "Armenians realize they are no longer welcome, especially because of their support for Assad."

Throughout the regions I traveled to document these vanishing Christian communities, their loyalty to dictators—less than fierce, but nonetheless a steadfast allegiance—came up often. In Iraq, there was fidelity to Saddam. In Egypt, to Mubarak. Strongmen were seen as viable alternatives to the chaos that ISIS or the Muslim Brotherhood, or even Hamas, which now controls Gaza, would bring. The state brings order, several Syrian Christians told me. Obey the state, obey the law.

"Obama made a mistake asking Assad to step down," Khalil Jouayed told me firmly. Not only was it not the American president's right to interfere in a sovereign country's political process, he said, but it was a matter of what was right for Syria. Assad, he told me—as did many other Christians—is the glue that keeps the many religions together.

The Assad family belongs to the Alawite sect of Shia Islam, a small group compared to Syria's Sunni Muslims, who make up around three-quarters of the population. Because the Alawites are such a small minority, the regime has cleverly manipulated and relied on other minorities to strengthen their power base. Political posts are often based on demonstrated party loyalty and group identity.

Both Hafez and Bashar al-Assad have used regulations on religious freedom to bolster or restrict different groups for political benefit.[30] Although Christians are banned from building missions and from converting Muslims, they have a right to worship freely, so long as they continue to support the regime. Meanwhile, the regime has imposed greater restrictions on Sunni religious freedom, including guidelines on the selection of imams and limits on political participation.[31] In the early days of the war, in the late spring of 2011, I remember going to Sunday services in Damascus and finding a circle-the-wagons mentality among the congregants. Most people would not talk to me at all about politics; the priests who did were firmly behind Assad.

When the subtle differences in treatment for religious groups exploded into sectarian violence beginning in 2011, many Christians felt trapped between two evils. On the one hand, they have suffered from indiscriminate government bombing, especially in Aleppo, which is home to around 40 percent of the country's Christians. Although the majority of the damage from the Russian-led airstrikes (and Bashar al-Assad's illegal barrel bombs) has fallen on rebel-held territories in the eastern half of Aleppo, opposition forces also lobbed shells into the western part of the city, where most of the Christians lived. When bombs fall, they do not discriminate.

Early on in the protests, many Christian organizations attempted to be neutral. They called for de-escalation and dialogue, citing passages from the Bible about peace and brotherhood. As the violence spread, however, many Christians moved or returned to homes in government-controlled areas in order to avoid both government bombing and attacks from opposition militias and terrorist groups.

Bishop Antoine Chbeir of Latakia, the coastal area that is the homeland of the Assad clan, is a Maronite Catholic originally from Lebanon. Maronites have their origins in northern Syria, where St. Maron performed miracles in the fourth century, he told me in 2020. His diocese covers four provinces: Homs, Latakia, Tartus, and Hama. Some among his approximately forty-thousand-strong flock are Maronite refugees who fled the fighting in Aleppo, many ending up in Tartus, a regime-held coastal city that boasts a large Russian naval base. According to the Associated Press, "In 2017, Moscow struck a deal with Syrian President Bashar Assad to extend its lease on Tartus for 49 years. The agreement allows Russia to keep up to 11 warships there, including nuclear-powered ones."[32]

Despite the war and the refugees leaving Syria, Bishop Chbeir still believed, as did many faith-based leaders I'd spoken with, that only Assad and his regime could prevent this religiously and ethnically diverse country from fracturing. "Syria is a tolerant community," he said. "The relationship between Christians and Muslims is good, thanks to the Alawite rulers." He attributed this to the fact that Alawites are "not a Muslim sect but part of a Muslim community that was persecuted by Sunnis, considered heretic." As such, he felt that they understand the plight of minorities in the region and are willing to protect them from the Sunni majority.

The catastrophe of Syria today, the bishop argued, is the economy as well as the war, and US sanctions exacerbated the economic situation. "Now the situation is catastrophic in Syria," he told me. He said the United States was continuing to wage war, but with sanctions instead of arms. The sanctions, he explained, had "stripped the value from Syrian wages," meaning that many people were unable to afford basic commodities.

Bishop Chbeir believed that despite the persecution of Maronites, and Christians in general, the church was resilient and would prevail. "The history of the church is a history of persecution. We will go on fighting," he said. But he stressed that in order for Christians to stay in Syria, they needed jobs, education, security, and health services. At the moment, in a country broken by war, those things were nowhere to be found.

Speaking to the bishop and others like him reminded me that the regime rhetoric tended to refer to rebel groups as Islamists and jihadists who hoped to institute Sharia law, subjugate women, and crucify nonbelievers and non-Sunnis. The rise of ISIS in Raqqa in 2014 and the violent images that came out of it—of Jordanian soldiers being burned alive in cages, of Christian and Yazidi women being sold in the markets like cattle to be sex slaves, of children being forced to watch beheadings—were terrifying and, unfortunately, very real.

But ISIS was not always a component of the Syrian opposition. Many others had risen up peacefully, without arms, marching in the streets of Homs and other cities in 2011 in the hopes of getting rid of Assad and gaining the right to freedom and dignity. Along the way, the Free Syrian Army, once the most effective armed opposition to the regime, was supplanted by louder, more prominent Islamists who were highly skilled at branding and promotion. "Now, they've lost their minds," one high-ranking State Department official told me in 2021. "The old opposition is gone."

I saw foreign fighters and the rise of radicalism during the earliest days of the jihadists, when passing checkpoints on the Turkish-Syrian border. One of the foreign languages I heard sounded like Chechen. Gradually, the moderates were pushed out, and more foreign combatants arrived. The Salafist dogma became entrenched. Even some of my Muslim friends in Aleppo became more and more radicalized. The kidnapping of journalists and aid workers began, and it became impossible to operate in western Aleppo without the looming threat of being taken and sold from one jihadi group to another. This turn of events culminated in the horrific public beheading of James Foley and Steven Sotloff, two American journalists, in Raqqa in August

2014. Foley was a former altar boy from New Hampshire, and Sotloff, a student of Arabic, was just starting his career as a freelance reporter. Fear escalated within Syrian Christian communities around this time, and amplified.

Because of the Assad regime's history of co-opting religious minorities into its power base, Syrian Christians feared that opposition groups would automatically associate them with the regime.[33] They were right to worry. Terrorist groups such as Jabhat al-Nusra and ISIS inflicted tremendous damage upon Christian communities as part of an ethnic and religious cleansing campaign, destroying over eighty churches nationwide, selling Christian women into sex slavery, and kidnapping prominent archbishops and priests.[34]

One afternoon in northern Iraq, I watched a distressing video on a cellphone of a live "market" where Christian and Yazidi women and children were being sold to the highest-ranking ISIS fighters. The video belonged to a Yazidi "rescuer" who operated under grave danger trying to save women from Raqqa and bring them back to their families.

I could not believe that a slave market was taking place in the twenty-first century. It seemed grotesque, medieval, savage. The women were young—many of them girls really, in their teens—with long unbraided hair swinging near their waists. They were in shock, tears running down their faces, powerless. The fighters were older, bearded, and armed. When conducting a rescue operation, the rescuer would pretend to be a hairbrush salesman, knocking on the doors of the girls' new "homes" when the ISIS fighters were not there and arranging to bring them back to safety. Sometimes they were successful, often not. The ones I later met in Dohuk, in the Kurdistan Region of northern Iraq, who had survived the brutality still had deep psychological scars, having endured the most unimaginable cruelty.

In 2016, while ISIS was still at its zenith, I spent time at Yazda, a remarkable NGO that helped women, including

Yazidis, who had been sex-trafficked to Raqqa.[35] It was a clean, almost cheerful place, with drawings on the wall that rescued girls and women had sketched to celebrate their release from captivity. I was amazed at their resilience after having suffered so much and their willingness to speak with me openly about what had happened to them. One woman who had escaped and made it back to Kurdistan and safety told me she had contemplated suicide over and over rather than let the men touch her.

Unlike many other victims of systematic rape or sexual violence during wartime, these women were generally willing to talk about their experiences. Partly this was because the Yazidi emir, their highest spiritual leader, had issued an edict that they must not be shamed and must be embraced back into the community. In all my years of working with rape victims in the Balkans, in Africa, and in Syria, I had never seen such openness, which I believed would lead to greater healing. In Bosnia, decades after the rape camps were closed, many of the women, including those who had given birth to babies as a result of their assaults, still found it unbearable to remain in their communities or to talk about what had happened. In Kosovo after the 1999 war, where entire villages were used as sex farms, the women could not bring themselves to use the word "rape." Instead, they told me they had been "touched," and that if their husbands found out, they would be abandoned. In Syria, one woman painfully told me that her psychiatrist had advised her to tell her fiancé. She did, and he promptly left her, stating that she was "soiled."

ISIS violence led many Syrian Christians, particularly intellectuals and young people, to flee the country.[36] Again, the numbers are impossible to determine. But right before the war, Syria was home to around 1.1 million Christians out of a population of approximately 22 million. As of 2015, about 700,00 had left.[37] Some reports indicate that around 160,000 Christians have fled Homs, leaving only 1,000 or so behind.[38]

But any kind of count during wartime is bound to be inexact, so these are very rough estimates. Evidence suggests that Christian and Alawite refugees often do not register with local UN refugee agencies because they do not want to be associated with the Syrian government. While working for the UN Refugee Agency in Iraq, Jordan, Turkey, and Egypt in 2014, I encountered very few Christians who had fled. It seemed that the Christians who had escaped villages near Mosul that year, running from ISIS, largely sheltered with relatives or other Christians who opened their homes to them. As a result, counts of Christian refugees are often underestimated. Nonetheless, it is clear that the number of Christians remaining in the country is very low, representing a precipitous drop from before the war.

EXODUS

By the end of 2019, the Christian community of Syria had scattered to different parts of the earth, fleeing the war that had left their country broken. In the summer of 2020, the Caesar Syria Civilian Protection Act, US legislation sanctioning the Syrian government for war crimes, went into effect.[39] It was named after a Syrian military photographer known to the public only by his code-name, Caesar, who had shared with the world thousands of horrific photographs documenting torture in Assad's military prisons and hospitals. He had sent duplicates of the photos, which depicted mutilated and burnt bodies, to a Syrian opposition group, which in turn shared them with Human Rights Watch in August 2013. Caesar later escaped the country. The Caesar Act, signed into law at the end of 2019, was the United States' attempt—a bit late, in my view—to hold the regime accountable for the atrocities.[40]

But it could not have come at a worse time. In the midst of the COVID-19 pandemic, Syria was in an economic freefall. It was impossible for ordinary people to survive. A state employee in Syria was paid the equivalent of $200 per month in March 2011. Because of the collapse in the value of the currency, that salary is now equivalent to approximately $15 to $20 a month. This is barely enough to cover basic groceries.[41]

Sona Tatoyan, a daughter of Armenian Syrians living in the United States, called the sanctions from the Caesar Act barbaric. "People are starving. There is no medicine in the hospitals," she said. "What is happening now affects the Syrian people more than it affects the government. The people in government will still be able to eat."

According to Dr. Annie Sparrow, an assistant professor in global health for the Icahn School of Medicine at Mount Sinai in New York, writing in *Foreign Affairs* magazine in 2018, the regime had transformed itself into a war economy, a killing machine massacring its own people and using money meant for humanitarian aid to do so. Sparrow, who spent much of the war fighting for justice in Syria, claimed the regime had used most of the $30 billion it received in international humanitarian aid to skirt sanctions and fund its war effort.[42]

For the Christians of Syria, the summer of 2018 was a time of reckoning. Those who had left, including Khalil Jouayed, the Melkite Greek Catholic from Aleppo, believed they had done the right thing by supporting Assad, who gave the Christian community structure and continuity. Jouayed left Aleppo with his wife and two sons in 2018 for Los Angeles, where he had been a university student at the University of California, Los Angeles, years earlier, as part of his studies with the University of Geneva. He emigrated after living through the worst horrors of the war. There was a great poignancy in his voice, a regret that he had lived through so much violence only to leave before the end.

"As Christians," Jouayed told me, "I believe we are *le sel de la terre*, the salt of the earth, as Jesus said, and if we become limited to a few hundred Christians, we lose that. I hope we will flourish again. Without Christian Orientalism . . . " he paused, and became emotional. "Many people here," meaning Los Angeles, "have one leg here and one leg there. But me: I will never cut ties with Syria, with Aleppo, my home. I am Syrian first." And now the tears truly came, and he did not try to stop them. "Forever."

As for what would happen to Christians once the war ended, he had no good answer. If the jihadists took over—which I pointed out was unlikely, given that Assad had taken nearly all of the country's territory back—he reckoned that radical factions like Jabhat al-Nusra and Hay'at Tahrir al-Sham would provoke "massacres, even genocides": "Let's say the Islamists take power through democracy," he said bitterly. "Islamists, once they take power, do not believe in democracy. For them, Sharia and the Quran are the only laws . . . " he drifted off. "So comparing two bad options, you take the least bad one."

"Syria's best hope to overcome this ugly war is to be a secular state," he concluded.

Sarkis Balkhian, who works with Syrian Armenian refugees in Yerevan, reckoned that the old Aleppo, the symbol of multifaceted Syria, would never return. Back in 2012, many members of the community packed small suitcases, took their children, and drove from Aleppo to Turkey to Georgia, and finally reached Armenia, assuming they would be gone only for the summer. But then the checkpoints went up. Aleppo deteriorated. Kidnapping of local Armenians began. People were dying from arbitrary bombing by rebel forces in the regime-held neighborhoods where they had lived. Six months of exile turned into six years and counting. Balkhian thought the

Syrian refugees in Lebanon might return if the situation in Lebanon continued to worsen, but he doubted that those who had ventured farther, to Sweden, to the United States, to Canada, would ever return to the ancient city. "Too much has happened," he said.

Despite spending most of his childhood in Aleppo, Balkhian said he never wanted to live in a ghettoized Armenian community in an Islamic country. While Syria before the conflict was far more progressive and secular than the Gulf countries, it was still an Islamic country with all of the difficulties that brings for religious minorities. Yet, like Jouayed, Balkhian believed the invasion of Iraq had changed the dynamic of the region. More Iraqi refugees poured into Syria, and "Assad himself was radicalizing Muslims to send them to fight the Americans in Iraq." He considered the idea of moving back to Syria impossible.

We spoke for some time about the country where he was born and raised, the irrevocable changes, the shifts in demographics and sectarian divides. He believed his Armenian community would endure in the short term, despite the most recent blow of economic hardship. But in the long run, his outlook for Christians was gloomy. "I do believe they will vanish," he said, "and they are in the process of vanishing." He paused. "Not just in Syria, [but] throughout the region."

Growing up, Thomas Bedrossian, the former journalist and now lawyer, always felt different from the majority population as both an Armenian and a Christian. By the time he left Syria in 2012, at the beginning of the war, the violence had yet to reach him. He "didn't even see a broken window from real bombing," he said. And yet, he knew something evil was coming.

When I asked him to envision a future for Syria, he paused. "It's so frightening, I really don't want to see it," he said. "Essentially, there are two versions. One is it goes more Sunni, so

it's less diverse and less independent, merely a ghost of its past."
The other version, he said, is that Assad clamps down harder on
the Sunnis, a recipe for another insurrection—something like
Iraq, which continues into a forever war.

As for Assad, would he ever be tried for war crimes? Bedrossian laughed. "How can he? Syria would have to turn him over
to the International Criminal Court. That will never happen.
Assad is the head of the state in what is practically a full presidential, or even a semi-monarchical, system. It is unlikely to
expect Syria to hand over its own officials to be tried in foreign
courts, let alone the sitting president," he explained.

He was still for a moment. "That will never happen because
Assad is Syria." He paused, and then repeated it. "Assad is Syria."

Sona Tatoyan is tired of Syria being discussed in binary
terms. The conflict is so much more complex and nuanced than
a simple story of rebels versus the government. In her view, the
widely held Western narrative of modern-day Syria is built off
of reductive, insulting tropes. She stated emphatically, "There
are no good guys. Anyone who tries to make one thing the pen-
ultimate evil is doing a disservice to the Syrian people."

"It's a lot easier to topple and destroy things," she went on,
"but how do we rebuild them? There needs to be a plan for what
comes after."

4

EGYPT

IT DIDN'T LOOK MUCH LIKE A PLACE OF WORSHIP.

On a back street near Hassan Basha, a remote village in Minya Governorate in Upper Egypt, the doors of the low concrete building were locked and bolted. It resembled an abandoned house, aside from the plaque written in Arabic and English: Assembly of God Church. The street was dusty. Donkeys pulled a few carts piled with vegetables, but otherwise, the road was empty.

A man named Zaki Abdullah, a leader of this small village's Christian community whom I had met earlier in the day, had led me to the entrance. He struggled with the key and heavy chain and finally pushed the door open. The inside was grimy, chilly, and contained a small altar, a few folding chairs, and some scattered pews. It appeared not to have been used in months.

"It's not easy keeping it up," Abdullah said. "But nothing about being a Christian is easy in Egypt."

163

This is particularly true in Minya, the capital of the Minya Governorate, about four hours' drive south from Cairo along the Nile. Christians make up an estimated 33 percent of the governorate's population—which makes them the largest concentration of Christians in any of Egypt's twenty-seven governorates—and they are frequently targeted for their faith.[1] Discrimination against Christians takes many forms. Christians are often prevented from having their own places of worship, and congregants are often directly attacked or bombed.

In May 2017, masked gunmen attacked Coptic pilgrims in a bus convoy en route to Saint Samuel the Confessor Monastery near Minya. At least 28 people were killed. A month before, at the debut of the Lenten season that precedes Easter, hundreds of Christians were forced to flee their homes in the North Sinai after ISIS issued an edict forbidding the celebration of Easter. The Christians dispersed, but it hardly mattered: on Palm Sunday, ISIS bombed two churches in other parts of the country, killing 45 and wounding 125, largely as a symbol of their power.[2]

"When there is a bombing, it is always a coded message to Christians throughout Egypt," one young worshipper told me: "'You are not welcome here.'"

About a year and a half after the first bus attack, in November 2018, ISIS militants targeted another bus convoy en route to Saint Samuel—on the same road, in fact, as the first attack. Minya is the hardest-hit governorate, the place where Christians feel the most under threat. This time, the gunmen killed 8 and injured more than 13, all Coptic Christians.[3]

There are too many more incidents to list, a drum roll of violence and killing, including some that occurred while I was in Egypt in December 2019 and January 2020: a bloody catalog of bombings, kidnappings, and burnings of houses and churches. In the decades that I have been coming to Egypt, during the reigns of Hosni Mubarak, the Muslim Brotherhood's Mohamed

Morsi, and now General Abdel Fattah al-Sisi, I would always seek out Christians. I wanted to know how they lived as a minority in an authoritarian country where political upheaval was so frequent and so visible.

All the Christians I've spoken to over the years have had some version of their own sinister incident, something that had happened to a family member or someone in their village or parish. No one in this Christian community, I was told, is untouched by persecution. It's not just Islamic fundamentalism that is harming them. Abdullah told me that societal persecution is at times far more damaging than bombings. It is the constant sense of alienation and inferiority, the laws and the taboos.

"Sometimes it's not even a direct attack," Abdullah told me. "They don't have to throw a bomb at you. They just always manage to make you feel like a lower caste." He said it was something he recalled from his earliest childhood memories: being called names, being made to feel different. One woman told me she always felt that people stared at her "as though she wore a different kind of clothes."

Egypt contains the largest population of Christians in the Middle East and was a majority-Christian nation until the fourteenth century. The Egyptian Christian community makes up around 10 percent of the population.* The largest share belongs to the Coptic Church, although there are also Evangelical Baptists, Catholics, Presbyterians, Greek Orthodox, and other denominations. The most reliable estimates suggest that between six million and ten million Copts reside in Egypt. But it's difficult to determine real figures; the most recent census was in the 1960s, and the Sisi government, in power since a 2013 military coup, is reluctant to encourage sectarianism by dividing the population by religion. Sisi has enough problems enforcing his authoritarian rule; he has imprisoned journalists, activists, and human rights lawyers in an effort to, as he describes it, instill security and eradicate the Muslim Brotherhood.

The Muslim Brotherhood is Egypt's oldest, largest, and most influential Islamist organization. Founded in Egypt in 1928, the Brothers have sprouted offshoots across much of the Arab world. They have long had a solid base of support from the working classes owing to their organized opposition to the British occupation—and especially for providing social services that the state failed to deliver. After decades of state repression, the Brotherhood reached its apex following the 2011 Tahrir Square demonstrations and the subsequent ousting of Hosni Mubarak. Mohamed Morsi, a leading member of the Muslim Brotherhood, was democratically elected president the next year.

After the military overthrew Morsi's government in 2013, and Sisi rose to power, the government banned the Brotherhood, declaring it a terrorist organization. (Morsi died in prison in June 2019.) Still, the Brotherhood maintains a strong presence in the country, as do much more extremist groups, such as ISIS in the Sinai.

Hostility toward Christians has periodically erupted into deadly sectarian mob attacks, including more than a dozen during Hosni Mubarak's tenure (1981–2011). Even though Sisi, who was Mubarak's director of military intelligence, as well as defense minister for Mohamed Morsi, vowed to protect Christians, there is a long-standing pattern of government negligence, or even complicity, in the face of these attacks. Victims, moreover, have typically been denied justice through the courts.

In the years since the Arab Spring, the attacks on Copts have become more frequent, often triggered by perceptions that the community has aligned itself with the government. Pope Tawadros II, the head of the Coptic community, stated that more than forty churches were damaged or destroyed around the country in August 2013.[5] The military refused to protect the churches before or during the widely anticipated attacks and did not hold the attackers accountable.

But to put things in context, on a scale of suffering, Christians in Egypt are not in the same position as other Christians throughout the Middle East. They are, by and large, "discriminated against, rather than persecuted," in the words of one US State Department official. They are not in danger of being eliminated entirely, like the Chaldeans or the Assyrians in Iraq.

Still, the threats to their lives are very real. ISIS brought a new danger to Egyptian Christians when its loyalists carried out murders and suicide bombings in the Sinai Peninsula and around the country. The NGO Open Doors counted a total of 128 Christians killed in Egypt because of their faith in 2017, describing it as an "unprecedented persecution."

More recently, ISIS has been battered down in Egypt, yet it remains a threat and a source of anxiety for the Christian community. And on a daily basis, Christians suffer from other institutional and generational forms of discrimination. Despite Sisi's pledge to protect Christians, his relationship with Christians is a complicated one. Over the Christmas holidays, the government insisted on wrapping Cairo's churches in enormous red, white, and black Egyptian flags, as if they were gigantic Christmas presents. Soldiers patrolled outside. On the one hand, it symbolized a kind of protection. But worshippers in the upscale Cairo neighborhood of Heliopolis told me they saw it more as a kind of threat: you are Egyptians first, Christians second.

"We are endangered. As a minority, we need to be protected," said Kamel Zakher, who owns an import/export business in central Cairo and writes about the plight of Christians. We sat in his downtown office, the windows open to the cacophony of Middle Eastern street life: cars and buses honking, vendors shouting, music blaring from small radios. His office on the second floor was drab, with a crucifix on one wall and a portrait of the Virgin Mary on another. He opened a book he had written about the history of Christians in Egypt.

"For this community to fall down, it means all of Egypt will have to fall," he said. "Christians are a part of Egypt, as ancient as the country. If you touch any Egyptian, you touch a Christian. Christians are not considered Christians first, but Egyptians first."

He described to me his own secular upbringing and said the difference between Christians in Egypt and anywhere else in the Middle East is that in Cairo, Christians and Muslims tend to live together in the same neighborhoods. Sometimes they even shared the same apartments.

"I remember in the 1970s sharing a large apartment with a Muslim family," he said. "They had one door, we had the other, but every floor had a family like that, sharing. That has changed." During the Nasser years, he said, many Christians fled, beginning an exodus that he fears is continuing today.

He expounded on the complicated position of Christians in relation to the Egyptian government and Islamic groups. Despite their long ties to the land, Egyptian Christians have been turned into pawns—sacrificial lambs, in a sense—in the struggle between Sisi and extremist groups. These groups are attempting to make a mockery of Sisi's claims to be bringing peace and security to the country. Zakher told me he thinks the Muslim Brotherhood and other Islamist groups want to come back, and they are using the Christians to "irritate the government."

Zakher said the bombing of the churches, and the subsequent displays of Christian persecution in the media, are a way of showing Sisi's powerlessness in the face of the extremists.

"It sends a very clear message to the European Union and the United States that the Egyptian government is powerless," he said. As Sisi's legitimacy is based on a claim to provide peace, security, and stability, he clearly hates this.

Still, Zakher told me, it's a "no-brainer" whom the Christians support between Sisi and the Brotherhood. "We are endangered," he said simply, meaning that they will side with whoever can offer the most protection.

Begemy Naseem Nasr, the priest of the Church of St. Mary in Minya, has come to a similar conclusion. "The Islamic State has repeatedly vowed to go after Egypt's Christians as punishment for their support of President Abdel-Fattah el-Sisi," he told *The Guardian* in 2018. "They want to embarrass Sisi and show that the state is unable to protect the Copts."

Sisi's actions and the troubling security situation led many people I spoke with to voice mixed feelings about how the government was run. Some felt that Sisi's more extreme actions have been justified by the current state of the country and are convinced by his declarations of protection for Christians.

"He has promised to take care of us," one retired nurse told me in a resigned voice as I visited her home near Heliopolis. "And he is fighting terrorism."

But Egyptian Christians remain second-class citizens in terms of the justice system and society. "We can't get elected into powerful positions," the retired nurse added. "There are no Christians in the army at high ranks."

Egypt's former president Mubarak, a Muslim who ran the government from 1981 to 2011, and Shenouda III, the Coptic pope from 1971 to 2012, had an extremely close relationship. In exchange for his support, Shenouda received access to power; Mubarak, for his part, largely retained the support of the country's approximately eight million Copts.

Sisi, knowing the importance of the Christian vote—in Cairo, many of the Christians are not only wealthy, but part of the educated elite—has pledged to protect minorities generally. He has changed election laws to allow more Christians into the national legislature, and he has eased restrictions on building

new churches and renovating old ones. The new Egyptian constitution grants non-Muslims (primarily Christians and Jews)
greater autonomy in setting their own civil and religious laws,
which allows them to rely on the tenets of their own religions
rather than Sharia law.

But a real gulf remains between what the government says
and what local community leaders actually do.

In the rural areas, such as Minya, local councils, headed by
elders, often convene to settle land disputes or local arguments.
They call this *Qa'ada Arab*, which literally means "men sitting."
It is a traditional system of justice that has been used for centuries. The problem is that when a Christian is in a dispute with
a Muslim, the system yields unfair results. The elders, Muslims
themselves, inevitably side with the Muslim.

"They are always unfair; a Muslim always gets treated better," Abdullah told me.

I went to have lunch with a Muslim family in Wasif Village in
Minya. With me was my son's godmother and one of my closest
friends, Mariann Wenckheim, a Viennese businesswoman who
is deeply spiritual. It took us hours to arrive, traveling by car on
winding back roads where most of the traffic was donkey carts.
My host was a young man—I will call him Abubakar to protect
his identity—an office worker from Cairo who was home for the
holidays. He said he grew up constantly aware of the mistreat-
ment of Christians, and other members of the family described
themselves as "Muslims who have always helped Christians."

Theirs is not a wealthy family. Their house is one story with
two rooms—an open living room, where rolled sleeping mat-
tresses are piled in a corner against concrete walls, and a back
kitchen with a gas stove. The door and windows were open
to the December winds. We sat on hard cushions on the floor
as Abubakar's mother and sisters prepared a lunch that I was
ashamed to eat; they must have spent most of their weekly

earnings buying the chicken, beans, vegetables, and bread. Cows and ducks wandered outside. There was a dirty canal in the center of the village where everyone came to dump their garbage. Flies, even in winter, swarmed around us, settling on our faces as we ate.

"It makes no sense to brush them off," Abubakar said, laughing at me.

He was proud to serve the meal that his mother made, although she and his sisters declined to eat with us once they had brought the platters of food and placed them in the middle of the room.

"People in small villages like this, places that are so far away from Cairo, don't like anyone who is different," Abubakar explained, passing the plate of bread. "My school was a long way from here, but I wanted to go, I wanted to get an education. I took a bus that took hours to reach it. At one point I had a ponytail. I got beaten up because of that, because I was different. So Christians are *really* different. People in small places don't like anyone who is not like them."

As we were finishing lunch, a Christian man named Khalaf arrived. Born and raised in Hassan Bayaf, the neighboring village, he told me he was fifty-four years old. Although he ran a jewelry store in town, he was considered a kind of unofficial mayor. He called himself an engineer and said he could fix anything: telephones, computers, old television sets. He had heard there were foreigners in the village, and he was curious to meet us.

"Nothing is a secret here," he said, placing a cushion on the floor and joining our circle. Khalaf wanted to talk about justice, "how Christians are always punished if something goes wrong."

He said he believed the most important tool to counter Christian persecution was education. "We have to open people's minds," he averred, taking a plate of chicken. "You see how

small these places are. This is how small people's minds are."
He said the persecution of Christians in the villages was subtle.
Sometimes, his Muslims friends would say to him, as the *adhan*,
the call to prayer, was ringing out, "Why don't you pray? Why
don't you come pray with us?" There were times when he left
the house with his wife while her head was uncovered and the
village men had sent her home for a hijab.

"I'm a guy who likes to use my brain," he went on. "But in
Egypt, there is one thing you cannot do, you must never do:
question religion. The Quran, the Bible. In these villages, people think with their manhood, not their mind." Most of the stories of village life were "really stupid," he said. "Then the law
has no gray. It's either good or bad, principles or honor. Nothing
else. People get punished for stupid, simple things."

It was never really straightforward, he explained. He told
a long, winding story of how events got misconstrued in village life, then revealed that his house had been burned down by
Muslims in 2011. When he complained to the other Christian
leaders, they had advised him to keep quiet. He refused. "Now I
am banished from my own church," he said.

Still, as we finished up lunch and the women gathered the
plates and went to the kitchen to finally eat alone, Khalaf said
he was at peace with being a Christian. "I just wish I wasn't
treated like a second-class citizen," he muttered.

We went for a walk along the canal to see some of his Christian friends. We passed by a child selling large balloons of spun
sugar. We stopped in Khalaf's jewelry shop, where he showed
me the silver rings and bracelets he sells, laid out on a neat tray.
He explained the intricacies of the telephones he fixes, and he
pointed out the armed guard outside his shop. "This is because
my house was burned."

He brought me to see Abdullah, his Protestant friend, who
would later let me into the locked church. "He is kind of like the

local imam," Khalaf told me. Khalaf's wife, Magda, told me she has been beaten on the streets several times for being Christian. She sat on the floor, her long, dark hair flowing down her back, peeling a huge bowl of garlic cloves, and repeated the story of the house burning. Abdullah has a wife in Tennessee and speaks some English. They told me there are often divisions, especially in the small villages, between the different Christian sects: Orthodox, Protestant, Catholic, Evangelical.

We ended up at the locked church. Abdullah said that if there were more Christians in the village, they might be better protected. They might not have to lock up the church. They might not need armed guards. When we finally went inside the tiny, dusty church, I asked him, "If you have to live and pray like this, to constantly be afraid, what does it mean to you, to be a Christian?"

He looked utterly surprised by my question. He talked about following rules and caring for others. But most of all, he said simply, "It means being free."

HISTORIC ROOTS

Since Mary and Joseph fled to Egypt with the infant Jesus, the country has played an outsized role in the history of Christianity. Some experts believe that St. Mark—who was said to have founded the Coptic Church of Alexandria and was the first Coptic pope—wrote one of the four gospels in Alexandria, where he was assassinated some years later. The Christian community enjoyed rapid growth in the following centuries, and almost all Egyptians converted by the fourth century. At that point, the national Egyptian Christian church formed, resisting attempts at unification with the Eastern and Western churches.[6] The church served as a type of opposition to the Roman authorities and gave birth to a number of Christian traditions, including Gnosticism, Arianism, and Christian monasticism.[7] The independent nature of Coptic Christianity had its roots in its use of the Coptic language, a remnant of the ancient Egyptian language from the time of the pharaohs.[8]

In the year 641, Muslim invaders from the Arabian Peninsula managed to wrest control of Egypt from the Byzantines with only four thousand troops, a remarkable feat. Some experts speculate that the invaders received help from the Christian population, who saw the Arabs as a potential improvement upon centuries of Roman rule.[9] The invasion, however, transformed the Christian community into a *dhimmi* group, entitled to protection but forced to pay *jizya* and wear specific colors of clothing. They were also barred from carrying weapons, and often from building new churches. Muslim rulers tried to influence the clergy and keep Christians out of the civil service. Meanwhile, the Coptic Church established its dominance over the Greek Orthodox Church at a time when communication with the rest of the Christian world became more difficult.[10]

Conversion to Islam happened at a slower rate in Egypt than in some of its neighboring countries, but Christians became a minority a few centuries later. When the Mamluks came to power in 1250, they hoped to solidify their legitimacy by cracking down on Egypt's *dhimmi* communities. This wave of persecutions caused a rapid decline of the Coptic community in the fourteenth century.[11] Under Ottoman rule, interest in protecting Christians continued to decline, and a combination of conversions and immigration from the Arabian Peninsula boosted Egypt's Muslim majority to 75 percent of the population by 1700.[12]

The tide turned for Christians after Napoleon's 1798 invasion of Egypt, when Muhammad Ali and his descendants took control of the Ottoman province. Dress codes for Christians came to an end in 1817, and the *jizya* was last collected in the 1850s.[13] The country experienced a cultural and economic renaissance, often with Christians at the helm of new innovations. A Christian of Armenian origin, Nubar Pasha, served as Egypt's first prime minister starting in 1878. He was not democratically elected—with the British interfering in Egyptian politics at the time, he was essentially appointed by them. Although he disagreed with British policies, he nevertheless complied with them. He said bitterly, "I am not here to govern Egypt, but to administer the British government of Egypt." Meanwhile, a Christian family, the Taklas, founded *Al-Ahram*, still the country's most widely circulated daily newspaper. Christians became wealthier, and they were the most prominent members of society, partially as a result of the favoritism shown them by their British overlords.

Christians also played leading roles in developing and modernizing Egypt in a host of areas, including theater, cinema, banking, manufacturing, and education.[14] In the political realm, Makram Ebeid Pasha, a Coptic Christian, served as the secretary-general of the powerful Wafd party in the early twentieth century. In the economic sector, more than forty of the country's largest landowners were Christian.[15] The leading role that many Christians played in politics and civil society contributed to the formation of Egypt's collective identity as a nation rooted in diversity and tolerance. Egyptians were "one people worshipping the same God in two different ways," said Kyrillos VI, patriarch of the Coptic Orthodox Church from 1959 to 1971.[16]

The period also saw greater European involvement in Egypt, including a growing missionary presence from Europe and the Levant. Both Catholic and Protestant missionaries challenged the traditional power of the Coptic Church, leading to different denominations in Egypt that still exist today. By 1895, the Coptic Catholic Church based in Cairo was deemed a patriarchate, one of six in the Eastern Catholic tradition.[17] Soon, Egyptian Muslims and Christians came together to call for an end to British occupation, and by 1919, Egyptian nationalists were flying flags emblazoned with both the Muslim crescent and the Christian cross.[18]

After Gamal Abdel Nasser overthrew the monarchy in a military coup in 1952, his government instituted a series of reforms that fundamentally altered the Christian position in society. Egyptian Christians "increasingly withdrew from society in the second half of the twentieth century," according to political economist Tarek Osman, who attributed the Christian retreat to three factors: economics, Arabization, and violence against Christians.[19] Nasser's socialist land reform policies stripped away the power and influence of many affluent Egyptian Christians, resulting in a wave of emigration.

Nasser is perhaps best remembered as an ardent Arab nationalist. Although he tried to emphasize the secular nature of his nationalist philosophy, in order to appeal to non-Muslims in Egypt and Lebanon, many Christians saw the shift to a shared Arab identity as a move toward Islamism and a threat to their position in Egyptian society.[20] As rich Christians emigrated, middle-class Christians turned inward, and many went so far as to join the priesthood.[21] The decline in monasticism reversed after 1948; now only around 30 Coptic monasteries and 1,600 monks across Egypt remain.[22] While the Coptic church, viewed as authentically Egyptian, expanded its influence, many other denominations suffered from the anti-foreigner sentiment that proliferated during Nasser's rule. Most of their numbers declined to a few thousand.[23]

The relationship between the Christian community and the state, which was cordial under Nasser, soured under Anwar Sadat in the 1970s. A new pope, Shenouda III, consecrated in 1971, began to divide dioceses after the deaths of their bishops, in order to reduce the power of the Holy Synod, the church's governing council.[24] With Shenouda III at the helm, the Coptic

Church expanded its role in everyday life by introducing social services, associations, and social groups. Sunday schools saw an uptick in participation, and Christian "clusters" emerged in certain businesses and universities.[25] In trying to distance himself from Nasser and his secular Arab nationalism, Sadat introduced Islamizing policies that often ran counter to Christian desires. After a series of confrontations, the final showdown between the two leaders came in 1981, when a dispute over Sadat's proposal to introduce Sharia law led the president to strip the pope of his state-recognized authority and banish him to a monastery.[26]

The Islamization of Egyptian society continued under Sadat's successor, Hosni Mubarak. While the Mubarak regime tried to counter this trend by appointing Christians to parliament and cabinet posts, and by declaring Christmas and Easter to be national holidays, Egypt nevertheless experienced another great wave of emigration in the 1990s and 2000s.[27] According to Osman, writing in 2013, "a certain sectarianism has taken its toll on the fabric of Egyptian society. It is felt in the Christians' withdrawal into economic enclaves, the emergence of Christian neighbourhoods, in clearer dividing lines in university classrooms and professional syndicates, in the near impossibility of any Christian politician winning an election in any constituency with a Muslim majority, in job advertisements 'for Muslims only,' in dress codes (especially after the exponential increase in the number of veiled women in Egypt), even in slang."[28] From the 1970s to the mid-2000s, Christian leadership in private enterprise declined from 35 to 25 percent. The share of university professorships held by Christians went from 25 to 15 percent, and that of highly educated professions, such as doctors and engineers, decreased from 30 percent to 15 or 20 percent. Like so many other Christians in the Middle East, many Egyptian Christians feel like their future lies elsewhere.

PERSECUTION ALONG THE NILE

It was the Christmas season in Egypt. When I woke up at dawn in my modern hotel in Cairo overlooking the Nile, I heard church bells ringing. The scene outside my window, I realized, could have taken place thousands of years ago: there were boats moving slowly down the muddy river, and a few fishermen were out on the banks.

I'd been coming to Egypt for many years, but this was the first time I had heard the bells. Later, when I passed some of the churches, I had to climb over enormous multicolored ribbons, part of the decorations Sisi's government was using to gift-wrap them. These lay amid statues of the Virgin Mary, blonde and blue-eyed, holding an equally fair-skinned baby Jesus. The statues seemed so at odds, so distant, from the streets.

"Even in Cairo, far from Minya, we always feel different," said Christine, a twenty-nine-year-old office worker who grew up in Minya but moved to the capital to work. It was New Year's Eve. (In Egypt, Christmas is celebrated according to the Eastern Orthodox calendar, on January 7.) Christine fiddled with her long, highlighted hair—uncovered, as most Christian women do not wear a hijab—and ordered a hot chocolate with whipped cream. We were in a crowded restaurant in Heliopolis, noisy with an office party celebrating Christmas. The men wore button-down Oxford shirts; the women were dressed like Christine, in a mini skirt, sweater and boots. Egyptian rap music blared.

Christine studied the table and told me they were Christians—when I asked her how she knew—Was it something physical?—she shrugged and said, "You just know."

Mostly, she defines her experience as a Christian as a sense of alienation, of detachment from mainstream society. "You get used to it, but it's a sense of always feeling you do not belong," she said, blowing lightly on her drink to cool it. She felt most comfortable in social groups with other Christians. She told me that after she worked for a few years and saved some money, she would move back to Minya to marry and settle. There, she felt able to live her life among people who understood her.

"I feel better when I am with my own people," she said. But even in Christian areas, she admitted, life as a young woman was not easy. People do not accept those who are different, she said, those who want to stray beyond the expected. She talked about growing up and the complications of village life, including the divisions between Christian sects. "I once went to an Orthodox Mass and was asked to leave," she told me.

Christine is smart and forward-thinking. She wanted to find a way to combine her life as a Christian with being a modern Egyptian woman. She told me about the importance of her religion and how it figured into her daily routine. "It's who I am," she said. Educated in Jesuit schools in the center of Minya, Christine remembered when radicals burned down her school auditorium. She was young at the time, and, standing outside, watching the flames, she remembered feeling angry; but, even more than that, she was confused. Why was it happening?

"There are seventy-three churches I remember being burned down in my childhood alone," she said. "Seventy-three is a lot." She was worried about an attack happening that night—New Year's Eve 2019. (There was, in fact, an attack that night in Minya, as we would later hear.) "But really, there are attacks against Christians every single week," she said. "We don't count."

She said that often the police didn't cooperate, or that people sometimes didn't even bother to report the crimes. Word about most of the incidents was passed down through the community.

"Some get reported. Some people are too afraid to report them," Christine said. "But I have to tell you, the underlying sense of inferiority is our greatest persecution. For instance, just walking down the street, I've had Muslim men grab me by the hair and try to drag me because I don't have a headscarf on."

"But," she added, "I think the strongest societal deprivation is a political one. Muslims really don't want us to have a voice."

Christine believed that the majority of the church burnings, kidnappings, and other incidents happened around election time because they were meant to convey a message: that Christians should be afraid, that they should stay home and away from the polls. The Muslim Brotherhood gave the farmers sugar and rice during voting season after the Egypt's January 25 Revolution, she pointed out, and many of the Brothers lived in small villages, where they controlled everything. To her, the Brothers were the biggest threat to society, not Sisi.

"Everyone knows who they are," she said. "They pressured us to vote for them." Meaning, she was forced to vote for people she did not actually believe in, because she felt too frightened to do otherwise.

The legal system itself limits what Christians can do. Severe restrictions on building or securing places of worship prevent Christians from gathering to pray, for example, making the denial of lawful places of worship the greatest form of legal persecution in the country. Though Egypt approved applications for more than five hundred churches in one two-year period (out of three thousand filed), Christians of all backgrounds—not only the Copts but also the Protestants and Greek Orthodox—still faced hurdles getting permission to build or even meet in an existing building to worship together. As a result, there were simply not enough churches—one man told me that he had to walk more than six miles to get to church.

Although the Copts are the main target of persecution, other Christian groups complain that they, too, are persecuted. These groups also have long histories in Egypt, usually connected to

missionaries who headed to the Holy Land in the nineteenth
century.

The Synod of the Nile, or the Evangelical Church in Egypt,
has over 300 congregations and an estimated 250,000 followers,
the descendants of those who were converted in the nineteenth
century by the American Evangelical Presbyterian Church of
Egypt. The Evangelical Theological Seminary, now in Cairo,
was founded in 1863; at that time, it operated out of a house-
boat that sailed between Aswan and Cairo, training leaders in
villages along the way. At one point, the churches were full. Today, there are believed to be barely one hundred Presbyterian
churches in Egypt, many of which don't even have pastors.

Discrimination affects the private lives of Christians. By
law, Muslim women cannot marry Christian men (or any other
non-Muslims, for that matter). If a Christian woman chooses
to marry a Muslim man without converting, meanwhile, her
children will still be Muslim, and she cannot inherit from her
spouse unless she converts. These marriages are only recognized by the state when signed by clerics, who are often hesitant
to support such unions. Even if an interfaith couple manages to
obtain permission to wed from both the church and the state,
most families will still shun the Christian bride.

In rural areas, interfaith relationships are still very much ta-
boo, sometimes with violent consequences. In Karama, a village
in the Minya Governorate, in 2016, Suad Thabet, a seventy-
year-old mother of a Christian man who was rumored to have
had an affair with a Muslim woman, was dragged from her
house. She was stripped naked by a mob of several dozen people,
many of them armed, then pulled through the streets as they
shouted "Allahu Akbar" (God is great). The mob torched seven
Christian houses. Several of the attackers were later arrested for
taking part in the violence.

The trial was repeatedly delayed. It was heard twice in late August 2020, but the criminal court in Minya refused to decide the case and sent it back to the appeals court in Beni Suef. Some believe it was an attempt to delay the verdict. According to Christian Solidarity Worldwide, a human rights group based in the United Kingdom that promotes religious freedom, "while not deadly, the attack [in 2016] on Thabet by Muslim villagers in Minyan province whom she had known for years stands out as one of the most shocking."[29]

A few months later, in December, despite the high profile of the case and a personal apology from President Sisi, the three men accused of the assault were acquitted and found not guilty. No one was held accountable. The attackers remained at large.

"To God I will bring my case," Suad said after the trial. "He will bring me justice." Meanwhile, she has had trouble sleeping since the attack. She moved closer to a monastery to feel safer.[30]

Although the status of Christians in Egypt might be better than that of their coreligionists in Iraq, it is certainly not an enviable one.

GARBAGE CITY

One of the poorest neighborhoods in Cairo is called Mansheya Nasir. Nestled at the base of the Mokattam Hills, it is the slum settlement where the Christian "Zabbaleen" garbage collectors live and work. The Zabbaleen arrived from villages in Upper Egypt in the 1940s and began raising animals there. But they also began an unusual sideline: collecting and sorting the rubbish. Hence the neighborhood's nickname, "Garbage City."

Adham al-Sharkawy, a Christian born and raised in the community, agreed to meet me at a local coffee shop. When he was seventeen, in 2009, he was the subject of a documentary called *Garbage Dreams* made by Mai Iskander, a graduate of New York University's Tisch School of the Arts. Iskander had followed the lives of three teenage boys in the community, and Adham became something of a star after his appearance. In the film, he describes his life sifting through piles of trash and his desire to fly away to a different world, a place that is clean and fresh and new. The film became symbolic of the persecution of the Christian Zabbaleen.

At the coffee shop, Adham ordered a flavored coffee, offered to pay for it himself, and spread his hands on the table. His long fingers, I noticed, were scarred from digging through glass, aluminum, paper, tin cans, and other trash.

"Without us, Cairo wouldn't be clean," he said. He believes it was his fate to be born where he was, to do what he does now. He lives with garbage. When he was small, other boys who were not part of the community called him "Garbage Boy." He grew up with the identity of someone who lived with trash.

The afternoon we met was a perfect Egyptian winter day: cobalt blue skies, a slight breeze. Adham was cheerful and articulate. He spoke good English. After we talked for a while, he offered to bring me inside the world of the Zabbaleen so I could see it firsthand.

So we went. What struck me first about the settlement was the piles of trash, stinking of poverty and rot. "I don't notice the smell," Adham said. There were around eight thousand tons of garbage inside the community on the day I visited, Adham told me as we wound through the narrow streets. He showed me how it is all separated, cleaned, dried, and sorted. Skinny dogs sniffed at piles of rubbish that looked like a mix of cloth, tin, and plastic. Children sat on the back of trucks piled high with colored plastic bottles.

Adham told me about his family and his early life. The only son of a family with five children, he was right in the middle, between two older sisters and two younger ones. He felt like he was rooted in his community, but he also yearned to leave

Egypt. He hinted at family tragedy, and about his inability to rise in the world because he was Christian—and because he was a Zabbaleen (or "Recycler," as some of them prefer to be called). The Zabbaleen community is estimated to number anywhere from thirty thousand to seventy thousand people. They manage about 40 percent of Cairo's garbage, perhaps fifteen thousand tons a day.

"Everyone knows everyone in this community," Adham told me, "and everyone collects garbage." He said that 80 percent of what they collect is recycled, as opposed to the approximately 30 percent recycled abroad, and the rest goes to landfills.

"We are famous for what we collect and how we can break everything down to be recycled," he explained. But he added that the Egyptian government and the Cairo City Council, resentful of the Zabbaleen's resourcefulness, had started using foreign contractors, namely Italian and Spanish firms, as a way of punishing the Christian minority.

"They see our way as old-fashioned," he said bitterly.

Adham was seven years old when he started working with the garbage. Children here actually attend "recycling school," where they learn how to separate plastic, cloth, and paper, as well as how to "fight for a better future and develop a new trade."

But Adham is tired of living in Garbage City. During the making of Iskander's film, he got the chance to visit Wales and see how other communities recycle, and he came away with the impression that the Zabbaleen had entrepreneurial skills that could help the rest of the world become more sustainable. It's frustrating to have so little impact, such a small voice, he told me.

"Some of them have become recycling entrepreneurs," Adham said, speaking of those who profit from the world he was born into. He is desperate to leave a society where he feels he is always labeled a second-class citizen. Some of his relatives have been murdered, and he remembers being called a "Roman" as he walked to school as a child. Having things thrown at him. Always being made to feel different.

Pigs aid the Zabbaleen in the trash collection project, and as we wandered through the streets of Garbage City, Adham told me about a time in 2009 when the government had all the pigs killed under the guise of preventing swine flu. The flu, which had spread to humans and had been running rampant in other parts of the world, had arrived in Egypt; eventually it killed some 284,000 people worldwide. In Egypt, nearly 300,000 pigs were slaughtered. Adham says it was not the fear of disease that caused this response; rather, he believes it was another blow at the Christians, a conspiracy to undermine their business. "It was just a way of taking away the Christians' livelihood," he said darkly. It was a way of keeping Christians subjugated by ruining their economy.

Adham took me to the local Church of St. Simon the Tanner, named after a tenth-century saint. As the legend goes, the Coptic pope of that era, named Abraham, was engaged in religious debate with a Jewish holy man and a Muslim caliph. The latter challenged Abraham to move a mountain, as Jesus had said his disciples were capable of doing, or he would have all the Copts killed. After three days of prayer in Cairo's iconic third-century Hanging Church in the center of Old Cairo, Abraham had a vision of the Virgin Mary, who bade him to go to the market. He was led to a tanner, who was named Simon. At Simon's urging, Abraham called out three times, "Oh Lord Have Mercy," while making a sign of the cross toward the mountain. The mountain moved, and Abraham and his followers were saved.

Today, the Church of St. Simon, one of the largest in the Middle East, is carved into that same mountainside. It was built in the 1970s, a millennium after St. Simon's miracle was said to have taken place, and is named in his honor. It is massive, seating twenty thousand worshippers in an amphitheater built inside of a cliff. As we wandered through the cave church, Adham showed me a crypt with the relics of St. Simon.

Outside there was a kind of playground for families, with games for children and picnic benches. People appeared to be having fun, but there was something grim about a Sunday outing on the outskirts of a city of trash.

"I don't want my children to grow up like this," Adham reflected. He asked me to try to help him find a way to get out of Garbage City.

Adham belongs to one level of Christian society, and he made it clear that there was no long-term future for a Christian community among the garbage. It was not a livable future. But some Egyptian Christians are born into very different lives. Did children educated at the French *lycée* in Heliopolis still feel discrimination as Christians? Did their connections and wealth shelter them from its worst effects? Or was the sense of imminent persecution so much a part of their lives—the systemic prejudice, the laws of marriage, of land ownership, of inheritance—that they barely noticed? I continued to seek out Egypt's Christians to find answers to these questions.

THE DIVIDE

Christmas ended. I found myself back in the wealthy northwestern Cairo suburb of Heliopolis, where Cairo International Airport is located. In ancient Egypt it was a major city. Since the 1880s, Heliopolis has been the seat of the Latin Vicariate, the city's link to the Holy See. It is where Egyptologists first arrived on the old train lines. It is also the site of St. Mark's, one of the oldest Coptic churches, on Cleopatra Street, and the Catholic Basilica of the Holy Virgin on Al-Ahram Street. There is much wealth here, even now. In the 1990s, I remember coming to report on a group of private school kids who had been arrested for blasphemy because they had partied in an abandoned building known as The Baron. It was the height of the Islamic witch hunts, and while they were far from the "devil worshippers" the government prosecutor was portraying them as, listening to death metal and painting their fingernails black landed them in court, facing possible death sentences. I talked to their families and was startled by their affluence, the opulence of their homes, compared to other parts of Egypt. It was akin to the vast divide between students in Manhattan attending elite and expensive private high schools and those unlucky students struggling simply to attend classes in the Bronx during the COVID pandemic.

A friend brought me to see her aunt, a retired teacher, who lives in a fourth-floor apartment on a busy street. It was a warm day. The electricity had been on and off but it was working at the time, and she welcomed us into her home, which was decorated with a fake Christmas tree, an Advent calendar, and silver and gold garlands. We sat on reclining chairs and I noticed that among the photographs of her children on the walls, there was also a mounted wooden crucifix. There were religious cards scattered throughout the apartment, as well as small bottles of Holy Water. Her religion was ingrained into her daily life, into the decor of her apartment.

She did not want to give her name, so we agreed to call her Mary. She told me about growing up in the 1960s and how much easier it was to be a woman, to be a Christian, in the Nasser years. To Mary, Nasser, who presided over Egypt from 1956 until his death in 1970, took the country forward, changing it from an underdeveloped state to a leading one in the Arab world. She explained that he had introduced socialism, that he had stood up to the West and Israel, and that he had protected the Christians. Her vision of her youthful life under Nasser seemed almost like a childhood fantasy: it was a world where everything worked and life was perfect.

Yet, although Nasser never encouraged violence against the Copts, and during his watch there was little of the violence against the Christian community that took place under later presidents Sadat and Mubarak, Mary acknowledged some unpleasant memories. Like Adham, she remembered being called a "Roman" and having rocks thrown at her. When she was ten, she said, as the Nasser years were drawing to a close, she remembered being in a shop with her grandmother. "A Muslim man grabbed me," she recalled, shuddering slightly, "and held out my crucifix, which I was wearing on my neck. He said, 'You must convert.'"

And that, she said, was the beginning of the end of the time when life was "good for Christians." Mary was at university studying when President Anwar Sadat came to power in 1970 after Nasser's death. "I didn't even realize I was a Christian until the Sadat days," she said, describing how things changed radically for her when Sadat arrived. She remembered her family beginning to emigrate: to Canada, New Zealand, the United States, London.

In September 1981, the *Christian Science Monitor* wrote of an "increasingly antagonistic relationship between Mr. Sadat and the Coptic patriarch, Shenouda III."[31] The main reason for the patriarch's opposition was the amendment to the Egyptian constitution making Sharia law the source of legislation. Despite government assurances that personal status and inheritance laws for non-Muslims would remain intact, many Copts expressed their dismay with the change, and their reaction culminated in a four-day protest fast called by the patriarch. When Sadat allowed the Muslim Brotherhood more freedom in exchange for their backing against his political rivals, the Coptic leader organized marches against the flourishing Islamists and spoke against the president's tolerant stance.[32]

By 1981, Sadat had accused Shenouda III of "fomenting sectarian trouble between Copts and Muslims."[33] Thereafter, he cracked down hard on the Christian community. He also rescinded a previous presidential decree that had recognized Shenouda III as the leader of the Coptic Orthodox Church, instead putting him under house arrest.[34]

"That was the beginning of the end," Mary repeated, getting up to make tea and serve Christmas cookies. "That was when they began to allow the jihadists to operate freely. The Christians' lives became hellish."

As I left, she said, "It's getting harder for all Egyptians, but really for Christians now. Much harder for the man in the street, the everyday man, rather than the government." But being Christian, she reminded me, was about forgiveness. She wanted to live in peace with her Muslim neighbors. She did not want war or revolution. She wanted a shared community. But she also didn't want to be forced to wear a hijab. She'd heard that in some Cairo neighborhoods—El Marg, Imbaba—young Christian girls were being forced to cover their hair.

"If I could change one thing about the relationship between Christians and Muslims here, it would be education," she said, echoing Khalaf. "Education and culture."

Another young woman, Mina, who was born in the Mubarak era in the 1980s to a well-off middle-class family, with an engineer for a father, told me that when she was growing up, she had lived in a Muslim neighborhood. On Saturdays, the family would walk to church together.[35]

"We had to go to school on Sundays, which is the Christian day of worship," she explained, "in order to follow the Muslim calendar of the weekend starting on Thursday and ending on Saturday night." This, she said, was a source of great contention among her family and the Christian community.

"It wasn't fair. Sunday is a sacred day to us," she said. She remembered that en route to the "Italian church" (St. Joseph's Roman Catholic Church in Zamalek, on an island in the Nile) where the family worshipped, Muslim children came out and threw rocks at her.

"My father said to keep walking, not to engage," Mina said. "But it hurt. More emotionally than physically, that someone throws rocks at you for going to worship your God." Like others I talked to, she said at school she was mocked for being a "Roman." There were other hurtful things.

"The Muslim kids told others not to share food with us. They said Christians smelled bad." When she went to university, she was part of a group made up mainly of Christians, "but we never talked about it."

Another afternoon, I arranged to meet Big Pharaoh, a popular blogger who rose to fame during 2011's January 25 Revolution in Tahrir Square. He had become something of an icon for the movement with his outspoken views. His actual identity is not known to the public, although many people know who he is. Several people recommended I see him, largely because he is an example of a Christian who is well integrated into society. He sees himself as an activist first, a Christian second.

Tall, articulate, and well dressed, Big Pharaoh is the son of two Christians, a father from Egypt and a mother from Syria. He looked as though he could be Italian or French, two languages he spoke well. He was educated in British schools and had a slight accent.

"In Egypt, it's more about class and money than religion," he said bluntly. "I never had any trouble growing up Christian."

Big Pharaoh told me his real name but asked me not to use it when we met in the ostentatious faux-Ottoman lounge of the Marriott Hotel in Zamalek, which has an underground casino attached to it. The casino draws hordes of people from the region. In pre-COVID times they would arrive for the New Year's festivities with their aunts, cousins, grandmothers, nannies, babies, and piles of Louis Vuitton luggage stacked perilously high on trolleys. Big Pharaoh and I ordered mint tea in a small ceramic pot, honey, and round Egyptian biscuits. We sat on leather sofas and observed the commotion. I asked him if he felt that Christians had equal social standing with Muslims in Egypt. He paused, sipped some tea, then explained that standing like his own in society was pretty rare. He had a good life. He came from a well-off family, had a good job, and had gone to the English School in Heliopolis.

Obviously, privilege helps, and his life is very different from Abdullah's in Minya or Adham's in Garbage City. But did privilege and an elite education mean one was exempt from marginalization? "Still, Christians do not get treated the same by society at large," he said. "I know I will never become president of this country. I know I could never become a high-level police officer."

I asked him about the concept of Christians supporting dictators, largely for their own protection. He smiled. "I would be comfortable saying Christians did support Sisi," he said, due to the "dichotomy of the army or disorder."

For Big Pharaoh, the basic issue was less about religion and more about social justice. "Look, you can't have democracy without social equality," he said. Christians in his social and economic class "live in a bubble." They didn't have much in common with those who live in rural areas with no churches. Their concerns were about Sisi's crackdown on freedom of expression, the lawyers and protesters rotting in prison, or the fact that Tahrir Square failed "because the revolutionary force failed to materialize into political options."

He did fear the persecution of Christians, even if it did not touch him personally, but what he feared more was greater disorder. Though he had supported the Tahrir Square protests, in the hope they might bring about lasting change, he thought the country could not sustain another major crisis.

"My biggest fear is another upheaval, another revolution," he told me. "This country cannot stand another upheaval. I don't want that. If I could choose between armed regime or upheaval, I'd say regime. The other would be messy, bloody. The lower social classes revolting against the state."

He worried about hunger strikes in Egypt, too, saying, "If you give people no hope and they have the ability to mobilize, it could happen."

The power of the Egyptian military interferes with nearly every aspect of Egyptian life. They are even wrapped up in the movie business, with the security bodies becoming increasingly involved in the industry. One of the country's top producers is Egyptian businessman Ahmed Abou Hashima, who is close to President Sisi and the military.[36] Big Pharaoh reflected on the post–Tahrir Square generation of activists and the dashed dreams of the Egyptian revolution. "In 2010 and 2011, we were full of hope," he said. "Then it all started to go down with the rule of the Muslim Brotherhood. The only good they did was show people who Islam is and how Islam rules."

The new generation of protesters—particularly, in the post-COVID world, the ones following on the heels of Black Lives Matter in the United States—are "more rebellious, more individualistic, more materialistic," he noted gloomily, as we watched more Gulf Arabs arrive at the hotel to celebrate. "That is why the status quo of Egypt, of Sisi's reign, will continue in the short term, not the long term."

Another, even loftier, perspective came from an elegant Christian woman in her late sixties whom I had met at a seasonal cocktail party she was hosting in her home. It could have been in Paris or London. A former banker, she had magnificent art and a balcony overlooking the Nile, with jasmine trees winding around the wrought-iron bannisters. She served vodka cocktails in crystal glasses, and servants circulated with platters of smoked salmon and crudités.

Hers was a grand and famous landowning Christian family with strong ties to Europe. But their riches had slowly eroded, beginning in the Nasser years, as socialism became more widespread. First the government took away their land, then it took their factories, and their majestic houses. Then their rights were taken, and finally their privileges. This woman left for France in the early 1960s, during "the most difficult times," but her family remained, in one way or another, connected to society in Cairo.

Her memories of the best years of her life in Egypt recalled the great American photographer Lee Miller, who documented Cairo's grand society in the 1930s and called it the "black silk and pearls set." It was a postwar life, where the wealthy could send their children to the south of France in the summer, where British boarding schools and universities were de rigueur. And then, abruptly, it stopped. *Fin de race*, the French call it (immortalized by Voltaire), a terrible, shuddering term that inspires visions of the ends of generations, failed empires, and worlds that will never return.

Perhaps because this woman's life was cocooned in her lovely apartment high above a noisy street in Cairo, perhaps because she saw the inevitable happening—that Christians would eventually, somehow, disappear from her native land—she faced the fate of her people in Egypt with a clear, undramatic resignation.

"It's finished," she said calmly. "The way it was."

THE GHOSTS OF TAHRIR SQUARE

The plight of Christians in Egypt is tied up with the larger political landscape in the country today. To understand the challenges Christians are now facing, we have to go back to the seminal event of this generation, those extraordinary weeks of the revolution at the beginning of 2011, when a crowd of protesters liberated their country from an authoritarian regime by sitting in a square and refusing to leave.

The morning of January 25, 2011, the so-called Day of Rage, was a clear, cold Egyptian morning. The mass of protesters had gathered in Tahrir Square, an area in downtown Cairo not far from the Nile, to rail against corruption, nepotism, rising food prices, and blatant inequality under the thirty-year rule of President Hosni Mubarak, a former air force officer.

"I felt like I was in a dream," recalled Omar, a young Egyptian activist who was part of the January 25 Revolution.[37] Today he lives quietly in the United States, and when we spoke about the revolution days, he seemed wistful. But in 2011, he spent weeks living in Tahrir Square in a state of euphoria. He and his friends truly believed they were building a democracy from the ashes of a dictatorship.

Dr. Rasha Abdulla, a professor and chair of media studies at the American University of Cairo, told me that people attached themselves to the movement in a seamless, organic way. "I recall marching down the street and hearing the crowds urging people on their balconies to come down and join us," she said. "So the crowd got bigger and bigger and bigger—and gained more power."

Despite an Internet blackout at one point, the protests flourished. People used landlines to report back to friends in London or Dubai, who would then use Twitter or Facebook to post the latest news from the square. The crowds grew even more.

The dramatic events over the next few weeks in Tahrir Square in many ways sealed the fate of modern Egypt, and also of the rest of the region. By February 11, after eighteen solid days of demonstrations, Mubarak was gone. The power of the crowd, which hailed from a broad socioeconomic sweep across Egypt—student and youth groups, trade unions, farmers—had prevailed. The street had effectively unseated an entrenched dictator who had used and abused his power and had allowed his cronies, mostly retired military officials, to become the business elite with a monopoly over key economic sectors. It was the people versus Mubarak, and miraculously, the people won.

But transitions following revolutions are difficult. In the aftermath of Mubarak's departure, the military's top leadership, known as the Supreme Council of the Armed Forces, took control of the government. They initially promised a democratic transition, but it took them more than a year to give power to a freely elected parliament and president from the Muslim Brotherhood, led by Mohamed Morsi.

The Brothers made plenty of mistakes, and they did not keep promises. The military, meanwhile, felt threatened by them and at risk of being sidelined. By July 3, 2013, the Brothers were ousted from power by a new military-backed dictatorship led by the former defense minister, Abdel Fattah al-Sisi. Under his regime, as of this writing in 2021, there is no political opposition, and repression is at one of the harshest levels in decades.

Many of the Christians I spoke to complained about the general state of human rights in Egypt today. Under Sisi, there has been a widespread campaign to arrest possible opponents of the regime. Journalists have been stifled and imprisoned, civil society has been threatened, and human rights activists, lawyers, and students have been under siege. A state of emergency is renewed every three months, giving the police expanded powers and allowing for the continued operation of emergency courts. The military controls most levels of society, from public infrastructure to the film industry.

In addition to the government's draconian measures in the name of security, the other issue that affects everyone, Christian or Muslim, is the continuing economic crisis. At the urging of the International Monetary Fund (IMF), which Egypt had been attempting to woo to attract a $12 billion loan, the country recently floated its currency and ended fuel subsidies. While these were probably necessary steps to allow growth in the long term, the short-term effect has been to make everyday life harder for all Egyptians, particularly the poor. Even more painfully, the astronomical increases in the prices of all goods, commodities, and services have placed them way beyond the average Egyptian citizen's budget. Over 35 percent of the population lives below the poverty line, while Sisi and the members of his inner circle live lavishly.

"I have no idea how people in places like Minya, which is really poor, buy things like tomatoes, let alone bread," Omar told me. "For the poor now, it has never been worse."

Ghannam, a PhD student living in Washington, DC, who participated in the 2011 protests, agreed. "I have no idea how people live. Consumer behavior has changed: middle-class people used to buy meat once a week. Now it's dried cauliflower as a replacement for meat. . . . . Now they are saying cauliflower absorbs too much oil—and oil is too expensive. so they can't even afford that!"

Any attempts at change as radical as the Tahrir protests are brutally crushed. In September 2019, an exiled actor-turned-businessman known as Mohamed Ali living in exile in Spain began detailing on YouTube how billions of Egyptian pounds were being squandered on luxury residences for President Sisi and senior military officials. Ali's posts went viral. He seemed like the whistleblower people had been waiting for.

In the stifled economy, Ali's messages resonated. People tried to rise up. By the end of September, "small but passionate protests" (in the words of one protester) began. Protesters objected to the corruption, and Sisi's alleged building of elaborate homes for himself and his cronies was dubbed "Palacegate."

For a brief moment, they seemed to be reliving the glory of January 25, when the street had changed history. The protesters had only one demand for Sisi: step down.

But the Egyptian military today is a different breed than during the Mubarak days. In the past seven years, it has consolidated and grown. The protesters never really had a chance. The military and police responded with a heavy-handed detention campaign that involved a reported 3,763 arrests, at least 448 of them of individuals aged twenty-five or younger.

Mohamad Elmasry, a professor at the Doha Institute for Graduate Studies in Qatar, told *The New Arab* newspaper why the September protests could not succeed. "In 2011, the Mubarak government wasn't able to handle the shock of a sustained protest movement," he explained. "The Sisi government is considerably more brutal than the Mubarak government ever was. In particular, the Sisi regime shows no mercy to protesters. Thousands have been killed in the streets and tens of thousands have been arrested, with many of those tortured in prison and given draconian sentences."[38]

Still, the protests moved something in Egyptians that had been dormant since Sisi took power. "I see Mohamed Ali as a catalyst and a trigger for people to go out and protest, rather than a direct cause," said Dr. Sahar Khamis, an Egyptian American professor of communication at the University of Maryland. "I feel that the extreme repression that Egyptians are experiencing now, coupled with severe economic hardships such as high poverty and unemployment rates and the new wave of uprisings sweeping the region, are all triggers for Egypt's next uprising."

Most people want to see Sisi go, but equally, the people I talked to were frightened, with good cause. Forced disappearances are becoming common. Foreign journalists have been deported. Christians are afraid to speak up. Everyone has some horror story connected to disappearances, prison, or torture.

No one is immune from police brutality, even foreigners. In 2016, an Italian PhD student at Cambridge University, Giulio Regeni, was researching Egyptian trade unions when he was abducted by the police. His corpse was found on the Cairo-Alexandria road. His dead body and face were so badly mutilated by torture that one human rights lawyer told me discreetly that Regeni's own mother could not identify him.

The September 2019 protests died quietly, and those activists who were left of the old-school January 25 Revolution were skeptical. Michael Wahid Hanna, a Senior Fellow with the Century Foundation in New York, explained, "They saw it as overblown and dangerous and, if it succeeded, it would provoke the state even further."

EGYPT TODAY

Given his thuggish policies, it is staggering that Sisi has managed to garner such support from Western and Arab allies. The primary reason is that fearful leaders see him as the only force capable of keeping the Muslim Brotherhood out of power, and as someone who cracked down on al-Qaeda in the Sinai and prevented ISIS from gaining a foothold in Egypt. The Emiratis, following Sisi's 2013 coup, gave his government vast sums in aid. Sisi was trained in the United States, attending the US Army War College in 2006 for a yearlong master's degree program that has become a way station for up-and-coming Egyptian officers.

And there is plenty of support from Christians for Sisi. One afternoon, I climbed the stairs to the office of a well-known publisher, Youssef Sidhom, who runs the Coptic newspaper *Watani*. *Watani* was established by his father, Antoun Sidhom, in 1958, and it has a wide following among Christians in Egypt and abroad.

Youssef is openly pro-government, and he makes a convincing argument against the Islamists and in favor of Sisi. "The majority of Christians feel secure in this regime," he said. "This doesn't mean they don't look for change."

When I met with him, he ordered coffee, pushed aside the layout for the next edition of *Watani*, and guided me through a lecture on Egyptian national law regarding minorities, starting with the 1856 Hamayouni Decree during the Ottoman Empire. The measure gave the empire's Christian inhabitants the right to build churches.

The building requests, however, had to be approved by the sultan. "It was meant to be a law that was fair," Youssef said. "But in fact, it was used as a way of restricting the building of churches."

I spent a few hours with Youssef as he talked of the Nasser years ("There were no real problems"), the rise of the Islamists under Sadat, and the 1967 and 1973 wars with Israel. Like Mary from Heliopolis, he blamed much of the persecution on Sadat's courting of Islamists. It was after the 1978 Camp David Accords between Sadat and Israel's prime minister at the time, Menachem Begin, Youssef said, that "Christians began to be stung with rhetoric that was hateful to anyone who was not Muslim—1978 was when the real attacks against Christians began. This was the first time Christians experienced hatred."

But it was under Mubarak, he said, that Christians had the "toughest time of all." Mubarak started being "very cautious not to provoke the Islamists, so he turned a blind eye to the atrocities Christians were being subjected to." Apart from being denied high-ranking state jobs, they were also denied building permits (again, to build churches). Youssef told me that as a result, some 3,700 Christian churches were built illegally in the 1980s. In addition, the educational system was changed to omit the Christian era from history books. "There was nothing about the six centuries before Islam," Youssef said. "It falsified our history being taught to children."

Youssef summarized Egypt's recent history all the way to Tahrir Square and the rise and fall of the Brotherhood, concluding, "There is now no place for the Muslim Brotherhood." He seemed more optimistic about the future than anyone else I spoke to.

Youssef did not want to look at Sisi's human rights record, as he basically saw this as a Western intrusion onto Egyptian sovereignty. Nor did he really want to hear that Donald Trump liked to describe Sisi as "his favorite dictator."

"The Western media is always looking for a way to hit hard at Sisi's attempts to control terrorism," was his response, ending the discussion.

European countries and international organizations, such as the UN's Office of the High Commissioner on Human Rights, try to hold Sisi and his government accountable, particularly on their treatment of prisoners, but the human rights record remains pretty dire. Observers' requests to enter prisons are consistently denied, so documentation of abuses is difficult for these organizations to obtain.

Shortly before he left his post as assistant secretary-general for human rights at the UN, I met with Andrew Gilmour, a man who is renowned for speaking truth to power. He is now executive director of the Berlin-based Berghof Foundation, which focuses on peace building. While at the UN, Gilmour—and indeed anyone working on human rights—tended to have a particularly difficult relationship with Egypt. Part of his mandate was to work with people who had suffered reprisals by the government for being human rights defenders and cooperating with the UN. The Egyptian government had a consistent record of carrying out such reprisals. "Each year, the UN Secretary-General features Egypt in his reports on this topic," Gilmour told me. "One of the saddest cases we reported on was Ibrahim Metwally, a man whose son was arrested, and presumed tortured and murdered, in 2013, as a result of which Metwally started working on the issue of judicial disappearances. In September 2017, he was about to take a flight to Geneva to speak to the UN about it, when he was arrested on charges of 'terrorism,' which no serious person believed for a moment. He too disappeared for a while, before emerging, obviously tortured, but remaining in prison for years. Knowing the nature of the regime in his country, when warned that he might be arrested, he told a friend, 'Yes, I know, but let them arrest me—that way I may feel closer to my lost son.'"

Despite this, most of the world seems to take little notice of Sisi's reign of terror, ignoring it and brushing it aside in the same way that President Trump dismissed the Saudi regime's murder of journalist Jamal Khashoggi in 2018. "Western policymakers have turned their attention away, dismissing the country and the people whose protest movement once inspired the world as a 'failed attempt,' 'a sad story,' or 'no longer a priority,'" said Mai El Sadany, the legal and judicial director for the Tahrir Institute in Washington, DC. "Others have made excuses for the government's policies, relying on a tired understanding of the region that has long changed, and a false choice between security and rights."

I've worked in Egypt off and on for nearly three decades. During my most recent visit, I was startled to see how much more paranoid I felt working as a reporter than I had ever felt in the past. The offices of Mada Masr, an independent Egyptian online news platform overseen by Lina Attalah, a journalist who was also an activist during the Tahrir days, were raided a few weeks before I arrived. Journalists were arrested. When I met with people in Cairo, they asked me to conceal their identity. Nearly every person I spoke to for this chapter asked that their name be changed. Everyone wanted to speak on encrypted cellphone channels rather than by email. Others

did not want to talk at all, and understandably so: the consequences could be prison, or worse.

When I met with people outside the country, they told me
how worried they were for their families still in Egypt. They
also sought reassurances that their names would be carefully
hidden. It reminded me, in a bleak sense, of working in Iraq
back in the dark days of Saddam, when Iraq was referred to as a
"Republic of Fear." In seven years in power, Sisi has managed to
instill a vast collective trauma on his own people.

What happened to the dream of the January 25 Revolution is
a painful debate among Egyptians, both those in exile abroad
and those in Cairo. It's important to both Muslims and to the
Christian minority. Everyone remembers those days with wist-
fulness. Every January and February, when memories stretch
back to those afternoons and nights in the square—the sit-ins,
the solidarity, the hope—it feels even more painful.

Dr. H. A. Hellyer, a British scholar of mixed English and Arab
parentage at Cambridge University and the Carnegie Endowment
for International Peace, published a book examining the Tahrir
phenomenon, *A Revolution Undone: Egypt's Road Beyond Revolt*,
in 2016. He believes that the January 25 Revolution had massive
potential: "It represented an incredibly inspiring historical moment in Egypt, but also affected other peoples around the globe,"
he wrote. It was a unique moment, where people truly believed
that change was coming, and that they could help bring about an
equitable and accountable government. But, Hellyer added, "its
promise was eventually squandered . . . one hopes not forever."

Part of the reason for the ultimate failure of the revolution
to create change was the fallout among the many actors on the
ground—secular, Islamist, liberal, leftist—who failed to stick
together against the forces that wanted a return to the status quo. In the early days of the protests, an array of forces,

including self-identified leftists, liberals, and the Brotherhood, among others, united against the ruling power. Yet Ghannam, the former protester now studying in DC, is sure that the Brotherhood, even then, was plotting to push out the secular opposition and take power itself.

"They had their own plans," she said, "to be with the military, not against them."

Youssef Sidhom, the editor of *Watani*, agreed, telling me that what "started as a genuine pluralistic outburst turned out to be a fierce race toward power." The various groups that opposed Mubarak and his regime were unable to resolve their ideological and strategic differences without excluding one another. The Brotherhood, for all their grassroots support, were no match for the *ancien régime*, which simply bided its time.

Hellyer thinks the most obvious mistake was that few people recognized how much of the state apparatus (or rather, the military and security apparatus) was left behind when Mubarak was removed. The protests had not eroded the intricate system he presided over; although they had given the system a massive jolt, the system rebounded.

"The regime was shocked and shaken to the core," Hellyer said, "but it was able to recover, regroup, and eventually, engage in counter-revolutionary moves when it saw the opportunity to do so."

"So the post-uprising consensus lasted for a very short period of time, while the anti-revolutionary or counter-revolutionary alliance managed to build up momentum," Hellyer said. "Past a certain point, it became a 'zero-sum game' for the most powerful actors, which eventually meant the most powerful actor—i.e., the army—taking over completely." The military ousted Morsi and suspended the new constitution in 2013.

For a while, the disbelief that the revolution had failed was replaced by blaming foreign powers, especially the Saudis and the

United Arab Emirates. Both loathe the Muslim Brotherhood—
and the feeling is now mutual—due to Riyadh and Abu Dhabi
views of the region, in contradistinction to the Brotherhood's
outlook. Hellyer explained, "We've seen a lot of claims that the
ending of the democratic experiment and the military takeover
in 2013 depended on foreign intervention, manipulation, or
acquiescence."

Hellyer disagrees that these other nations are primarily to
blame, however, even though he agrees they were involved in
Egyptian affairs. "I have to emphasize—this was intrinsically
an Egyptian story, even if it was one other nations tried to impact," he said. The reality is more complicated, and muddier. "The
events were fundamentally driven by considerations and calcu-
lations on the ground by Egyptian actors, whether one agrees
with or opposes them," according to Hellyer. "Of course outside
forces were interested and tried to influence—but the fundamental consequences were a result of bad domestic decisions, not
external ones." In other words, the revolution failed primarily because of choices made in Egypt by the most powerful actors: the
military, the Brotherhood, and the revolutionary forces, in that
order. Among them, unsurprisingly, there had never been a solid
agreement or consensus on how to engineer the transition period
following Mubarak's removal.

Some blame a lack of transitional justice. The courts and ju-
diciary were still largely made up of "regime loyalists and social
elites," according to Sahar Aziz, a law professor at Rutgers University. "Most senior judges also were deeply suspicious of the
forces pushing for transitional justice—the revolutionary youth
and (at first) the Muslim Brotherhood—and thus acted to support political continuity and a strong state. Consequently, most
Mubarak regime defendants got off with undue leniency or were
exonerated."[39]

But most of the blame has been squarely placed on the Muslim Brotherhood, which made its first mistake by appearing to align itself with the military. Ghannam remembered how surprised and "hurt" she was when the Brothers started emulating the old regime. "The way they conducted things was very similar to Mubarak," she said. "People were terrified that they had no intention of building democratic institutions—they just wanted to be in power. And that is what the military used to rally people against them. . . . They sold out the secular opposition and joined the military camp. But the military camp played them."

None of this was inevitable, though. Had the Muslim Brotherhood created a tighter, more inclusive, and more efficient government, and had the population not acquiesced so easily when Sisi and his military overthrew Morsi's government in 2013—perhaps the dream of January 25 might have become reality.

In 2020 on the anniversary of January 25, Tahrir Square was under partial lockdown. But it wasn't because of COVID; it was because of the threat posed by the chance of renewed protests. The square is under partial lockdown on the anniversary of the revolution every year. Tanks and checkpoints were set up at strategic sites. But it was a needless exercise. Most of the original leaders of the revolution are dead, in prison, in exile, or mentally and physically broken. The ones who have survived are tormented by guilt, or question what went wrong after that golden moment when they realized Mubarak was stepping down.

The memory seems to be growing dimmer. On the fifth anniversary, only a few protesters came out, handing out flowers and waving Egyptian flags. By 2020, it was barely a handful. By 2021, the tenth anniversary, while the world was still in the midst of a terrible year of pandemic, Martin Chulov of *The Guardian* mused on the changes from a decade before:

A decade on, the launchpad of Egypt's revolution—a seminal part of the uprisings which became known as the Arab spring— is a very different place, as is the country. The strip of grass has been concreted over and on it stands a newly erected obelisk, pointing skywards in a trenchant reminder of times of staid certainty. Traffic moves sedately around a roundabout now free of protesters or attempts at defiance. Secret police are positioned, not so secretly, nearby. There is little talk of revolution, and attempts to stir the ghosts of Tahrir Square are met with the heavy hand of the invigorated military state that entrenched itself in the revolution's wake.[40]

At a New Year's Eve party in Zamalek, the lush island in the Nile where many diplomats and foreign journalists live, I met a vibrant young woman named Sally Touma. A psychiatrist by training and a Christian, Sally's complaints were largely about the state of women in Egypt from a socioeconomic viewpoint. I remembered, when I was a young student many decades earlier in London, meeting the great Egyptian feminist Nawal el Saadawi, also a psychiatrist. El Saadawi came from a small, conservative village and had spent a lifetime fighting against the scourge of female genital mutilation and the subjugation of women in Egyptian society. Some have called her the Simone de Beauvoir of the Middle East. El Saadawi was circumcised as a child, cared for her eight siblings after her parents died, and put herself through medical school at a time when women did not study science in Egypt. She has researched the plight of Egyptian women, especially their physical and psychological states resulting from oppression. She was brave, outspoken, wild. She took on the Islamists, she combined feminism with pan-Arabism, and when she was detained in prison in 1981 on trumped-up charges, she wrote her memoir on toilet paper using a smuggled eyebrow pencil as a pen.

She died March 21, 2021, as I was editing this book. I was stunned when I opened the *New York Times* over my morning coffee and saw a photograph of al Saadawi—in a neon pink shirt, a shock of white hair—next to her obituary.[41] She seemed like one of those forces of nature who never could die: she was so alive. I remembered walking with her down Haymarket in London on a wintry day. Wrapped in an old tweed coat, she lectured me on how patriarchy and poverty—not Islam, in the case of Arab women—oppress females. This was the basis of her magnificent book published in 1977, *The Hidden Face of Eve*. "I should be more aggressive, because the world is becoming more aggressive and we need people to speak loudly against injustices," she told the BBC in 2018.[42]

Sally Touma, who had been a leading force in the 2011 Tahrir Square demonstrations, spoke about the same kinds of struggles that el Saadawi did. For Sally, the oppression was less about Christians versus Muslims than about class and economics. She called herself a "Marxist Christian," or a "Revolutionary Socialist."

"Christian women are the dark bottom of a pit," she said, ticking off the challenges on her fingers: Can't get into power. Muslim country. Impoverished. Sisi a devout, preaching leader. "But my issue is class," she said. "Not religion."

On the last day of 2019, I drove deep into the Nitrian Desert, west of the Nile Delta, on the road to Alexandria, heading to the Monastery of Our Lady Baramus, also called Paromeos Monastery, in the Wadi el Natrun. I was again with my son's godmother, Mariann, an Austrian Roman Catholic, with whom I had spent much time sitting quietly in European churches. We had lit candles together, and had often discussed the faith we had been raised with and were trying to adapt to modern life. My friend is one of the most spiritual people I know, yet without judgment for those who do not have faith. She simply lives her life on a path that always incorporates God.

We arrived at the monastery in the early morning. The desert next to the highway was golden dust. The invitation we had received from the monks had reminded us that we would have to leave before late morning, so that the monks could continue their solitary prayers. I had slept for the first part of the drive under a blanket I had liberated from my hotel and awoke to the sight of the white stone bell tower of the monastery's oldest church rising in the sky. There are five small churches and chapels at the complex, and the largest is dedicated to the Virgin Mary.

At the gate, we went through several security checks before a police car escorted us inside. I was reminded that despite the isolation of the monastery, the monks were still, in many ways, endangered.

It was a beautiful, peaceful place, washed with white paint, with neat rows of small flowers and carefully tended bushes bursting with greenery. Until forty years ago, no roads led here. Only camels could make the trip. The monks lived in nearby caves and came to take their meals together at wooden tables in silence.

At the entrance, a small man in dark robes greeted us and then guided us through the ancient halls and lush gardens. He was very familiar with Christian persecution, his monastic forebears having warded off attacks from bandits, Berbers, Bedouins, and Romans. They barricaded themselves inside the walls, drew up the ladders, and were often besieged for months on end, living on bread and water.

"They stayed inside and prayed," said the monk, who also did not want to give his name. I asked if I could call him Michael. He nodded.

So it is with Christians in Egypt today, he reminded me. There is fear, of course. They remain besieged, perhaps even more so under General Sisi than under Mubarak.

But the monk was not worried. "We've gone through worse," he said. "The more we are persecuted, the more we pray."

For an hour or more, he explained to me in great detail the difference between the many Christian churches—Coptic and Roman Catholic, Syriac and Greek Orthodox—and what separated people, how their rituals and saints differed. He carefully explained the ritual of Transfiguration, and the small differences in Orthodox and Catholic beliefs about the third person of the Trinity, the Holy Spirit.

The monks had come to the desert for the sole purpose of gaining enlightenment: to live according to the monastic principles. Yet now, the monk lamented, they found themselves busy performing social tasks for the wider Christian community. He regretted that the monastery had become so easily accessible. He had joined it to be a hermit among hermits, and he yearned for that time again.

He also said that the monastery had undergone part of its modernization when a German engineer discovered water in the ground a few years earlier. Thanks to the new well, the monks had transformed the ascetic eremite retreat into a lush oasis. Rather than feeling barren and uncomfortable, the monastery now feels welcoming and warm, well kept and much loved. This stands in stark contrast to Cairo and the villages closest to the monastery, where people continue to inhabit buildings that are falling down around them.

In a quiet chapel, Michael let me stand on the fringes for a while as three Coptic priests chanted their prayers, which he warned me would be several hours long. I had asked if I could stay for some time to pray quietly, and he had agreed.

The tiny room was lit by sunlight and full of the overwhelming scent of incense. The wall space was full of icons. The three monks mostly ignored me as they chanted and prayed. After some time, Michael came and motioned for me to follow him, and I joined Mariann, who had been standing outside the chapel waiting for me. The place had a powerful effect on both of us. Later, she wrote to me: "You were in heaven in that chapel, listening to the monks' prayers and chants. I stood outside and noted the wind that gently blew between the clay buildings and the beautiful shadows the sun projected on the tactile walls."

Michael showed us an icon of the Black Madonna. He reminded us that it is believed that Mary, the Mother of Jesus, arrived in Egypt with Jesus when he was about two years old, escaping King Herod. Then he led us to a simple guest house for tea.

At the guest house, there were a few Christian families gathered with their children on sofas. They seemed quietly content. The monk said he had been thirty years old when he had decided to live a life of faith, choosing this calmness with so few distractions. Before that, he had studied mathematics. Now, he has a simple room not far from the monastery. He reads the gospels, he prays, he eats. He talks with his brothers. He is not aware of Black Lives Matter protests in New York or what might happen in Cairo. His faith is all-encompassing.

When I left Cairo, the words of one of the many people I interviewed echoed in my head: "I don't think this is the end of the story. The story is not over." And I thought of Zakher describing with delight how his household, half Muslim and half Christian, had evolved in the 1970s, when sectarianism was not as rife. He had assured me that Christians' right to the land was essential—"We have an important link to the land. In every prayer, we pray for the country and its future. What happens here is extremely important for us"—but even more than that, he told me about meals shared, laughter and jokes.

"I think it's important this generation remembers," he said, "that we used to live together in the same house."

EPILOGUE

QUARANTINE, APRIL 2020

Years ago we had the church, which was a way of saying, we had each other.

Jack Nicholson, playing Frank Costello
in Martin Scorsese's film *The Departed*

HERE IN THE ALPS, WE ARE GETTING READY FOR EASTER. THE LAMB WE ORdered from the farmer down the road will be slaughtered today. In my life before confinement, I would have balked at having any kind of role in the death of an innocent animal. In Iraq, I had seen the ritual slaughter of lambs before Muslim holy days. The goriest was in Karbala, the holy city for Shia Muslims, before Eid al-Adha. I felt sick for days.

But in my new lockdown life, I am not thinking of the animal. I'm thinking of how long the meat will last, feeding six of us in our mountain retreat. A friend keeps reminding me that we are hardly in the *Hongerwinter* of 1944 in the Netherlands, when many people, Audrey Hepburn included, subsisted on tulip bulbs and sugar beets. But our diet and our habits are dictated by something larger than us right now: the coronavirus. You eat what you can get from the farmers nearby, and you don't complain.

213

The Holy Week of my childhood in America was a laborious event. I went to a Catholic school run by harsh Irish Dominican nuns, and there were endless daily Masses, some in Latin. There was chanting, the recitation of memorized prayers, and much naughty note-passing among my friends. We knelt on wooden kneelers for what seemed like hours. The dreaded nuns patrolled the aisles, their glowering red faces within their wimples.

Holy Thursday was the evening Mass commemorating Jesus's washing of the disciples' feet, complete with the local priests and altar boys administering the Holy Water. My brothers were altar boys. Back then, before sex scandals wracked the Catholic Church, local priests were akin to town doctors, deeply revered figures. Still, how odd to see them in their dark clothes with bare feet. In 2020, Pope Francis offered the Mass to an empty basilica. He did not wash feet. Coronavirus and social distancing altered—and in some cases eradicated—many traditions, at least for a while.

My childhood Good Fridays were somber. We could not eat meat. At 3:00 p.m. sharp, the hour Our Lord died, the sky, in my memory, always went ominously dark. The nuns would stop class and we would sit in silence. And yet I also remember those absurdly off-kilter moments that punctuated Holy Week. Sometimes, we would watch campy films that were meant to seem inspirational and somehow authentic: a dashing young Richard Burton in *The Robe*, or a Charlton Heston epic, *Ben Hur*. How we laughed at a skirted John Wayne, playing a Roman soldier in *The Greatest Story Ever Told*, as he stared intensely at the crucified Jesus and declared, in his best Old Western drawl, "Truly, this man was the son of God."

Much is different during this strange plague year. There is one TV in the large room of our old farmhouse here in the Vercors, which we use only to catch up on the news, called *infos*, at

8:00 p.m. I find it hard to watch anything but sobering facts. The broadcasts are entirely devoted to talking heads pontificating on the raging virus. I feel guilty watching *The Office* or *Narcos*. Occasionally, there are long shots of empty Paris streets, and once, a report on a security guard at an empty Eiffel Tower. I cannot get my head around the fact that a few weeks ago, many thousands were living, and now they are gone.

My friend Anna, who is spending her confinement in the center of Paris, has been sitting every morning in the beautiful garden of a retirement home for priests on Boulevard Raspail. Like her fellow Parisians, she is allotted one walk a day. Outdoors at these times, she has found solace in birdsong. For a few moments, she has found, she can pass the time without a single thought of the virus. This morning she called me in tears. As she was sitting there, absorbing the serenity, heavily shrouded emergency workers emerged, carrying out the body of a dead priest. She was hoping he might have passed away due to natural causes. But no: he had died, she learned, during Holy Week, from complications due to COVID-19.

It brings me comfort and consolation this Easter Week to follow a few rural traditions. The local church, as it happens, is closed down. Even in the best of times, this area is so isolated that the Mass moves from village to village each Sunday, as there is only one priest for all of them. So instead of attending Mass, I've been walking to a small chapel at the edge of a forest. I make small crowns of yellow wildflowers, which I place on the head of the statue of Our Lady. I light a candle. I pray for those who are sick and for those who have died. Ordinarily, I am not a prayerful person. I am a proud sinner, in fact. But faith is coming back to me in these dark times.

I will also try my hand at preparing traditional food. My mother, whose family comes from Naples, is one hundred years old and living in semi-isolation in a rural New Jersey town.

When I was small, her Easter Week involved a ritual that had been passed down for generations: the making of a traditional salty Easter pie known, among other names, as *pizza rustica*. It's a Neapolitan dish, something like a stuffed pizza filled with cheese and sausage, which is prepared in advance and then cut into cold slices. Because the more religious Neapolitans fasted for forty days before Easter—no dairy, no eggs—this pie was a generous way to break the fast. "When the peasants would go to the fields to work," Yola, my favorite aunt, would tell me, "they took slices and wrapped them in clothes." She would always make a point of adding, "Not that our family were peasants."

The sourcing for the ingredients was the most difficult part: the perfect Parmesan, the right prosciutto. My spirited aunt, when she was alive, was the designated pie maker. A successful businesswoman long before female emancipation, Yola had a beautiful kitchen, which had been built in the 1940s, interestingly enough, by a French architect modeling it after a Provençal farmhouse. Her *batterie de cuisine* was similar to the one I am using now: old farmhouse tools for cooking, tin funnels, cracked wooden spoons, my grandfather's elaborate brass wine opener brought from Naples in the 1920s.

I would stand on the side watching as Yola and my mother sifted flour, grated endless triangles of Parmesan, and chopped onions. I was not allowed to do much other than stir. Over the years, as the relatives who had linked me to my past passed on, one by one, the task was left to my brother Joseph. He was also an excellent cook, and he lived near my mother. But his attempts at *pizza rustica* were inconsistent; sometimes the crust would be too soggy, or the cheese would have hardened too much.

Joseph died tragically in 2015. Even now, six years on, I grieve him: I am not sure where he has gone. My mother, who had lost two other children, went into a time of deep grieving and after his death ordered her remaining children to buy the pie from a local Italian bakery. "My days of making it are over," she said. The bakery version was good, but never the same.

As a war reporter, the greatest tragedies I've witnessed and recorded have been those involving families that were thrust apart by events outside of their control: a child who was pushed onto the last bus leaving a falling city, lines of refugees who lost their family members in the crowds. So many of us are now separated by coronavirus.

I feel so distant from my mother, from our holidays together. And so, this year, in confinement, I will once again make Easter pie. There is no ricotta in this part of France, but we do have crème fraiche from the cows. The only Parmesan available comes in nasty plastic packs at the supermarket, which is only open a few hours a day. And prosciutto does not exist, though there is lardon from the pigs and good French sausage. But, with my mother's help, I am going to try. I will FaceTime her and try to sift flour as she talks me through it.

Many years ago, and I am not even sure when or why, I wrote these words in an essay: "Easter is meant to be a symbol of hope, renewal, and new life." It is the only time in my career that something I wrote went insanely viral. It now appears on greeting cards, posters of baby chicks, and photographs of white lilies and pastel sunsets. Yes, many people have expressed similar sentiments over the centuries. But for some reason, this one fragment from an essay caught on. Childhood friends wrote that their families had seen it, with my byline, in their church bulletins in South Carolina, in Georgia, in the United Kingdom, in the Philippines.

This year, I yearn for symbols of hope. Here in Grisail, our tiny village at the base of Le Mont Aiguille (where, legend has it, mountaineering was born in 1492), we are trying to be hopeful. My son's second godmother, who is Jewish—her father is a Holocaust survivor and her mother grew up in an Orthodox family in Brooklyn—told me that what strikes her so profoundly during this week of Passover is that the most religious people feel God will protect them. The ultra-Orthodox in Jerusalem refuse to comply with government restrictions because they say God is on their side. I've read the same testimony from pious Iranians and from evangelicals, some of whom are still flocking to church in the midst of a pandemic.

Why, I wonder, are members of these disparate belief systems drawn to such prayer rituals when the act of congregating in public is a risk to their very being? They go, in my view, because they believe their God will save them—when, in reality, their true protectors are God, sound medicine, and the wisdom of social distancing, all working hand in hand. They also go because whether one is religious or not, in the time of plague or fearsome torment, hope is all we have.

THE VANISHED

Christian communities in countries beyond the subject of this book continue to suffer from persecution and attacks, from the more than three hundred Sri Lankan churchgoers who were killed in bombings on Easter in 2019 to the tens of thousands of Christians estimated to be languishing in North Korean concentration camps on account of their faith (most of whom will die there). Turkey's president recently announced that Hagia Sophia, the largest cathedral in the world and the center of Eastern Orthodox Christianity for nearly one thousand years, would again be converted into a mosque, another blow for that country's ancient but disappearing Christian community.

What fascinated me as I researched and wrote this book, and continues to fascinate me now, is how believers manage to hold onto their faith. "Faith has to do with things that are not seen and hope with things that are not at hand," wrote St. Thomas

Aquinas, the Italian theologian and philosopher, in the thirteenth century.

There is always something that emerges from dark times: a belief, a prayer, a shift in society, a change, a hope that life will get better. Omar, the young Gazan whose story I told in this book, wrote to tell me his mother had died during the lockdown and he was unable to travel back to Gaza to fulfill her final, dying wish to see her son. I wrote to him with the only consolation I know for those who suffer profound loss. It was a quote from Thornton Wilder's great book on faith, *The Bridge of San Luis Rey*, that has sustained me through the death of many of those I've loved, including my two brothers: "There is a land of the living and a land of the dead and the bridge is love, the only survival, the only meaning."[1]

The dead, and especially those we love who pass, are never far from us; this I have always believed. Life in wartime taught me that. But what I was really thinking as I wrote, trying to comfort a grieving young man who had already suffered so much in his life—four wars, his beloved brother being killed—was that there is something that will sustain us, and that is faith. The moving visit of Pope Francis to Iraq in the midst of COVID in 2021 was a testament to it.

Nearly every Christian I interviewed for this book used the same word over and over, in different languages, to express why they continued to believe, despite, despite, despite: it is, they said, because of love.

As for the Christian communities in this book that faced such strife, from the Copts and their burnt churches in Egypt to the besieged nuns of Maaloula to Iraq's beleaguered congregations, did their faith somehow cancel out the evil that had been done to them?

Hope is what has sustained the Christian communities for many years, even as they have been inundated by invaders, disease, poverty, and the waves of emigration that have left their neighborhoods empty and devoid of their rich, centuries-old cultural and spiritual life. Churches were razed to the ground near Mosul, but I saw people attending them anyway, squatting on broken pews in half-built structures, still whispering prayers that they truly believed would elevate them to something higher than their immediate desperate circumstances. Christians believe, as they are taught in the gospels, that there is a life beyond, one that is without pain, without longing, without sorrow. I do not follow the gospels as closely as I should, nor would I call myself devout, but I do think of myself as a believer.

And I know when I think of others whom I have lost—my brothers, my friends who died in wartime—we will meet in a place where there is no more pain. Perhaps I am naive, but that is what I have taken from my many years working on this book and all that I gathered in the decades leading up to it. I learned something profound from all of the people I encountered in Syria, Iraq, Gaza, or Egypt who prayed quietly and without any kind of assurance that they would be delivered or redeemed. Still, they continued to pray.

So in many ways, this is a book about dying communities, but it is also about faith. I wrote it so that the people I documented would never disappear. They are here on these pages, and therefore they live forever. But I also wrote it as a way of acknowledging that their faith, in many ways, is more powerful than any of the armies I have seen trying to destroy them.

ACKNOWLEDGMENTS

PARIS, JULY 2020

I'VE BEEN A FREELANCE WAR REPORTER AND HUMAN RIGHTS INVESTIGATOR FOR most of my thirty-five-year career: often a lonely road, certainly riddled with economic and spiritual uncertainty. I am indebted to the organizations that made it possible for someone such as myself to do the kind of fieldwork needed to write about the worlds and communities of people who might, in one hundred years' time, no longer be on this earth.

The Council on Foreign Relations gave me their Edward R. Murrow Fellowship in 2017, which enabled me to have an office overlooking Park Avenue to write and the time to return to the Middle East to fill in the gaps of my fieldwork. The John Simon Guggenheim Foundation was beyond generous with its help, awarding me a fellowship in 2019 that allowed me to return to the region and finish the final draft, and also with their kind words about my project. The American Academy of Arts and Letters unexpectedly gave me its Blake-Dodd Prize for my lifetime body of work, somehow making me feel that all these years of trudging through war zones with a notebook have not been in vain. Type Investigations, formerly The Investigation Fund at The Nation Institute, then run by Esther Kaplan, gave me three separate grants to travel to the region and investigate why Christians were disappearing. I am forever grateful to organizations such as these that allow academics and journalists to keep going. A special thank you to IWMF (International Women's Media Foundation) and Elisa Lees Muñoz for their remarkable work and help throughout my career.

Thank you to Nicole Tung, a wonderful, gifted photojournalist and producer, who accompanied me on many of the journeys described in this book. I first met her when she was a newly graduated New York University journalism major in Libya, wandering along with just a camera and great courage.

Nicole, who is originally from Hong Kong, is warm company, but she also possesses sharp wisdom. Her sense of justice and compassion, her eye for stories, and her huge talent make her an ideal teammate in the field. She also always packs an enormous medical kit and knows how to do most emergency first aid, as well as how to spot a land mine or identify which weapons a checkpoint soldier is carrying. She rarely complains of cold, hunger, or sitting in the back seat during long and bumpy car rides in conflict zones. Her sense of fairness to her colleagues is renowned. She is a star in every way.

Harper's Magazine under John R. MacArthur, Ellen Rosenbush, and editor James Marcus published my first report on Christians in the Middle East, called "The Vanishing," which became the seed for this book. It was James who first gave me the idea to return to Iraq and record these ancient people. Chris Beha, now editor at *Harper's*, commissioned me to go to Egypt and record the Copts and their struggle and published later pieces. *Air Mail*, *Vanity Fair*, *Granta*, *The Critic*, and the *New York Review of Books* also published portions of this book in earlier drafts; thank you to David Friend, Sigrid Rausing,

Michael Mosbacher, Matt Seaton, Graydon Carter, and Alessandra Stanley.

I am very grateful to my talented and sensitive editors Alexandra Pringle and Clive Priddle, Michelle Welsh-Horst and Katherine Streckfus, Allegra LeFanu in London, and my agents Kim Witherspoon and David Forer. Thank you to Jocelynn Pedro, Jaime Leifer, Miguel Cervantes, and Anu Roy-Chaudhury at PublicAffairs.

Misia Lerska, a thoughtful young student at Wellesley University, who is both Polish and French, had long conversations with me about the book early on and helped research French and other material. Other hardworking interns were Lara Adoumie, a Syrian-American now at University of California, Los Angeles, School of Law, and Alex Toutounj, a Georgetown grad of Lebanese/Syrian Christian descent whose grandparents were raised in Egypt. Sophie Huttner and Nathalie Bussemaker from Yale College and Dorothy Scarborough from Amherst College were all skilled readers and researchers. Dorothy had a charming penchant for rooting out the most obscure and fascinating trivia—such as comparing the car I drove in Iraq to the same model Hillary Clinton took to meet Bill in Washington in 1987.

I am deeply indebted to Professor James Levinsohn, the visionary and talented founding director of the Jackson Institute for Global Affairs at Yale University. When Jim recruited me from the Council on Foreign Relations to be a Senior Fellow back in 2017, I had no idea how Jackson would change my life. The intellectual rigor and curiosity, the brain power and camaraderie of the other Fellows, and the constant flow of information of the community were vital for a writer who had spent a lifetime working alone in the field.

But this book could not have been completed without the help of two extremely gifted Jackson graduate students, Zachary White and Robin Schmid. Robin explores gender issues in public policy; Zach is focused on Turkey and the Caucasus. They both fearlessly jumped into a book about Christians in the Middle East with the enthusiasm and devotion of the most courageous Sherpas leading a hapless and tired climber up Mount Everest.

When my son, Luca, was born in 2004, after I'd spent so many years roaming the world's darkest places, as part of that rare and strange breed known as "career war reporters," one of the letters of congratulations I received came from the great war photojournalist Jim Natchwey.

"You've done your bit," he said. "Now pass the baton."

Even with a newborn baby, I wasn't quite ready to pass the baton—I went back to war-torn Iraq when my son was only six months old—nor am I now, sixteen years later. But teaching at Yale has taught me that we are training a whole new generation of youth who will go out and make the world a better place as human rights officers, journalists, humanitarian doctors, and lawyers. I have utter confidence they will do the greatest things with their lives, and I am beyond proud of their contributions.

Which brings me to other people whose names should be on the cover: the hundreds of people in Egypt, Syria, Iraq, and Palestine who helped me by telling me their stories. The late Karen Blixen (Isak Dinesen) once wrote, "All sorrows can be borne if you put them into a story or tell a story about them."

My life's work has been to tell stories for those who did not have the ability to tell them themselves for fear of persecution, subjugation, and sometimes even death. Most of them cannot be listed here due to that fear, but here are some who can:

GAZA

Father Mario da Silva

Matthias Schmale, Director of UNRWA Operations in Gaza

Gaza Sky Geeks and #wearenotnumbers
Raffaella Iodice
Dr. Caitlin Procter
Chris Gunness
Omar Al Khatib
Ahmad al-Naouq
B'Tselem
Hagai el-Ad
Bel Mooney
Omar Shakir
Human Rights Watch
Amnesty International
Médecins Sans Frontières (Jacob Burns)
Amjad Tandesh
Dr. Jihad El-Hissi
Grisha Yakubovich
Pilar Crespi
Stephen Robert
Dr. Mahmoud Sabra
Dr. Yasser Abu-Jamei
Dr. Ahmed Yousef

EGYPT
Mary Rogers
Mariann Wenckheim
Mirit Mikhail
Cecilia Udden
Father Exodoums
Ambassador Jonathan R. Cohen
Sally Touma
Youssef Sidhom
"Big Pharaoh"
Aly el Tayeb

Omar Monies
Hamada el Rasam
Michael Wahid Hanna
Dr. H. A. Hellyer
Dr. Rasha Abdulla
Zaki Abdullah
Kamel Zakher
Monique el-Fazy
Adham al-Sharkawy
Sona Tatoyan
Thomas Bedrossian
Khalil Jouayed
Sara Hamdy

SYRIA
Jenifer Fenton
Idrees Ahmad
Sarah Leah Whitson
Sarkis Balkhian
Dr. Radwan Ziadeh
Nadim Shehadi
Kenan Rahmani
Dr. Riad Adoumie
Lara Adoumie
Ambassador Robert Ford
Liz Sly
Ludovic Hood
Bishop Antoine Chbeir
Dr. Omar Muhammed

IRAQ
Mona Mahmoud
William Warda

Ambassador Fareed Yassin

Alice Walpole

Joseph Pennington

Peter Galbraith

Tamara Chalabi

Sam Chalabi

Zaab Sethna

Tim Spicer

Ammar Dawood

Hanaa Edwar

Ali al-Saffar

Louay al-Khattib

Haris Zafar

Sajed Jiyad

Ali al-Malawi

Erin Evers

Nathan Sobey

Duncan Spinner

Dr. Mowaffak al-Rubaie

Mustafa Salim

Catherine Philp

Sam Morris

Mathew Van Dyke

Sara Hamdy

Thanks also to the songwriter Eric Bazalian, who was kind enough to allow me to use the lyrics of his beautiful song "One of Us" in Chapter 3.

Finally, a special thanks to my only child, Luca Girodon, who grew up with a wandering mother who packed him in a basket and often took him along for the ride, whether he liked it or not. He had an unconventional but always loving childhood. As a baby, he slept in drawers; he slept on blankets on the floor; he slept in an empty suitcase; he slept under my desk; he learned how to be patient in airports and how to get through checkpoints and eat food from all over the world.

He had to share his mother's attention not only with her books and assignments but also with dissidents, activists, and human rights defenders, who often joined us at our dinner table from Syria, from Iraq, from Afghanistan, the Balkans, and Africa. When Luca was old enough, I sometimes hired him to be my "notetaker" on research trips to Palestine and elsewhere, thinking it was a way of keeping him entertained while providing him an education about the world that one doesn't learn in school. I read once that Margaret Mead had done that with her daughter, Mary Catherine Bateson, and I reckoned it must be a great mothering technique.

Notetaking or not, Luca grew up to be a remarkable young man, my heart's joy. But he's also been my balance, my north star, and the clear strong light that always draws me home from wherever it is I am wandering.

NOTES

INTRODUCTION

1. Derek Thompson, "Elite Failure Has Brought Americans to the Edge of an Existential Crisis," *The Atlantic*, September 5, 2019, www.theatlantic.com/ideas /archive/2019/09/america-without-family-god-or-patriotism/597382; "Religious Landscape Study," Pew Research Center, Religion and Public Life, n.d., www .pewforum.org/religious-landscape-study/age-distribution.

2. Sarah Pulliam Bailey, "More Than Half of Americans Have Prayed for the End of Coronavirus, Poll Finds," *Washington Post*, March 30, 2020, www .washingtonpost.com/religion/2020/03/30/prayer-coronavirus-church-faith -americans; "Most Americans Say Coronavirus Outbreak Has Impacted Their Lives," Pew Research Center, Social and Demographic Trends, March 30, 2020, www.pewresearch.org/social-trends/2020/03/30/most-americans-say-coronavirus -outbreak-has-impacted-their-lives.

3. "Middle East–North Africa," Pew-Templeton Global Religious Futures Project, n.d. www.globalreligiousfutures.org/regions/middle-east-north-africa.

CHAPTER 1: IRAQ

1. Reem's name has been changed to protect her identity, as has Munzer's.

2. Genesis 2:10–14 (ESV). See also Andrea Wulf, "Paradise Lust," *New York Times*, August 5, 2011, www.nytimes.com/2011/08/07/books/review/paradise-lust -by-brook-wilensky-lanford-book-review.html.

3. Ezekiel 39:27 (ESV).

4. Emma Green, "The Impossible Future of Christians in the Middle East," *The Atlantic*, May 23, 2019, www.theatlantic.com/international/archive/2019/05 /iraqi-christians-nineveh-plain/589819.

5. Anthony Shadid, "Church Attack Seen as Strike at Iraq's Core," *New York Times*, November 1, 2010, www.nytimes.com/2010/11/02/world/middleeast /02iraq.html.

6. Tim Judah, "Passover in Baghdad," *Granta*, July 2003, https://granta.com /passover-in-baghdad.

7. P. J. Tobia, "Why Did Assad, Saddam and Mubarak Protect Christians?," *PBS NewsHour*, October 14, 2011, www.pbs.org/newshour/world/mid-easts-christians -intro.

8. Ibid.

9. According to the BBC,

> The term "jihadist" has been used by Western academics since the 1990s, and more widely since the 11 September 2001 attacks, as a way to distinguish between violent and nonviolent Sunni Islamists.

> Islamists aim to reorder government and society in accordance with Islamic law, or Sharia.

> Jihadists see violent struggle as necessary to eradicate obstacles to restoring God's rule on Earth and defending the Muslim community, or umma, against infidels and apostates. If the umma is threatened by an aggressor, they hold that jihad is not just a collective obligation (fard kifaya), but an individual duty (fard ayn) that must be fulfilled by every able Muslim, just like ritual prayer and fasting during Ramadan.

> The term "jihadist" is not used by many Muslims because they see it as wrongly associating a noble religious concept with illegitimate violence. Instead, they use delegitimizing terms like "deviants."

"What Is Jihadism?," BBC, December 11, 2014, www.bbc.com/news/world -middle-east-30411519.

10. "Iraqi Christians Report a Decade of Blood," *San Diego Union-Tribune*, August 30, 2014, www.sandiegouniontribune.com/sdut-iraq-ISIS-christian -chaldeans-genocide-2014aug30-htmlstory.html.

11. Daniel Williams, *Forsaken: The Persecution of Christians in Today's Middle East* (New York: OR Books, 2016), 80.

12. "Remarks by the Vice President at the 'In Defense of Christians' Solidarity Dinner," American Presidency Project, October 25, 2017, www.presidency .ucsb.edu/documents/remarks-the-vice-president-the-defense-christians-solidarity -dinner.

13. "Remarks by Vice President Pence to Advance Religious Freedom," White House, Office of the Vice President, July 26, 2018, www.whitehouse.gov/briefings -statements/remarks-vice-president-pence-ministerial-advance-religious -freedom.

14. Green, "Impossible Future."

15. An independence referendum for the Kurdistan Region of Iraq was held on September 24, 2017, with preliminary results showing approximately 93.25 percent of the votes cast in favor of independence.

CHAPTER 2: GAZA

1. Palestinian Central Bureau of Statistics (PCBS), "Preliminary Results of the Population, Housing and Establishments Census, 2017," State of Palestine, February 2018, www.pcbs.gov.ps/portals/_pcbs/PressRelease/Press_En_Preliminary _Results_Report-en-with-tables.pdf.

2. Muhammed Al-Jamal, "Christians in Gaza: History and Struggle," Holy Land Christian Ecumenical Foundation, August 21, 2013, https://hcef .org/790793540-christians-in-gaza-history-and-struggle.

3. Zena Tahhan, "Hamas and Fatah: How Are the Two Groups Different?," *Al Jazeera*, October 12, 2017, www.aljazeera.com/indepth/features/2017/10/hamas -fatah-goal-approaches-171012064342008.html.

4. "Gaza: Journalist Facing Prison for Exposing Corruption," Amnesty International, February 25, 2019, www.amnesty.org/en/latest/news/2019/02/gaza -journalist-facing-prison-term-for-exposing-corruption-in-hamas-controlled -ministry.

5. J. P. Kirsch, "St. Philip the Apostle," *The Catholic Encyclopedia*, vol. 11 (New York: Robert Appleton Company, 1911), www.newadvent.org/cathen/11799a.htm, quoting John 6:5 (KJV).

6. "Palestinian Christians in the Holy Land," Institute for Middle East Understanding (IMEU), December 17, 2012, https://imeu.org/article/palestinian -christians-in-the-holy-land. But IMEU adds, "According to Israeli government figures, as of 2009 there were about 154,000 Christian citizens of Israel, or about 2.1% of the population. Of those, approximately 80% are Palestinian Arabs, including 44,000 Roman Catholics, while the rest are non-Arab immigrants, mostly spouses of Jews who came from the Soviet Union in the early 1990s."

7. *Report by His Majesty's Government in the United Kingdom of Great Britain and Northern Ireland to the Council of the League of Nations on the Administration of Palestine and Trans-Jordan for the Year 1937*, December 31, 1937, archived at United Nations Information System on the Question of Palestine (UNISPAL), https://unispal .un.org/UNISPAL.NSF/0/7BDD2C11C15B54C2052565D10057251E.

8. Paul Halsall, "Huneberc of Heidenheim: The Hodoeporican of St. Willibald, 8th Century," Fordham University, October 1, 2000, https://sourcebooks.fordham .edu/basis/willibald.asp.

9. "Gaza Crisis: Toll of Operations in Gaza," BBC, September 1, 2014, www.bbc .com/news/world-middle-east-28439404.

10. "Two Years On: People Injured and Traumatized During the 'Great March of Return' Are Still Struggling," United Nations Information System on the Question of Palestine (UNISPAL), April 6, 2020, www.un.org/unispal/document /two-years-on-people-injured-and-traumatized-during-the-great-march-of-return -are-still-struggling.

11. Peter Beaumont and Oliver Holmes, "US Confirms End to Funding for UN Palestinian Refugees," *The Guardian*, August 31, 2018, www.theguardian .com/world/2018/aug/31/trump-to-cut-all-us-funding-for-uns-main-palestinian -refugee-programme.

12. "The 2014 Palestine Human Development Report: Development for Empowerment," United Nations Development Programme, April 2015, www.un.org /unispal/document/auto-insert-204688.

13. Oliver Holmes and Hazem Balousha, "Gaza's Generation Blockade: Young Lives in the 'World's Largest Prison,'" *The Guardian*, March 12, 2019, www.theguardian

.com/world/2019/mar/12/generation-blockade-gaza-young-palestinians-who
-cannot-leave.

14. "Gaza Strip Demographics Profile 2019," Index Mundi, December 7, 2019, www.indexmundi.com/gaza_strip/demographics_profile.html.

15. Omar's name has been changed to protect his identity.

16. "We Are Not Numbers," Facebook, "About" page, www.facebook.com/pg /WeAreNotNumbers/about/?ref=page_internal.

17. Abdel's name has been changed to protect his identity.

18. Omar Ashour, "Egypt's Notorious Police Brutality Record," *Al Jazeera*, March 28, 2016, www.aljazeera.com/indepth/opinion/2016/03/egypt-notorious -police-brutality-record-160322143521378.html.

19. Gaza Sky Geeks website, https://gazaskygeeks.com.

CHAPTER 3: SYRIA

1. Janine di Giovanni, "Why Assad and Russia Target the White Helmets," *New York Review of Books* (blog), October 16, 2018, www.nybooks.com/daily/2018/10/16 /why-assad-and-russia-target-the-white-helmets.

2. M. Zuhdi Jasser, "Sectarian Conflict in Syria," *PRISM* 4 (2014): 58–67.

3. Ibid.

4. Razek Siriani, "Syria," in *Christianity in North Africa and West Asia*, ed. Kenneth R. Ross, Mariz Tadros, and Todd M. Johnson, 102–113 (Edinburgh: Edinburgh University Press, 2018).

5. Ibid.

6. Ibid.

7. Janine di Giovanni, "Lebanon: About to Blow?" *New York Review of Books* (blog), February 8, 2018, www.nybooks.com/articles/2018/02/08 /lebanon-about-to-blow.

8. Acts 9:3–19 (NIV).

9. Siriani, "Syria."

10. An earlier version of this passage appeared in my article for the *New York Times*, "Mountaintop Town Is a Diverse Haven from Syria's Horrors," published November 21, 2012, and found at www.nytimes.com/2012/11/22/world/middleeast /maloula-is-a-diverse-haven-from-syrias-horrors.html.

11. Patrick J. McDonnell and Nabih Bulos, "Syria Fighting Leaves Maaloula, a Historic Christian Town, in Ruins," *Los Angeles Times*, April 16, 2014, www.latimes .com/world/middleeast/la-fg-syria-christian-town-20140416-story.html.

12. Sohaib Enjrainy, "Syrian Christian Village Besieged by Jihadists," *Al-Monitor*, September 5, 2013, www.al-monitor.com/pulse/security/2013/09/syria -christians-maaloula-jihadists-opposition-army.html.

13. McDonnell and Bulos, "Syria Fighting."

14. Siriani, "Syria."

15. Ibid.

16. Agha Ibrahim Akram, *The Sword of Allah: Khalid bin al-Waleed—His Life and Campaigns* (Oxford: Oxford University Press, 2004).

17. Siriani, "Syria."

18. Ibid.

19. Ibid.

20. Ibid.

21. Alexis Heraclides and Ada Dialla, "Intervention in Lebanon and Syria, 1860–61," in *Humanitarian Intervention in the Long Nineteenth Century: Setting the Precedent*, 134–147 (Manchester: Manchester University Press, 2015), https://doi .org/10.2307/j.ctt1mf71b8.12.

22. Ibid.

23. Ibid.

24. Kerim Yildiz, "Syrian History, 1918–2005," in *The Kurds in Syria: The Forgotten People*, 27–42 (Ann Arbor, MI: Pluto Press, 2005), https://doi.org/10.2307/j .ctt18fs50d.8.

25. Ibid.

26. Siriani, "Syria."

27. Ibid. ·

28. Ibid.

29. Thomas's name has been changed to protect his identity.

30. Otmar Oehring, "On the Current Situation of Christians in the Middle East," in *Contemporary Conflicts and Value-Driven Policy*, ed. Gerhard Wahlers (Berlin: Konrad Adenauer Stiftung, 2015), www.jstor.org/stable/resrep 09943.

31. Jasser, "Sectarian Conflict."

32. Yuras Karmanau, "Russia Plans to Invest $500 Million in Its Only Navy Base Outside the Former Soviet Union—Here's What It's Like There," Associated Press, in *Business Insider*, December 18, 2019, www.businessinsider.com /base-in-syria-helps-russia-expand-presence-in-mediterranean-2019-9.

33. Siriani, "Syria."

34. Ibid.

35. Janine di Giovanni, "How Yazidi Women Are Fighting Back Against ISIS," *Vogue*, October 26, 2016, www.vogue.com/article/sun-ladies-yazidi-women -isis-genocide-sexual-enslavement.

36. Siriani, "Syria."

37. Oehring, "On the Current Situation."

38. Jasser, "Sectarian Conflict."

39. Caesar Syria Civilian Protection Act of 2019, H.R. 31, 116th Cong., 1st sess., www.congress.gov/bill/116th-congress/house-bill/31/text.

40. "Syria: Stories Behind Photos of Killed Detainees," Human Rights Watch, December 16, 2015, www.hrw.org/news/2015/12/16/syria-stories-behind-photos -killed-detainees.

41. For more on the Syrian economy in the summer of 2020, see this excellent report from the Center for Global Policy: Elizabeth Tsurkov, "Syria's Economic Meltdown," Newslines Institute for Strategy and Policy, June 15, 2020, https:// cgpolicy.org/briefs/syrias-economic-meltdown.

42. Annie Sparrow, "How UN Humanitarian Aid Has Propped Up As-sad," *Foreign Affairs*, September 20, 2018, www.foreignaffairs.com/articles /syria/2018-09-20/how-un-humanitarian-aid-has-propped-assad.

CHAPTER 4: EGYPT

1. "Egypt: New Church Law Discriminates Against Christians," Human Rights Watch, press release, September 15, 2016, www.hrw.org/news/2016/09/15 /egypt-new-church-law-discriminates-against-christians.

2. "Egypt: Horrific Palm Sunday Bombings," Human Rights Watch, press release, April 12, 2017, www.hrw.org/news/2017/04/12/egypt-horrific -palm-sunday-bombings.

3. "Egypt Security Forces Kill 19 Suspects Linked to Coptic Attack," *Al Ja-zeera*, November 4, 2018, www.aljazeera.com/news/2018/11/04/egypt-security -forces-kill-19-suspects-linked-to-coptic-attack.

4. Harriet Sherwood, "Christians in Egypt," *The Guardian*, Janu-ary 10, 2018, www.theguardian.com/world/2018/jan/10/christians-egypt -unprecedented-persecution-report.

5. "'How Long Are We Going to Live in This Injustice?' Egypt's Christians Caught Between Sectarian Attacks and State Inaction," Amnesty International, June 24, 2014, www.amnestyusa.org/reports/how-long-are-we-going-to-live -in-this-injustice-egypts-christians-caught-between-sectarian-attacks-and-state -inaction.

6. Tarek Osman, "Egyptian Christians," in *Egypt on the Brink: From Nasser to the Muslim Brotherhood*, rev. ed., 158–178 (New Haven, CT: Yale University Press, 2013).

7. Samuel Tadros, "Egypt," in *Christianity in North Africa and West Asia*, ed. Ken-neth R. Ross, Mariz Tadros, and Todd M. Johnson, 68–79 (Edinburgh: Edinburgh University Press, 2018).

8. Robert L. Tignor, "Christian Egypt," in *Egypt: A Short History*, 105–121 (Princeton, NJ: Princeton University Press, 2010).

9. Osman, "Egyptian Christians," 158–178.

10. Tadros, "Egypt."

11. Ibid.

12. Osman, "Egyptian Christians."

13. Tadros, "Egypt."

14. Osman, "Egyptian Christians."

15. Tadros, "Egypt."

16. Osman, "Egyptian Christians."

17. Tadros, "Egypt."

18. Ibid.

19. Osman, "Egyptian Christians."

20. Ibid.

21. Ibid.

22. Tadros, "Egypt."

23. Ibid.

24. Ibid.

25. Osman, "Egyptian Christians."

26. Tadros, "Egypt."

27. Osman, "Egyptian Christians."

28. Ibid.

29. "Delays in Criminal Case of Christian Woman Beaten and Stripped by Mob," Christian Solidarity Worldwide (CSW), August 27, 2020, www.csw.org .uk/2020/08/27/press/4778/article.htm; Jane Arraf, "After 2016 Assault, A Coptic Christian Grandmother in Egypt Fights for Justice," National Public Radio, May 26, 2017, www.npr.org/sections/parallels/2017/05/26/529508192/after-2016 -assault-a-coptic-christian-grandmother-in-egypt-fights-for-justice. See also Hamza Hendawi, "Muslim Mob Attacked Christian Homes in Egyptian Province," Associated Press, in *Chicago Daily Herald*, May 26, 2016, www.dailyherald.com /article/20160526/news/305269984.

30. "Criminal Court Acquits Three Men Accused of Assaulting a Christian Woman," Christian Solidarity Worldwide (CSW), December 18, 2020, www.csw .org.uk/2020/12/18/press/4930/article.htm.

31. Olfat M. El Tohamy, "Why Sadat Cracked Down on Copts," *Christian Science Monitor*, September 22, 1981, www.csmonitor.com/1981/0922/092234.html.

32. David B. Ottaway, "Egyptian Copts Support Ousted Patriarch," *Washington Post*, September 7, 1981, www.washingtonpost.com/archive/politics/1981/09/07 /egyptian-copts-support-ousted-patriarch/f8f951b7-bd0e-4ea0-a874-6e16a39 abf16.

33. S. Mikhail, "Pope Shenouda III and the Coptic Church," *Index on Censorship* 12, no. 5 (October 1983): 50–50, https://doi.org/10.1080/03064228308533618.

34. Sara C. Medina, "Religion: Egypt's Copts in Crisis," *Time*, September 28, 1981, http://content.time.com/time/magazine/article/0,9171,953135,00.html.

35. Mina's name has been changed to protect her identity.

36. "World's Most Powerful Arabs 2019: Ahmed Abou Hashima," *Arabian Business*, 2019, www.arabianbusiness.com/423073-worlds-most-powerful -arabs-2019-2nd-abou-hashima.

37. Omar's name has been changed to protect his identity.

38. Florence Dixon, "'Sisi Shows No Mercy': Nine Years On, Egypt Awaits the Rest of Its Revolution," *The New Arab*, January 24, 2020, https:// english.alaraby.co.uk/english/indepth/2020/1/25/nine-years-on-egypt-awaits -conclusion-of-its-revolution.

39. Amy Hawthorne and Andrew Miller, eds., "Why Did Egyptian Democratization Fail?," Project on Middle East Democracy, January 2020, 3–4, https:// pomed.org/wp-content/uploads/2020/01/200128b_EgyptDemocracy.pdf.

40. Martin Chulov, "'The Release of Six Decades of Fear': Egypt's Lost Revolution," *The Guardian*, January 24, 2021, www.theguardian.com/world/2021/jan/24 /egypt-lost-revolution-hosni-mubarak-military-takeover.

41. Alan Cowell, "Nawal el Saadawi, Advocate for Women in the Arab World, Dies at 89," *New York Times*, March 21, 2021, www.nytimes.com/2021/03/21 /obituaries/nawal-el-saadawi-dead.html.

42. Zeinab Badawi, interview with Nawal el Saadawi on HARDtalk, BBC Sounds, May 23, 2018, www.bbc.co.uk/sounds/play/w3cswjdy.

EPILOGUE

1. The full quotation is, "We ourselves shall be loved for a while and forgotten. But the love will have been enough; all those impulses of love return to the love that made them. Even memory is not necessary for love. There is a land of the living and a land of the dead and the bridge is love, the only survival, the only meaning." Thornton Wilder, *The Bridge of San Luis Rey* (New York: HarperCollins, 1998 [1927]), 107.

SUGGESTED READINGS

BOOKS

Ahmad, Aeham. *The Pianist of Yarmouk*. Penguin, 2019.

Anderson, Jon Lee. *The Fall of Baghdad*. Penguin, 2005.

Armstrong, Karen. *The Bible: The Biography*. Atlantic Books, 2015.

———. *A History of God: The 4,000-Year Quest of Judaism, Christianity and Islam*. Ballantine Books, 1994.

Bailey, Kenneth. *Jesus Through Middle Eastern Eyes: Cultural Studies in the Gospels*. SPCK, 2008.

Barghouti, Mourid. *I Saw Ramallah*. Knopf Doubleday, 2008.

Chomsky, Noam, and Ilan Pappé. *Gaza in Crisis: Reflections on Israel's War Against the Palestinians*. Haymarket Books, 2010.

Cragg, Kenneth. *The Arab Christian: A History in the Middle East*. Mowbray, 1992.

Dagher, Sam. *Assad or We Burn the Country: How One Family's Lust for Power Destroyed Syria*. Little, Brown, 2019.

Dalrymple, William. *From the Holy Mountain: A Journey Among the Christians of the Middle East*. Henry Holt, 1997.

Eid, Kassem. *My Country: A Syrian Memoir*. Bloomsbury, 2018.

Emerson, Gloria. *Gaza: Year in the Intifada: A Personal Account*. Grove/Atlantic, 2000.

Filiu, Jean-Pierre. *Gaza: A History*. Oxford University Press, 2014.

Filkins, Dexter. *The Forever War*. Knopf Doubleday, 2008.

Giovanni, Janine di. *Against the Stranger: Lives in Occupied Territory*. Penguin, 1994.

———. *The Morning They Came for Us: Dispatches from Syria*. Bloomsbury, 2016.

Griswold, Eliza. *The Tenth Parallel: Dispatches from the Faultline Between Christianity and Islam*. Penguin, 2012.

Hevelone-Harper, Jennifer L. *Disciples of the Desert: Monks, Laity, and Spiritual Authority in Sixth-Century Gaza*. Johns Hopkins University Press, 2014.

Jenkins, John Philip. *The Lost History of Christianity: The Thousand-Year Golden Age of the Church in the Middle East, Africa, and Asia—and How It Died*. Harper Collins, 2009.

Khalifa, Khaled. *In Praise of Hatred*. Macmillan, 2014.

Lawrence, Thomas Edward. *Seven Pillars of Wisdom*. Wordsworth Editions, 1997.

Löwy, Gideon, and Gideon Levy. *The Punishment of Gaza*. Verso, 2010.

Maḥfūẓ, Najīb. *Palace Walk*. Anchor Books, 2011.

Osman, Tarek. *Egypt on the Brink: From Nasser to Mubarak*. Yale University Press, 2011.

Pappe, Ilan. *The Ethnic Cleansing of Palestine*. Simon and Schuster, 2007.

Pearlman, Wendy. *We Crossed a Bridge and It Trembled: Voices from Syria*. Harper-Collins, 2017.

Rasche, Stephen M. *The Disappearing People: The Tragic Fate of Christians in the Middle East*. Bombardier Books, 2020.

Rassam, Suha. *Christianity in Iraq: Its Origins and Development to the Present Day*. Gracewing, 2005.

Rowe, Paul S., John H. A. Dyck, and Jens Zimmermann. *Christians and the Middle East Conflict*. Routledge, 2014.

Russell, Gerard. *Heirs to Forgotten Kingdoms: Journeys into the Disappearing Religions of the Middle East*. Basic Books, 2014.

Sacco, Joe. *Footnotes in Gaza: A Graphic Novel*. Macmillan, 2009.

Said, Edward W. *The Question of Palestine*. Routledge and Kegan Paul, 1980.

Said, Edward W., and Christopher Hitchens. *Blaming the Victims: Spurious Scholarship and the Palestinian Question*. Verso, 2001.

Saleh, Yassin al-Haj. *Impossible Revolution*. Haymarket Books, 2017.

Shehadeh, Raja. *Palestinian Walks: Notes on a Vanishing Landscape*. Profile, 2007.

Warrick, Joby. *Red Line: The Unraveling of Syria and America's Race to Destroy the Most Dangerous Arsenal in the World*. Knopf Doubleday, 2021.

Wivel, Klaus. *The Last Supper: The Plight of Christians in Arab Lands*. New Vessel Press, 2016.

Yazbek, Samar. *The Crossing: My Journey to the Shattered Heart of Syria*. Rider Books, 2015.

———. *A Woman in the Crossfire: Diaries of the Syrian Revolution*. Haus Publishing, 2012.

ARTICLES AND REPORTS

Brownlee, Jason. *Violence Against Copts in Egypt*. Carnegie Endowment for International Peace, 2013, https://carnegieendowment.org/files/violence_against_copts3.pdf.

Byman, Daniel L. "Why Be a Pawn to a State? Proxy Wars from a Proxy's Perspective." *Brookings*, May 22, 2018, www.brookings.edu/blog/order-from-chaos/2018/05/22/why-be-a-pawn-to-a-state-proxy-wars-from-a-proxys-perspective.

———. "Why Engage in Proxy War? A State's Perspective." *Brookings*, May 21, 2018, www.brookings.edu/blog/order-from-chaos/2018/05/21/why-engage-in-proxy-war-a-states-perspective.

Cohen, Edy. "The Persecution of Christians in the Palestinian Authority." Begin-Sadat Center for Strategic Studies, May 27, 2019, https://besacenter.org/perspectives-papers/persecution-christians-palestinian-authority.

Eid, Kassem. "Opinion: I Survived a Sarin Gas Attack." *New York Times*, April 7, 2017, www.nytimes.com/2017/04/07/opinion/what-its-like-to-survive-a-sarin-gas-attack.html.

Fahmi, Georges. *The Future of Syrian Christians After the Arab Spring.* European University Institute, Robert Schuman Centre for Advanced Studies, June 2018, https://cadmus.eui.eu/bitstream/handle/1814/55924/RSCAS_2018_04.pdf.

Giovanni, Janine di. "From Sarajevo to Aleppo: Lessons on Surviving a Siege." *The Atlantic*, October 12, 2016, www.theatlantic.com/international/archive/2016/10/sarajevo-aleppo-daraya-syria/503843.

———. "The Vanishing." *Harper's Magazine*, December 1, 2018, https://harpers.org/archive/2018/12/the-vanishing-christians-in-iraq-syria-egypt.

Gopal, Anand. "Syria's Last Bastion of Freedom." *The New Yorker*, December 3, 2018, www.newyorker.com/magazine/2018/12/10/syrias-last-bastion-of-freedom.

Green, Emma. "The Impossible Future of Christians in the Middle East." *The Atlantic*, May 23, 2019, www.theatlantic.com/international/archive/2019/05/iraqi-christians-nineveh-plain/589819.

Haider, Huma. *The Persecution of Christians in the Middle East.* Institute of Development Studies, February 16, 2017, https://assets.publishing.service.gov.uk/media/59786a0040f0b65dcb00000a/042-Persecution-of-Christians-in-the-Middle-East.pdf.

Hanna, Michael Wahid. "Explaining Absence." Century Foundation, March 21, 2017, https://tcf.org/content/report/explaining-absence.

le Caisne, Garance. "'They Were Torturing to Kill': Inside Syria's Death Machine." *The Guardian*, October 1, 2015, www.theguardian.com/world/2015/oct/01/they-were-torturing-to-kill-inside-syrias-death-machine-caesar.

Masi, Alessandria. "How Amnesty Uncovered 'a Universe of Degradation' at Saydnaya Prison." *New Humanitarian*, February 17, 2017, https://deeply.thenewhumanitarian.org/syria/articles/2017/02/17/how-amnesty-uncovered-a-universe-of-degradation-at-saydnaya-prison.

Monier, Elizabeth. "Christians and Other Religious Minorities in the Middle East." *Century Foundation*, April 18, 2019, https://tcf.org/content/report/christians-religious-minorities-middle-east-questions-elizabeth-monier.

———. "Middle Eastern Minorities in Global Media and the Politics of National Belonging." *Arab Media and Society*, American University in Cairo, November 2017, https://doi.org/10.17863/CAM.14315.

Rondeaux, Candace, and David Sterman. "Twenty-First Century Proxy Warfare." *New America*, November 9, 2018, http://newamerica.org/international-security/reports/twenty-first-century-proxy-warfare.

Shea, Nina. "Do Copts Have a Future in Egypt?" *Foreign Affairs*, August 2019, www.foreignaffairs.com/articles/egypt/2017-06-20/do-copts-have-future-egypt.

"Syria: Attacks on Religious Sites Raise Tensions." Human Rights Watch, January 23, 2013, www.hrw.org/news/2013/01/23/syria-attacks-religious-sites-raise-tensions.

Ufheil-Somers, Amanda. "Iraqi Christians: A Primer." Middle East Research and Information Project, June 2, 2013, https://merip.org/2013/06/iraqi-christians-a-primer.

US Department of State, Office of International Religious Freedom. *2019 Report on International Religious Freedom: Israel—West Bank and Gaza*, 2019, www.state.gov/reports/2019-report-on-international-religious-freedom/israel/west-bank-and-gaza/.

———. *2019 Report on International Religious Freedom: Syria*, 2019, www.state.gov/wp-content/uploads/2020/05/SYRIA-2019-INTERNATIONAL-RELIGIOUS-FREEDOM-REPORT.pdf.

Weitz, Lev. "Religious Minorities in the Modern Middle East." Foreign Policy Research Institute, November 20, 2015, www.fpri.org/article/2015/11/religious-minorities-in-the-modern-middle-east.

Wood, Graeme. "The American Climbing the Ranks of ISIS." *The Atlantic*, January 2017, www.theatlantic.com/magazine/archive/2017/03/the-american-leader-in-the-islamic-state/510872.

———. "What ISIS Really Wants." *The Atlantic*, April 2015, www.theatlantic.com/magazine/archive/2015/03/what-isis-really-wants/384980.

INDEX

Ghosts by Daylight
A Memoir of War and Love

'Brave, heroically and elegantly told, and brutally honest'
Fatima Bhutto

Janine and Bruno first fell in love as young reporters in the besieged city of
Sarajevo. Years later – after endless phone calls, much of what the French call
malentendu, secret trysts in foreign cities, numerous break-ups, three miscarriages,
countless stories of rebel armies and a dozen wars that had passed between them –
they arrive in Paris one rainy January to begin a new life together.

The remnants of their separate lives, now left behind, are tentatively
unpacked into their shared apartment on the Right Bank: Bruno's heavy
blanket from Ethiopia, a set of long feathered arrows from Brazil, an ash
tray stolen from a hotel in Algeria, and Janine's flak-jacket and canvas
boots, still full of sand from the Western Desert in Iraq.

But having met in another lifetime – in another world – ordinary, civilian
life doesn't come easily. War has become part of them: it had brought them
together, and, though both are damaged by it, neither can quite leave it behind.
And the difficult journey that follows, through their mix of joy and terror at
becoming parents, Bruno's battle with post-traumatic stress and addiction, and
Janine's determination to make France her home, leads to an understanding of
the truth that people who deeply love each other cannot always live together.

A searing, profoundly moving love letter, beautifully written, *Ghosts by
Daylight* is a powerfully raw portrait of marriage and motherhood in the
aftermath of war.

'Janine di Giovanni writes with unblinking courage about war, death,
marriage, motherhood, loss, love, redemption, fear – indeed, about all the
world's most pressing risks and dangers ... Her writing here (as ever in her
remarkable career) is a great and important achievement' Elizabeth Gilbert

'Gripping and brilliantly done' *The Times*

'A vivid, heartfelt book that shows the extremes of life lived to the full' T*atler*

Order your copy:

By phone: +44 (0) 1256 302 699
By email: direct@macmillan.co.uk
Delivery is usually 3–5 working days.
Free postage and packaging for orders over £20.
Online: www.bloomsbury.com/bookshop
Prices and availability subject to change without notice.
bloomsbury.com/author/janine-di-giovanni

Madness Visible
A Memoir of War

'Janine di Giovanni is superb – an extraordinarily brave war
correspondent and a wonderful writer as well. What a combination!'
William Shawcross

Award-winning journalist Janine di Giovanni spent much of the 1990s
observing the cycles of violence and vengeance from inside Balkan cities
and villages, refugee camps and makeshift hospitals. This was a conflict
that raised challenging questions: what causes neighbours, whose families
have lived peacefully for centuries, to turn with mindless brutality against
one another? How do we measure the difference between bravery and
cowardice in a conflict so morally ill-defined? What becomes of survivors
when the fabric of an age-old community is destroyed?

Searching for answers, di Giovanni brings the reality of war into focus:
children dying from lack of medicine, women driven to despair and
madness by their experiences in paramilitary rape camps and soldiers
numbed by and inured to the atrocities they committed. In *Madness Visible*
she paints an indelible portrait of the Balkans under siege and shows the
true – human – cost of war.

'A terrifying account, soberly written ... Presents a stunning portrait of
the anarchy, cruelty and overwhelming confusion of contemporary wars'
Independent

'A moving book by one of our generation's finest foreign correspondents ...
some of the stories are so tragic that they are hard to get through ...
excellent' *Daily Telegraph*

'Always compassionate, never sentimental, di Giovanni gives voice to the
victims, perpetrators and architects of the conflict'
Marie Claire

Order your copy:

By phone: +44 (0) 1256 302 699
By email: direct@macmillan.co.uk
Delivery is usually 3–5 working days.
Free postage and packaging for orders over £20.
Online: www.bloomsbury.com/bookshop
Prices and availability subject to change without notice.
bloomsbury.com/author/janine-di-giovanni

The Place at the End of the World
Stories from the Frontline

**'Janine di Giovanni has described war in a way that almost makes me
think it never needs to be described again' Sebastian Junger**

At the start of her career Janine di Giovanni was advised, 'Write about the
small voices, the people who can't write about themselves.'

For over fifteen years, she has been doing exactly that. From a near-
abandoned hospital in Chechnya to bombed-out Tora Bora in Afghanistan,
from Saddam Hussein's derelict palace in Baghdad to the inner-city barrios
of Kingston, Jamaica, di Giovanni has covered almost every embattled
place in the world and the people caught in its midst. Like Myriem, who
lives on the West Bank, but can no longer use her farm because it falls on
the Israeli side of the security fence; and Sia, one of the child soldiers of
Sierra Leone, who talks blithely of shedding her violent past; and Abdul,
who was imprisoned by the Taliban at seventeen for not wearing a beard.

The pieces collected here begin with Algeria in 1998 and end with Iraq
in 2005. They are vivid, raw and impassioned – and they make war
terrifyingly real.

'Few writers can match her evocations of individual suffering in wartime'
Newsweek

'A gifted and humane reporter with a novelist's eye for detail'
Literary Review

'One of our generation's finest foreign correspondents'
Daily Telegraph

Order your copy:

By phone: +44 (0) 1256 302 699
By email: direct@macmillan.co.uk
Delivery is usually 3–5 working days.
Free postage and packaging for orders over £20.
Online: www.bloomsbury.com/bookshop
Prices and availability subject to change without notice.
bloomsbury.com/author/janine-di-giovanni